**Forthcoming from the *University of Notre Dame Press*
For Release: April 30, 2019**

ReFormations: Medieval and Early Modern

CHAUCER AND RELIGIOUS CONTROVERSIES IN THE MEDIEVAL AND EARLY MODERN ERAS

Nancy Bradley Warren

ADVANCE PRAISE

"This study traces the history of Chaucer reception in the context of Christian controversies spannin[g] centuries, from the time of Chaucer up to the English Augustan Age and the Puritan project in Ameri[ca] a compelling story that—to the best of my knowledge—has until now remained largely untold." —Jen[,] University of Vermont

ABOUT THE BOOK

Chaucer and Religious Controversies in the Medieval and Early Modern Eras adopts a comparative, bou...ary-crossing approach to consider one of the most canonical of literary figures, Geoffrey Chaucer. The idea that Chaucer is an international writer raises no eyebrows. Similarly, a claim that Chaucer's writings participate in English confessional controversies in his own day and afterward provokes no surprise. This book breaks new ground by considering Chaucer's Continental interests as they inform his participation in religious debates concerning such subjects as female spirituality and Lollardy. Similarly, this project explores the little-studied ways in which those who took religious vows, especially nuns, engaged with works by Chaucer and in the Chaucerian tradition. Furthermore, while the early modern "Protestant Chaucer" is a familiar figure, this book explores the creation and circulation of an early modern "Catholic Chaucer" that has not received much attention. This study seeks to fill gaps in Chaucer scholarship by situating Chaucer and the Chaucerian tradition in an international textual environment of religious controversy spanning four centuries and crossing both the English Channel and the Atlantic Ocean. This book presents a nuanced analysis of the high stakes religiopolitical struggle inherent in the creation of the canon of English literature, a struggle that participates in the complex processes of national identity formation in Europe and the New World alike.

Nancy Bradley Warren is professor of English at Texas A&M University. She is the author of a number of books, including *The Embodied Word: Female Spiritualities, Contested Orthodoxies, and English Religious Cultures, 1350–1700* (University of Notre Dame Press, 2010).

–CONTINUED–

THE UNIVERSITY OF NOTRE DAME PRESS

Established in 1949, the University of Notre Dame Press is a scholarly publisher of distinguished books and e-books in a number of academic disciplines; in poetry and fiction; and in areas of interest to general readers. The largest Catholic university press in the world the Press publishes fifty books annually and maintains a robust backlist in print. Visit our website at: undpress.nd.edu

ISBN 978-0-268-10582-2 • $45.00 paperback • 220 pages • Publication Date: April 30, 2019

Available in the following digital editions: Kindle, Nook, Kobo, Apple iBooks, and Google Play Books

Please send tear sheet to mail or email address below.

For additional information, please contact: Kathryn Pitts p: 574.631.3267; e: pitts.5@nd.edu

MARKETING DEPARTMENT, UNIVERSITY OF NOTRE DAME PRESS

310 FLANNER HALL, NOTRE DAME, IN 46556, USA

Telephone: 574.631.6346 • fax: 574.631.4410 • www.undpress.nd.edu • ndpress.1@nd.edu

UNIVERSITY OF **NOTRE DAME** | NOTRE DAME PRESS

NOTRE DAME, INDIANA 46556 • UNDPRESS.ND.EDU

Chaucer and Religious Controversies
in the Medieval and Early Modern Eras

ReFormations

MEDIEVAL AND EARLY MODERN

Series Editors:
David Aers, Sarah Beckwith, and James Simpson

RECENT TITLES IN THE SERIES

CHAUCER
and RELIGIOUS CONTROVERSIES
in the MEDIEVAL *and* EARLY MODERN ERAS

NANCY BRADLEY WARREN

University of Notre Dame Press

Notre Dame, Indiana

University of Notre Dame Press
Notre Dame, Indiana 46556
undpress.nd.edu

Copyright © 2019 by the University of Notre Dame

Library of Congress Cataloging-in-Publication Data

∞*This paper meets the requirements of ANSI/NISO Z39.48-1992
(Permanence of Paper).*

For Paul Strohm and in memory of Emerson Brown
The teachers who gave me my love of Chaucer

CONTENTS

LIST OF ILLUSTRATIONS

ACKNOWLEDGMENTS

As is the case for nearly everything I write, this book is the product of collaboration and conversation, and I am grateful to the many interlocutors who made it possible. Though it took me many years to feel comfortable writing about Chaucer, my love of Chaucer goes back to my earliest student days at Vanderbilt University, where I had the good fortune to take a Chaucer class with the late Emerson Brown in my very first semester. That class put me on the road to becoming a medievalist, and Emerson eventually steered me to Indiana University for my graduate study. There I had the opportunity to engage in further study of Chaucer, and so much else, with Paul Strohm. It is to these two wonderful teachers that this book is dedicated.

I began this book while I was a faculty member at Florida State University, and I must express my appreciation to the wonderful medievalist and early modernist colleagues with whom I shared my time there. They read, listened to, and commented on many early versions of material that became chapters of this project. Elaine Treharne, David Johnson, and Anne Coldiron were all especially generous, and the support of my then department chair Ralph Berry was invaluable. I also owe a particular debt to my early Americanist Florida State colleagues Dennis Moore and Joe McElrath, who guided my first forays into quite unfamiliar scholarly territory.

I wrote much of this book after I moved to Texas A&M to serve as department head. Having colleagues with whom I could be a scholar and not just an administrator did much to make administration more enjoyable and helped me refine my ideas. The Glasscock Humanities Center Medieval Studies Working Group has been a scholarly haven throughout my time at A&M. Particular thanks to Bob Boenig (who was also an excellent associate department head during part of my term), Larry Mitchell, Britt Mize, and Jennifer Wollock, all stalwart members of the Working Group and providers of excellent suggestions and excellent fellowship. Other colleagues at A&M also did a great deal to help me advance this project. Hilaire Kallendorf and Craig Kallendorf are both treasured friends and seemingly boundless intellectual resources, and Dennis Berthold, whom I knew as the soul of kindness from my first day as department head when he surprised me by taking me to lunch, was also a generous mentor in all things early American.

In my time in Texas I have also had the good fortune to get to know my "Texas Medievalist Crew." Tom Hanks, Andrew Kraebel, Susan Signe Morrison, Liz Scala, Leah Schwebel, and Barbara Zimbalist have been particularly fine conversationalists; I appreciate the invitations to share my work with helpful audiences at their institutions as well as the many good times and good meals. Other colleagues across the country, and indeed across the globe, have also done much to support my work on this project. As always, thanks are due to David Wallace, mentor, friend, and extraordinary reader of my work. Lynn Staley, too, provided, as she has so many times before, insights and encouragement. Bob Yeager did much to help me refine my thoughts on the early modern Catholic tradition of Chaucer reception, as did Michael Kuczynski. I so appreciate Diane Watt's having included me as a network partner in her Leverhulme Foundation–funded Women's Literary Culture and the Medieval Literary Canon project. The three meetings of that group, at Chawton House, Boston University, and University of Bergen, were invaluable scholarly communities that contributed much to this book's development. I greatly value all the friends I made through being part of that project; special thanks are due, though, to Laura Saetveit Miles and Sue Niebrzydowski for their conversations and contributions. My dear Judy Alexander, Tim Collier, and Amanda Alford McNeil listened to me chatter about Chaucer, nuns, and other things medieval and early modern through more than one marathon training season; they and all the members of Cypress Running Club are largely responsible for the preservation of my sanity! Possibly the latest adopter of social media one might find, I finally entered the world of Facebook in the course of writing this project. So, I want to thank all the old friends with whom I reconnected, and the new friends I made virtually, who have encouraged and supported me in that community as I posted both triumphantly and despairingly about the progress of this project.

Some parts of my discussion of the Prioress's Prologue and Tale appeared in different form as "Sacraments, Gender, and Authority in the Prioress's Prologue and Tale and *Pearl*," *Christianity and Literature* 66, no. 3 (2016): 85–403, copyright © 2016 SAGE Publications. Reprinted by permission of SAGE Publications. An earlier version of part of chapter 2 appeared as "Chaucer, The Chaucer Tradition, and Female Monastic Readers," in *The Chaucer Review* 51, no. 1 (2016): 88–106, copyright © 2016 The Pennsylvania State University Press; this article is used by permission of The Pennsylvania State University Press. An earlier, shorter version of the final chapter also appeared copyright © 2015 The Johns Hopkins University Press in *ELH* 28, no. 2 (2015): 589–613 as "'Flying from the Depravities of Europe, to the American Strand': Chaucer and the Chaucer Tradition in Early America."

Finally, I must end by thanking my family, as always. My husband and children cheerfully dealt with my frequent absences to travel to conduct research and with the complexities of living with a wife and mother who was also an administrator, scholar, and teacher; they did a great deal to help make our crazy family work. I am so grateful for the examples of compassion, kindness, and determination my sons present to me every day, and I am even more grateful for the gift of laughter they constantly give me. And to my parents, who have unfailingly supported my scholarly efforts materially, intellectually, and spiritually from the beginning, I can never say thank you enough.

Introduction

The bawdy Wife of Bath might seem an unusual figure with whom to begin a book about Chaucer and Chaucer reception that considers such subjects as Chaucer's female monastic pilgrims, English nuns' interest in works by Chaucer and in the Chaucerian tradition, the early modern creation of Chaucer as an orthodox Catholic poet, and Chaucer's significance for colonial American Puritan writers.[1] However, both within the environment of *The Canterbury Tales* and in the context of Chaucer reception, Alison of Bath plays a significant role in linking Chaucer to the sorts of religious controversy that are the central concerns of this project. Only ten lines into her Prologue, the Wife of Bath begins to stir up religious controversy with her first mention of scripture. She says that "Crist ne wente nevere but onis / To weddyng, in the Cane of Galilee," referring to someone (a cleric?) who cited this biblical story to her as an instructive "ensample" to illustrate to her that she "ne shollde wedded be but ones."[2] She then proceeds to rebut this claim with liberal recourse of her own to scripture. Taking a contrarian stance, she says:

> Men may deyne and glosen, up and doun
> But wel I woot, expres, withoute lye,
> God bad us for to wexe and multiplye;
> That gentil text kan I wel understonde.
> Eek wel I wot, he seyde myn housbonde

Shoulde lete fader and moder and take to me.
But of no nombre mencion made he.

(III 26–32)

Signaling just how controversial a figure the Wife is, the Pardoner reacts strongly to her masterful manipulation of Holy Writ to craft her unorthodox—but orthodoxly supported through use of scripture—arguments for the legitimacy of multiple marriages and against the church's idealization of virginity. He interrupts her to call her "a noble prechour" (III 165), thus raising the specter of one of the most problematic of later medieval religious figures: the female preacher of the Lollard movement, *the* major English religious controversy of Chaucer's period.[3] With her gleeful embrace of sexual pleasure and her endorsement of female mastery and sovereignty in marriage, the Wife of Bath calls to mind much else that is religiously suspect, if not downright unorthodox, in the later Middle Ages. Her views on these subjects, along with her troubling performance as a female preacher, highlight, furthermore, the degree to which gender is a central feature in religious controversies in the medieval and early modern periods.

In spite of its transgressive aspects, the Wife of Bath's Tale, which often circulated separately from her Prologue, was in the early modern period one of the most popular texts in the Chaucer canon, and its popularity stemmed largely from its status as a source of providential wisdom. Alison Wiggins notes that among early modern printed copies of Chaucer, the Wife of Bath's Prologue and Tale, along with the Tale of Melibee, were often the most heavily marked up by readers.[4] The old hag's wedding night speech to the rapist knight, instructing him on the virtues of age and poverty as well as on the nature of true gentility, was often excerpted from the Wife of Bath's Tale and quoted in commonplace books and other early modern texts (including, as I discuss in the final chapter of this book, Cotton Mather's *Magnalia Christi Americana*)—further evidence for the tale's popular reception as a font of sentential material of a highly orthodox and conventional kind.

The Wife of Bath, then, embodies both the orthodox and the unorthodox as two sides of a coin, inseparably joined. The variations in her medieval and early modern receptions—as heretical female preacher, as bawd, as voice of received wisdom—make clear the porous boundary between the categories of orthodoxy and heterodoxy. Some of the very opinions and practices that make her suspect to a figure like the Pardoner are the foundations of her authoritative status as a source of wise advice for early modern readers.

The union of the orthodox and the unorthodox in the figure of the Wife of Bath represents in microcosm the complex ambiguity of the figure of Chaucer and of the Chaucerian tradition in environments of religious controversy from his own time through the early modern era. From Chaucer's lifetime through the beginning of the Enlightenment, the processes of defining Englishness (including determining the cultural value of writing in the English vernacular), of constituting an English nation, are inextricably bound up with the processes of defining religious orthodoxy and establishing gendered hierarchies. We see this dynamic in the Lancastrian monarchs' implacable opposition to the Lollard movement, with its support for vernacular translations of religious texts and for women's religious leadership. It is visible in the upheavals of Henry VIII's break with Rome as well as in Mary Tudor's accession to the throne and return to Rome. The nexus of gender, religion, and English identity informs the complexities of the Elizabethan Settlement and the worries about succession that troubled Elizabeth's, and succeeding, reigns (Would the next monarch be Catholic or Protestant? Male or female?). As I consider in chapter 1, Chaucer himself traverses the porous boundaries between orthodoxy and heterodoxy and navigates the fraught interplay of gender and authority in the prologues and tales of his female monastic pilgrims. He explores the status of the English vernacular and the roles of women in religious cultures in an environment shaped by the advent of the Lollard movement and the emergence of innovative forms of female spirituality on the Continent. As the ideas of an English nation, English literature, and an English church develop over the course of the sixteenth, seventeenth, and eighteenth centuries, Chaucer proves to be a touchstone as others define the orthodox and the heterodox while negotiating the categories of masculine and feminine in religiopolitical conflicts from the "King's

Great Matter" to the "Stillingfleet Controversy" to the English Civil War and the Glorious Revolution, controversies to which I attend in the subsequent chapters of this book.

Throughout the early modern period Catholic and Protestant partisans compete to define the English medieval past as their own and to reap the benefits of its legacies, a competition in which gendered rhetorics feature strongly. Protestant polemicists negatively feminize the Catholic past, and for them Chaucer is a masculine figure who underwrites an enlightened, proto-Protestant version of the English Middle Ages upon which they can build a case for Protestantism as the authentically English faith. Catholic polemicists, similarly, see Chaucer as a figure who can save the English Catholic past from feminization. As an orthodox Catholic poet, he legitimates Middle English as a language for devotional writing and illustrates that the Roman Catholic Church in the fourteenth century was, as it is for these Catholic writers in their early modern present, the true English church. Chaucer thus enables partisans in religiopolitical controversies to lay claim to the valuable yet volatile commodity of the past and to manage its fraught gendered dimensions. Religiously informed interpretations of Chaucer also authorize particular visions of what religious partisans think that their present is, or should be.

Just as the Wife of Bath takes on a life of her own outside of her Prologue and Tale, so too Chaucer as a figure, and writings associated with him, take on lives of their own. We see the Wife of Bath escaping the confines of her Prologue and Tale within *The Canterbury Tales*, when the Clerk invokes her "and al hire secte" (IV 1170–71) at the end of his Tale and when the character Justinus in the Merchant's Tale cites her as an authority on marriage (IV 685–86). We see something similar happening within English literary culture at large, when she becomes the subject of a ballad entitled "The Wanton Wife of Bath." The ballad begins:

IN BATH a WANTON WIFE did dwell,
As CHAUCER he did write,
Who did in Pleasure spend her Days
In many a fond Delight.[5]

The ballad recounts the Wife's death and her soul's dialogue with Adam, Jacob, Judith, Solomon, and various other biblical characters at heaven's gate before she finally gains admittance (in some versions she goes to hell, where the devil will not admit her, before journeying to heaven). It places great emphasis not only on her sexual transgressions but also on her quick wit, her verbal acuity, and her ability to turn scriptural knowledge to her own ends to undermine traditional sources of authority, as she does in her Prologue.[6] Note, for instance, the exchange that occurs when the Wife of Bath's soul encounters David:

> King DAVID hearing of the same,
> Unto the Gate did go.
> Quoth DAVID who knocks there so loud?
> And causeth all this strife:
> You were more kind, good Sir, said she,
> Unto URIAHS Wife.

Over the course of the early modern period, the figure of Chaucer and texts in the Chaucerian tradition become, like the Wife of Bath, not just textual artifacts but potent cultural signifiers available for appropriation and transformation. The Chaucer who created the loquacious Wife of Bath, or the translating Second Nun and the feisty St. Cecilia she presents in her Tale, might well not have recognized himself as the orthodoxly pious author William Forrest invokes in his *History of Grisild the Second* to legitimate the restrained model of queenship and female virtue he crafts for Queen Mary, but nonetheless Chaucer and his writings were available to be used in this way. Because Chaucer's writings contain such a range of religious perspectives, from critiques of ecclesiastical corruption that gave him a reputation for being a Lollard sympathizer to unquestionably orthodox prayers to the Virgin Mary, his religious malleability makes him readily accessible to competing factions in religious controversies. Furthermore, his authority—literary, political, and spiritual alike—makes him a highly desirable resource for rival religious causes to mobilize. Precisely because Chaucer, and with him the medieval past he represents, are so malleable, however, writers who invoke him have to work particularly hard to stabilize their religiously inflected representations.

Much as, in the political sphere, Protestantism ultimately won the day as the English religion, so too a Protestant version of Chaucer largely dominated Chaucer reception from the sixteenth century through the eighteenth century. An understanding of Chaucer as a figure who had sympathies with the Lollard movement would significantly influence his early modern reception. The identification of Chaucer as a Lollard sympathizer or proto-Protestant was commonplace in the sixteenth century, and this understanding was, as James Simpson has observed, received as fact by 1570, when the second edition of John Foxe's *Actes and Monuments* was published.[7] In that text, Foxe says that Chaucer "saw in Religion as much almost, as even we do now, and vttereth in his workes no lesse, and semeth to bee a right Wicclevian, or els was never any."[8] Though the interpretation of Chaucer as a friend of the Lollards rested largely on the Plowman's Tale (which was not written by Chaucer but which Thynne added to the 1542 edition of the *Works*), the figure of the Wife of Bath, like those of the ecclesiastical figures Chaucer satirizes (the Monk, the Friar, the Pardoner, the Prioress), also lent support to such an understanding of Chaucer's religious allegiances.

The dominant early modern Protestant reception of Chaucer is quite evident in a heavily annotated copy of *The Workes of Geffray Chaucer Newly Printed, with Dyuers Workes Whiche Were Never in Print Before*, held by the Harry Ransom Center at the University of Texas. The seventeenth-century reader who marked up this copy is clearly in sympathy with interpretation of Chaucer as a proto-Protestant, as a satirist of ecclesiastical corruption and proponent of religious reform. The annotations also, though, bear witness to the multilayered complexities of English religious cultures and Chaucer's roles in them.

The annotator of the Ransom Center copy of the *Workes* is particularly taken with the figures of the Friar, the Summoner, the Pardoner, and the Prioress. Beside the picture of the Summoner, this reader writes, "Chaucer no dowt saw the knauysh abuse of fryres in those dayes." The reader further comments on the Summoner's Prologue, which presents the memorable parody of the iconography of the Virgin's Mantle in which friars swarm out from under the devil's tail.

The reader notes, "The ffrers are all lodged in dyuells ars by thowsand thowsande or millions"—something of an exaggeration, since the text actually indicates "Twenty thowsande freres on a route." Furthermore, this reader adds beside the Summoner's Prologue, "The dyuells ers the ffryers heritage." Making her or his own religious allegiances abundantly clear, the reader labels the Prioress's Tale "A leued superstitious papisticall fable." The annotator additionally signals her or his view of how Chaucer would have responded to Tudor-era religious debate by attributing to Chaucer himself criticism of "popery" and prelacy. Next to the image of the Pardoner placed between the Pardoner's Prologue and Tale, the annotator writes, "Chaucer in thys prologue (as in dyuerse other places) verray excellently describes the great craft and abhominable disceyt of popysh prelates, vernyshed over with a fayre face and color of fayned religion and fals pretended holiness."

There is one more annotation by this reader that is even more interesting in relation to the reader's imagining of an afterlife for Chaucer in English religious debates. Returning to the Summoner's Prologue and Tale, we find in the right hand margin the following: "Yff Chaucer had beyn alyue perhaps this geare might have made hym tos a fagot in queane marys days." With this annotation, the reader imagines a Chaucer whose proto-Protestantism would have been deemed heterodox under Queen Mary. The phrase "made hym tos a fagot" indicates that Chaucer's depiction of religious figures would have been seen as crossing the orthodox line under Mary's Catholic regime; Chaucer as a consequence would have been tried for heresy. Subsequently, he would "have carried his faggot . . . i.e. been absolved of heresy and borne a faggot as a symbol of that repentance."[9] Though relapsed heretics were executed by burning at the stake, publicly carrying a faggot was a frequent punishment after absolution following an earlier conviction.[10]

Even more fascinatingly, and further suggestive of the annotator's projection of Chaucer not only into Mary's day but into the religious ferment of his or her own seventeenth-century moment, is the annotator's use of the word "geare." According to the *Oxford English Dictionary*, one of the meanings current in the sixteenth and seventeenth centuries for the term "gear" is "discourse, doctrine, talk; also in deprecatory sense, 'stuff,' nonsense."[11] As Mark Rankin points out, the word

"geare" is "typically used by polemicists who wish to position themselves against either an evangelical Protestant or Catholic position."
The term, he indicates, is used to signal a derogatory attitude toward an
opponent's position in a religious context.[12] Indeed, St. Thomas More
uses this term in precisely this way in his *Dialogue concerning Heresies*,
as I discuss in chapter 3, and Rankin's view accords with examples
given to illustrate this meaning in the *Oxford English Dictionary*—for
example, "1624 W. Bedel *Copies Certaine Lett.* vi. 101 No maruell if
this geare could not passe the Presse at Rome."[13] So, it seems that the
annotator is not only imagining that Catholic readers in Queen Mary's
day would have seen Chaucer as heretical but also positioning him- or
herself on the side of Chaucer vis-à-vis a Catholic reader of his or her
own time, who would derogatorily label Chaucer's reform-minded depiction of corrupt ecclesiastical officials "geare." In other words, the
pro-Protestant annotator and the proto-Protestant Chaucer are aligned
with each other against Marian Catholic persecutors of Protestants as
well as against seventeenth-century Catholic sympathizers who would
condemn the critiques of "popish" superstition and corruption that the
reader interprets Chaucer to be making, critiques like the ones the
reader her- or himself makes in the annotations.

Though the pro-Protestant annotator of the Ransom Center copy of
Chaucer's *Workes* imagines Chaucer being judged heretical under
Mary's reign, there were Marian readers of Chaucer who received Chaucer positively. Indeed, as I demonstrate in chapter 3, it is in the Marian
period that a version of Chaucer as an orthodox Catholic English poet,
rather than a Lollard sympathizer, begins to emerge. The seventeenth-
century annotator also posits an oppositional relationship between
himself/herself and a contemporary Catholic reader of Chaucer. Such
an oppositional relationship between Catholic and Protestant interpretations of Chaucer characterizes the nature of Chaucer reception in the
later seventeenth and early eighteenth centuries, as I discuss in chapter 4.
Indeed, in the literary sphere, as in the political one, the Catholic was
never entirely erased or eliminated, and one important aim of this project is to examine the little-studied Catholic countertradition of Chaucer reception, a countertradition connected with alternative visions of
the English nation, English history, and the English literary canon.

The Ransom Center Library's annotated copy of the *Workes* provides a fascinating illustration of the ways in which Chaucer and the Chaucerian tradition were enmeshed in early modern English religious controversies. This book looks both backward and forward from this early modern scene of reading to explore Chaucer's roles in religious debates in his own period and afterward. The first chapter, entitled "Female Spirituality and Religious Controversy in *The Canterbury Tales*," considers the prologues and tales told by Chaucer's two female monastic pilgrims, the Second Nun and the Prioress. These characters, as well as their prologues and tales, suggest that Chaucer was engaged with contemporary female spirituality as a vibrant, contentious cultural force in which the innovative yet orthodox and the emergently heterodox blend, much as the orthodox and unorthodox merge in the Wife of Bath's Prologue and Tale. These female monastic pilgrims and their prologues and tales reveal Chaucer's awareness of and interest in the emergence of Lollardy—the greatest English religious controversy of his lifetime—as well as his cognizance of the burgeoning visionary, mystical, and prophetic spirituality of Continental holy women. In my reading of Chaucer's nuns, I demonstrate in particular the strong affinities between their prologues and tales, on the one hand, and texts associated with St. Birgitta of Sweden, on the other. Significantly, there are important respects in which Brigittine spirituality converges with the emergent Lollard movement. Thus, I explore the Prioress and the Second Nun as exemplars of multivalent, ambiguous female spirituality. Their texts correspondingly engage a constellation of issues that are central both to English debates about Lollardy and to debates about the legitimacy of Continental women's mystical, visionary, and prophetic experiences and writings. Central points of contention include the status of women's speech, especially women's religious and political speech; the legitimacy of women's teaching and learning; and the nature of the relationship between Latin and the vernacular in the religious sphere. This chapter thus foregrounds a focus on Chaucer, gender, and instruction—a combination of topics already present in the early modern reception of the Wife of Bath as a source of didactic material and wise advice—that runs through subsequent chapters.

The second chapter is entitled "Chaucer, the Chaucerian Tradition, and Female Monastic Readers." In this chapter, I shift my attention from the ways in which Chaucer represents nuns to the ways in which actual later medieval and early modern nuns used texts by Chaucer and in the Chaucerian tradition. Though little scholarly attention has been devoted to this topic, Chaucer's works, as well as works by Hoccleve, Lydgate, and Bokenham in which they attend to the figure of and the literary legacy of Chaucer, were owned in the later medieval and early modern periods by such large and culturally influential English nunneries as Denney, Amesbury, and Syon. I focus in this chapter primarily on Syon and Amesbury, because the manuscripts found in these nunneries' libraries comprise potentially surprising reading material for nuns; they include Chaucer's *Parliament of Fowls*, Lydgate's *Siege of Thebes*, and Hoccleve's *Regiment of Princes*. As I argue in chapter 1, Chaucer's Second Nun represents a sophisticated engagement on Chaucer's part with question of female religious authority, vernacular theology, and religopolitical reform. Amesbury and Syon in the later medieval and early modern periods were communities in which the learned, outspoken Second Nun would likely have felt right at home. The real-life sisters of these houses drew upon texts by Chaucer and in the Chaucerian tradition to develop rhetorical strategies and courses of action in complex political situations in which their communities were actively engaged, situations that included providing religious and political advice.

Chapter 3 turns to the Tudor period, in which the proto-Protestant identity for Chaucer that would come to dominate Chaucer reception was consolidated. This chapter, called "Competing Chaucers: The Development of Religious Traditions of Reception," first traces the early emergences of both a reform-minded Protestant Chaucer and an orthodox Catholic Chaucer in texts appearing in the late 1520s and early 1530s: Thynne's *Works* (1532) and Thomas More's *Dialogue concerning Heresies* (1529, second edition in 1531). In many respects, though, the Chaucer of both of these texts is a more moderate figure than the more polemically inflected iterations that would follow later in the sixteenth century and through the seventeenth and eighteenth centuries. The Chaucer of Thynne's 1532 edition is not as strongly reform-minded as the reader of the annotated Ransom copy of the *Workes* suggests, and

More's Chaucer, at least through much of the *Dialogue*, is not the rigidly orthodox Catholic figure that he becomes for William Forrest in the mid-sixteenth century or for later seventeenth-century Catholic controversialists.

Because the reception of proto-Protestant Chaucer was so dominant in the early modern period, and because it has been the subject of so much criticism, in the rest of chapter 3 I turn my attention to the development through the middle and later sixteenth century of the interpretation of Chaucer as an orthodox Catholic poet. Considering again in this chapter questions of gender, religion, and instruction, and focusing on the writings of William Forrest, particularly his *History of Grisild the Second* and the devotional poetry found in MS Harley 1703, I analyze the ways in which Forrest draws upon Chaucer to promote, in an era dominated by female monarchs, a model of queenship predicated on queens' possessing limited political agency. Forrest's rewriting of the Clerk's Tale for exemplary ends instructs Mary to concern herself with traditional pursuits associated with medieval female spirituality, including affective piety, contemplation, and charitable good works. Forrest also associates Chaucer with forms of Marian piety quite different from those found in the Second Nun's Prologue and the Prioress's Prologue and Tale, linking the maintenance of traditional Marian devotion with the maintenance of the political good of the realm.

Chapter 4 is called " 'Let Chaucer Also Look to Himself': Gender, Religion, and the Politics of Canon Formation in Seventeenth-Century England." In this chapter I continue to analyze the Catholic counter-tradition of the use and reception of Chaucer in the seventeenth and early eighteenth centuries. This chapter brings together some prominent canonical writers who are today rarely considered together but who in the seventeenth and early eighteenth centuries did converge in exchanges among debating Catholic and Protestant factions: Chaucer, Julian of Norwich, and John Dryden. Both Chaucer and Julian of Norwich were reintroduced to seventeenth-century audiences by Catholic writers. Dryden published translations of several of the *Canterbury* tales in his *Fables Ancient and Modern* (first published in 1699), choosing to translate the tales since the Middle English of the sixteenth-century editions had become too difficult for many of his contemporary readers.

Serenus Cressy published Julian of Norwich's revelations in 1670, a publication that sparked the polemical exchange known as the "Stillingfleet Controversy," in which, as I discuss, Chaucer plays a key role. In my analysis of the texts published as part of this debate, I consider the modes of textual encounter theorized by early modern Catholic readers who engage with Chaucer and Julian; gender and religion here again dramatically interact in the realm of religious controversy, since these textual encounters are predicated on complex, and complexly gendered, imbrications of bodies and words. The Catholic literary and political histories that Cressy, Catholic polemicists, and Dryden shape through their involvement with medieval texts also depend on interlocking sets of generative and genealogical relations in which words cause bodies—and the religiopolitical histories associated with those bodies—to have presence and be present in their contemporary world of a Protestant England.

The final chapter is called "'Flying from the Depravities of *Europe*, to the *American Strand*': Chaucer and the Chaucerian Tradition in Early America." This chapter focuses on three colonial American writers who had personal and textual connections to each other: Cotton Mather, Anne Bradstreet, and Nathaniel Ward. For all of these writers, the figure of Chaucer, Chaucer's works, and works in the Chaucerian tradition feature significantly in their involvements in and negotiations of religious and political conflict in both Old and New England in the mid-seventeenth century. Though it might be surprising, especially in relation to the staunch Puritan Cotton Mather, the Wife of Bath proves to be an important figure for all three writers, as once again gender and religion intersect in framing the terms of religious debate and political instruction. Mather, Bradstreet, and Ward engage with Chaucer and the Chaucerian tradition to negotiate relationships of past and present, old and new, as they establish positions of textual, political, and spiritual authority. For these writers, Chaucer and texts associated with him inform their processes of shaping distinctively colonial religiopolitical visions and developing modes of New English identity vis-à-vis Old England. As these colonial writers work to advance their faith and achieve political as well as cultural transformations grounded in their faith, Chaucer and the Chaucerian tradition ensure the reformed legitimacy of the religion practiced in the churches of New England as well as the English authenticity of reformed Protestant religion.

Throughout this book, I adopt a transnational and transperiod approach, situating Chaucer and the Chaucerian tradition in an international environment of religious controversy spanning four centuries. My aim is to present an innovative, nuanced analysis of the high-stakes religiopolitical struggle inherent in the creation of the English literary canon, a struggle that overlaps with efforts to establish religious and national identities on both sides of the Atlantic. In these controversies, Chaucer proves to be much more than the "Father of English Poetry" that Dryden so famously dubs him.[14] He also appears in the guises of a sacerdotal, priestly father; a source of sentential wisdom; a quasi-saint; and a figure who legitimates political dynasties.

CHAPTER 1

Female Spirituality and Religious Controversy in *The Canterbury Tales*

In the later fourteenth century, female spirituality was rife with controversy. Debates about the legitimacy of female mystical experiences and about the authority accorded to holy women as well as to the textual records of their experiences proliferated. While Chaucer's cognizance of the emergence of Lollardy, the greatest religious controversy of his day in England, is firmly established, few scholars have examined Chaucer's engagement with the modes of spirituality and traditions of religious writing that flourished among Continental holy women and made their way into England in the later fourteenth century.[1] Significantly, some of these developments in female piety have resonances with Lollardy, a convergence underscored not long after Chaucer's lifetime by the case of the fifteenth-century East Anglian mystic Margery Kempe. As is well known, Margery's piety was shaped by Continental holy women, and, importantly for my purposes, as I shall demonstrate shortly, she was particularly influenced by St. Birgitta of Sweden.[2] She was also repeatedly accused of Lollardy as a result of her devotional practices, especially her public religious discourse as well as her adoption of quasi-clerical postures of authority.

The female pilgrims in *The Canterbury Tales*—the Wife of Bath, the Prioress, and the Second Nun—all suggest ways in which Chaucer engaged with female spirituality as a vibrant, contentious cultural phenomenon within which the innovatively orthodox and the emergently heretical merge. As I discuss in the introduction, the Wife of Bath calls to mind the figure of the Lollard female preacher, even as her Prologue and Tale blend the orthodox and the unorthodox. The Second Nun and the Prioress, too, combine the orthodox and the at least potentially heterodox in their Prologues and Tales as they make manifest aspects of female spirituality that resonate simultaneously with both the Lollard movement and emergent developments in Continental female piety.[3]

Chaucer was ideally situated to be aware of the development of such multivalent forms of spirituality. Religiosity of a mixed nature was present in the Ricardian court circle, with which Chaucer was connected; some members of this group embraced ideas somewhat paradoxically shared by Lollards and Carthusian monks.[4] The aforementioned Margery Kempe provides a representative, albeit particularly flamboyant, example of the sort of fluidity characteristic of the religious culture of East Anglia, a region in which interest in Continental mystics and new forms of devotion flourished alongside an active, long-lived Lollard community.[5] This is the area from which Chaucer's family originally hailed, and it is also a region with which Chaucer had many dealings in his role as controller of customs for the wool trade, since Norwich was an important center of that trade.[6]

In this chapter, I explore the interplay of female speech, forms of female spiritual power, and the status of the mother tongue in the Prologues and Tales of Chaucer's two female monastic pilgrims, the Prioress and the Second Nun. The ways in which these issues feature in the Prologues and Tales of both of these characters grant these texts, like the *Book of Margery Kempe*, shared affinities with the Brigittine tradition and the Lollard movement. The Brigittine tradition emphasizes maternal intercessory and didactic power, the authority of the Virgin Mary (authority particularly associated with her participation in both Christ's Nativity and his Passion), and positive presentations of the vernacular as well as of female religious speech, much as do the Prologues and Tales of the Second Nun and the Prioress. Additionally, both the Second Nun's Prologue and Tale and the Prioress's Prologue and Tale present quasi-clerical roles for women reminiscent of those at least theoretically available to women in the Lollard movement, and, like Lollard texts, they promote the value of making religious knowledge available in the vernacular. I would emphasize I am not arguing that either Lollard or Brigittine writings are a direct source for anything in the Second Nun's Prologue and Tale or in the Prioress's Prologue and Tale.[7] Rather, I am suggesting that Chaucer was likely to have been familiar with, and his work on religious subjects accordingly shaped by, strikingly convergent heterodox developments in English religious culture and innovative yet orthodox developments in Continental female spirituality of which St. Birgitta was an important exemplar accessible to him at home and abroad.

St. Cecilia, St. Birgitta, and "Quiting" the Clerics: The Second Nun's Prologue and Tale

Chaucer's ecclesiastical satire exemplified by his portraits of the well-fed, hunting Monk and the greedy, fake-relic-peddling Pardoner have long been considered in relation to the Lollard movement. As we saw in the introduction, the portrait of the Pardoner prompted the early modern reader of the Ransom Center's copy of Thynne's 1532 edition of Chaucer's works to inscribe enthusiastic marginalia concerning Chaucer's proto-Protestant proclivities. Similarly, critics have for some time remarked on aspects of the Second Nun's Prologue and Tale that have Lollard associations. As I will discuss shortly, for a start, the Prologue emphasizes translation and the vernacular, subjects that took on Lollard coloring in England from the 1380s through the early fifteenth century. Not only is the St. Cecilia of the Tale a woman who speaks publicly and authoritatively on theological matters, but this saint also figures in Wycliffe's writings concerning lay celebrants: Wycliffe argues that St. Cecilia's turning her house into a church suggests that lay celebration—including that done by women—is possible.[8] William Kamowski notes that the Second Nun's positive images of the early church and its true miraculous powers resemble Wycliffe's perspectives on the purity of the early church in contrast to "its decadent fourteenth century descendent," especially when the Second Nun's Tale is set against the clerical corruption and abuses of the Canon's Yeoman's Tale.[9] Lynn Staley Johnson has also persuasively argued that the Second Nun's life of St. Cecilia intersects with many key aspects of Lollardy. She says that the tale perhaps *ought* to make Harry Bailey smell a "Lollere in the wynd" (II 1173), though ultimately in Johnson's interpretation of the Second Nun's Tale, St. Cecilia's gender, virginity, and sanctity, as well as Chaucer's claim that "he translated the work of another," all tone down the potentially heterodox dimensions of the tale.[10]

Critics generally have not, however, considered the relevance to the Chaucerian corpus of the Brigittine tradition, which emerged nearly contemporaneously with the Lollard movement and which also incorporates significant imperatives for ecclesiastical reform.[11] This lacuna is not particularly surprising, since the character in *The Canterbury Tales* who is perhaps most suggestive of Brigittine texts and spirituality, the Second Nun, does not have a portrait in the General Prologue or even a proper name. Just as Chaucer's European travels exposed him to such important Continental writers as Boccaccio, encounters that helped to shape his literary career, so too his journeys likely brought him into contact with texts and ideas that shaped his thinking about religion. Chaucer was particularly well placed to learn of the career and writings of St. Birgitta of Sweden. St. Birgitta spent the last twenty-four years of her life (1349–73) in Rome. During her years there, she lived adjacent to the English Hospice in the Campo dei Fiori, and it seems at least possible that word of her sanctity and her revelations circulated among English people traveling and working in Italy and elsewhere in Europe. Indeed, we know that "William de Guellesis, *scutifer Anglie*, met her in Cyprus, joined in her pilgrimages to the Holy Land and later came to Italy to testify to the fulfillment of her prophecies of punishment for the sins of the Cypriots."[12] The possibility that Chaucer, who, like William de Guellesis, was an Englishman abroad in the later fourteenth century, came to know of St. Birgitta and her writings in the course of his voyages is made even more likely by the fact that Birgitta's clerical supporters themselves traveled fairly widely in Italy, including to Genoa. In 1373, the year of Birgitta's death and the same year in which her extended canonization process was begun, Chaucer traveled to both Genoa and Florence.[13] He returned to Italy, this time to Milan, in 1378, the same year in which Pope Urban VI began official investigations of Birgitta's sanctity.[14]

Even if Chaucer did not learn of St. Birgitta and her revelations in Italy, he was well situated to get word of them in England. From 1374 to 1385 in his post as controller of customs, Chaucer was, as David Wallace has observed, in "daily contact with Italians."[15] These Italian merchants could easily have brought word of Birgitta's revelations and of the ongoing process of her canonization proceedings. Though it is probably less likely than his having acquired knowledge of the Brigittine tradition on the Continent, Chaucer might even have encountered written copies of Birgitta's revelations at home. At least one copy was in England before the end of the fourteenth century, used by Geoffrey, abbot of Byland, who wrote in the 1390s a defense of St. Birgitta's revelations (London, British Library MS Harley 612).[16] Chaucer was rather unlikely to have had the opportunity to see the copy used by Byland, who seems to have been at Oxford in 1393 and abbot by 1397, but its presence in England suggests at least the possibility that others circulated there as well.

Furthermore, a web of associations surrounding the circumstances of composition and circulation of the Second Nun's Prologue and Tale suggests connections not only to St. Birgitta but also to East Anglia, where Lollardy found an early following and where devotion to the Swedish holy woman was established soon after her death, and perhaps even before it. Mary Giffin argued many years ago that Chaucer initially wrote the life of St. Cecilia early in the 1380s for Richard II to give to the Benedictines of Norwich. Adam Easton, who was educated and professed at Norwich Cathedral Priory, was cardinal priest of Santa Cecilia in Trastevere, a position that he acquired perhaps as early as 1380. Giffin observes that a poem written to honor Easton's title of Santa Cecilia might have helped to secure his assistance in a thorny dispute with the papacy.[17] Easton was also one of the doctors selected in 1382 or 1383 (the exact moment to which Giffin dates the composition of the Second Nun's Tale) to examine the orthodoxy of St. Birgitta's writings. Easton had a particular attachment to St. Birgitta because he attributed his survival of imprisonment and torture by Urban VI to her intercession. By early 1390, he had completed the *Defensorium* of St. Birgitta as part of the canonization process, which was successfully concluded in October 1391.

Strikingly, many of the very charges against which Adam Easton had to defend Birgitta in her canonization proceedings mirror accusations regarding religious use of the vernacular and the acceptance of female preaching or teaching leveled at Lollards in England. Anxieties about vernacular translation of religious texts as well as about female religious authority emerged early and strongly as the Lollard movement became established in England. After 1382 the possession of English books was recognized as a primary sign of Lollard sympathies, and possession of a vernacular translation of the Bible was the most damning indication of heresy.[18] Whether or not Lollard women priests actually existed, some Lollards thought, as did Walter Brut, that women priests *could or should* exist, while orthodox clerics strongly feared they *did* exist. Walter Brut claimed in October 1393 that "women have power and authority to preach and make the body of Christ, and they have the power of the keys of the Church, of binding and loosing."[19] Furthermore, opponents of the Lollards like Thomas Netter had no doubt that Lollard women took up at the very least the office of preaching, a view to which cases of such women as Margery Baxter and Hawise Moon lend some credibility.[20]

Much as in debates about Lollardy, in St. Birgitta's canonization process the question of the legitimacy of the vernacular as a medium to convey religious content is at stake. The *adversarius* in the canonization process objects to Birgitta's claim that Christ, through an angelic intermediary, dictated the nuns' lessons to her "in lingua materna,"[21] saying that God would not make use of a vernacular tongue. In his defense of St. Birgitta, Adam Easton denounces this argument as "improbable,"[22] and elsewhere he defends Birgitta by presenting documented cases of Christ's speech to women. He particularly emphasizes the "dictamen Christi mulieribus de sua propria resurrexione eciam proprio ore suo" ([the] . . . utterance of Christ to the women by his own mouth concerning his own resurrection),[23] speech that presumably made use of the women's own mother tongues. Significantly, Easton compares Birgitta to St. Cecilia as a woman to whom Christ spoke:[24]

Et ista domina Birgitta fuit devotissima Domino Ihesu Christo elongando se ab omnibus delectacionibus huius mundi et persever-abat usque in finem in oracionibus peregrinacionibus et aliis operi-bus caritatis, abstinens se a viciis et peccatis, ergo est verisimile quod Christus sibi ore suo proprio loquebatur et dictavit eidem regulam monialium antedictam, et quod illam promulgaverit per eandem sicu loquebatur cum sancte Agnete Agata, cum Cecilie et aliis sponsis suis ut in vita earum plenius continetur.

———

(And [because] Birgitta was most devout to Christ, and removed herself from all the pleasures of this world, and persevered to the end in prayers, pilgrimages and other works of love, absenting her-self from faults and sins; it is probable that Christ, by his own mouth, spoke and dictated the rule to her, and that he promulgated it by her, just as he spoke with saints Agnes, Agatha, and with Ce-cilia and other of his brides as is fully contained in their lives.)[25]

Similarly, as in texts by Lollards and their opponents, the propriety of women's religious speech features as an important question in St. Bir-gitta's canonization process. Easton refutes the claim that Birgitta vio-lated the prohibition on women speaking in church by saying that she only engaged in private instruction; as James Schmidtke observes, in Easton's view, "Birgitta conforms to the special case of private instruc-tion described by Aquinas because the rule 'was not publicly taught in church, but instead to one community of nuns' [f. 232]."[26] Easton's de-fense of Birgitta largely does not deny traditional clerical perspectives concerning women's intellectual inferiority and the concomitant neces-sity for limitations on women's roles as religious instructors, nor does Easton reevaluate the inferiority of the vernacular to Latin. Easton ac-cepts the premise of female inferiority; the cardinal also asserts that the simple language and style of Birgitta's monastic rule are appropriate to women and nuns, whose intellectual shortcomings render them ill equipped to comprehend the subtle points of divine law.[27]

Despite Easton's claims concerning her rule, and despite the con-servatism of his defense, St. Birgitta, like several other Continental holy women, taught and undertook speech that could fairly readily be construed, if not exactly as preaching, at least as religious instruction, and she did so quite publicly, addressing not only women but also powerful men, including kings, bishops, and popes, in efforts to reform the church and society. To provide just one illustrative example, St. Birgitta gave advice, revealed to her by Christ, to Bernard de Rodez, archbishop of Naples, on how he should maintain his household and govern his diocese, instructing him, "If he wishes to be called a bishop in the justice of the divine judgment, he must not imitate the manners and customs of many who are now rulers of the Church."[28] She provides specifics on the proper size of his household (not "too large out of pride") as well as on the desirable character traits of his servants, who should "learn to flee from sins and vices and to love God above all things."[29]

Furthermore, Brigittine texts contain far more unambiguously positive associations of women with the vernacular in the religious sphere than those found in Easton's defense. In the version of her life by Archbishop Gregersson that was translated into Middle English, St. Birgitta's having the Bible translated into her vernacular is presented as a mark of her holiness, something to be praised alongside her asceticism, her devotion to the poor, and her keeping of virtuous company: "Sho fasted oft and keped hir fro delicious metes als mikill as sho might for persaiuinge of hir husbande and oþir: sho did grete alms, and had one house for þe pore, in þe whilke þare was one certain þat weshed þaire fete and cled and serued þaime oft time. Sho had grete will to comone with gude men and wise, and of holi menes liuinge, and of þe Bibill, þat sho does translate vnto hir modir tonge."[30] Birgitta's revelations, too, legitimate vernacular textuality generally and vernacular theology specifically, while at the same time presenting the vernacular as a medium in which women perform valuable spiritual work.[31] *The Myroure of Oure Ladye*, the Middle English translation of the Brigittine divine service made for the nuns of Syon, includes an account drawn from St. Birgitta's *Reuelaciones extravagantes* relating the way in which the Brigittine service and lessons came into existence. While Birgitta was in Rome, she prayed, and Christ told her he would send an angel to reveal the lessons to her. After the angel had revealed all the lessons in Swedish, he told her that he had (as the Middle English translation states) "shapen a cote to the quene of heuen the mother of God" and directed Birgitta, "Sowe ye yt togyther as ye may."[32] The image of a vernacular text as a garment for Mary, the Queen of Heaven and Mother of God, positively associates the vernacular with the feminine and the maternal. The angelic command that Birgitta sew together the coat conflates women's vernacular textual work with stereotypically female textile work.

Brigittine texts also contain frequent discussions of the Virgin Mary as one who translates the divine Logos into the human realm. In the Middle English version of the Brigittine divine service, the first lesson in the service for Sunday Matins reads, "Ryght so also had yt bene vnpossyble that thys worde that ys the sonne of god. shulde haue bene touched or sene for the saluacyon of mankynde. but yf yt had bene vned to mannes body."[33] Similarly, in book 1, chapter 35, of the *Liber celestis*, Mary tells Birgitta that Jesus "was conceived of a brinnande charite of Goddes lufe: oþir are conceiued be luste of fleshe; and þarfore John his awntis sone sais wele, '*Verbum caro factum est*'. . . A worde, and lufe, made him to be within me."[34] Through her maternal labor the invisible, incomprehensible Word of God is rendered into the comprehensible and redemptory "mother tongue," the human body Christ receives from her.

The Second Nun's Prologue, too, emphasizes vernacular translation in both linguistic and incarnational terms to legitimate the process and product. With an opening stanza that foregrounds vernacularity, the first section of the tripartite prologue proposes the labor of vernacular translation as an antidote to the "ministre and the norice unto vices, / Which that men clepe *in Englissh* Ydelnesse" (VIII 1–2, emphasis added). The third emphasizes "Englishness" with repeated references to the meaning of Cecilia's name in English: "It is to seye in Englissh 'hevenes lilie" (VIII 87), and "For 'leos' 'peple' in Englissh is to seye" (VIII 106). In the middle section, the "Invocacio ad Mariam," the Virgin Mary is the source of perfected vernacular language and an ideal exemplar of vernacular textual production.

Indeed, the Second Nun's Invocacio, the middle part of her prologue which opens with her saying to Mary, "To thee at my bigynnyng first I calle" (VIII 31), is as much about vernacularity and the legitimacy of translation as are the first and third sections of the Prologue. The Invocacio stresses Mary's maternity; specifically, it dwells on the process by which the divine, eternal Jesus becomes human. The Second Nun says:

> Withinne the cloistre blisful of thy sydis
> Took mannes shap the eterneel love and pees,
> That of the tryne compas lord and gyde is
>
> . . . .
>
>   . . . thou, Virgine wemmelees,
> Baar of they body—and dweltest mayden pure—
> The Creatour of every creature.
>
>   (VIII 43–49)

The emphasis on Mary's virginal, yet productive, body links female virtue and the virtue of the mother tongue, albeit obliquely, by foregrounding Mary's virginal and maternal labor as a translator. As Russell Peck has observed, that "the poet invokes the guidance of Mary in . . . translation is no accident. She is the greatest translator of all."[35] Mary's "wemmelees" body is the source of the vernacular text of Christ the divine Logos, which has been translated into the human "mother tonge" of "blood and flesh."[36]

Significantly, Chaucer's Second Nun, like the angel in Birgitta's revelation, also juxtaposes the textual and the textile to highlight the worthiness of the mother tongue, as she describes the work of translation that Mary performs in the Incarnation in terms of the creation of clothing. Mary is said to have "nobledest so ferforth oure nature, / That do desdeyn the Makere hadde of kynde / His Sone in blood and flesh to clothe and wynde" (VIII 40–42). Mary's textual work of incarnating the divine Logos made incarnate in her at the angel Gabriel's Annunciation is also textile work.

St. Cecilia's ceaseless activity in the Tale mirrors the Second Nun's own busyness in the Prologue, and the saint's labors, too, resonate with both maternal labor and the work of translation.[37] Although Cecilia does not, like the Virgin Mary, transform the divine Logos into human flesh, her speech recalls the translative process of the Incarnation in that she gives the Word of God a humanly comprehensible form. For example, when Tiburce is confused by Cecilia's account of the Trinity, she clarifies the doctrine by means of a concrete, human illustration, making the obscure knowable for Tiburce. She says:

> Right as a man hath sapiences three—
> Memorie, engyn, and intellect also—
> So in o beynge of divinitee,
> Thre persones may ther right wel bee.
> (VIII 338–41)

Additionally, Cecilia engages in a process of virginal, maternal "translation" of her own by producing converts; she multiplies Christians by transforming nonbelievers into believers through her linguistic efforts. We see this process at work with Maximus the "officer / Of the prefectes" (VIII 367–68) and with St. Cecilia's tormenters, all of whom are converted to Christianity by St. Cecilia's words:

> Whan Maximus had herd the seintes lore,
> He gat hym of the tormentoures leve,
> Ande ladde hem to his hous withoute moore,
> And with hir prechyng, er that it were eve,
> They gonnen fro the tormentours to reve,
> And fro Maxime, and fro his folk echone,
> The false faith, to trowe in God alone.[38]
> (VIII 372–78)

The Second Nun's Prologue and Tale thus present feminine labors, whether performed textually by a nun, corporeally by Mary, or spiritually by a saint, as related forms of productive, salutary, valuable work.[39]

Women's provision of instruction on religious matters, including the instruction of powerful men, is also an important type of labor featured in the Second Nun's Tale. Strikingly, in the Second Nun's Tale, "the rhyming couplet 'preche' and 'teche' [is] twice used to describe Cecilia's activities,"[40] recalling debates about Lollard women preachers and the *adversarius*'s objections to St. Birgitta's activities. The pairing first occurs when Cecilia is educating Tiburce about the Trinity. It later appears again in reference to her unceasing speech in the three days following the failed decapitation; the Second Nun says that St. Cecilia "nevere cessed hem the feith to teche / That she hadde fostered; hem she gan to preche" (VIII 538–39).

In addition to her discourses on doctrine with Tiburce discussed above, St. Cecilia engages in didactic interchanges with Almachius in which she resembles St. Birgitta as an authoritative woman who provides corrective instruction on spiritual matters to a male authority figure.[41] She lectures Almachius on his false worship of vain idols, calling him a "lewed officer and a veyn justice" (VIII 497) and telling him he is "blynd" in his adoration of "ilke stoon" that "a god thow wolt . . . calle" (VIII 501). She continues:

> It is a shame that the peple shal
> So scorne thee and laughe at thy folye,
> For communly men woot it wel overall
> That mighty God is in his hevenes hye;
> And thise ymages, wel thou mayest espye,
> To thee ne to hemself mowen noght profite,
> For in effect they been nat worth a myte.
>   (VIII 505–11).

This speech recalls some of St. Birgitta's directives to Queen Joanna of Naples. Birgitta sharply criticized the queen and publicized revelations offering her pointed instructions for reform. For instance, in book 7, chapter 23, of the *Liber celestis* "concerning a certain queen," Birgitta indicates, "A lady was seen standing in a shift spattered with sperm and mud. And a voice was heard: 'This woman is a monkey that sniffs at its own stinking posterior. She has poison in her heart and she is harmful to herself and she hastens into snares that throw her down.'"[42]

In their divinely endorsed religious teaching, both St. Birgitta and St. Cecilia "quite" those clerics—including Birgitta's defender Adam Easton—who deny, or at least strictly delimit, female authority in the spiritual realm. They also offer a rebuke to those like opponents of vernacular translation of Scripture who discount the legitimacy of the mother tongue as a medium for religious instruction. Indeed, I would also argue that the Second Nun herself engages in an act of "quiting" on the road to Canterbury. Consider the relationships between the prologues and tales of the Second Nun and the Nun's Priest. In the Ellesmere order, the Nun's Priest's Tale immediately precedes that of the Second Nun, and in some manuscripts it is connected to hers by a spurious link. In his barnyard fable, which focuses at some length on texts and the experience-versus-authority debate, the Nun's Priest inserts a long interjection in which he remarks, "Wommenes conseils been ful ofte colde / Wommanes conseil broghte us first to wo / And made Adam fro Paradys to go" (VII 3256–58). Although he tries afterward to pass off his misogynistic sentiments about women who dare to instruct men as "the cokkes words" (VII 3265), he seems a likely proponent of the very sort of views on the limits of women's intellectual and spiritual capabilities held by the *adversarius* (and even to a certain extent by Easton) in Birgitta's canonization proceedings. He also seems likely to embrace the delegitimizing of vernacular theology that would shortly after Chaucer's era be codified by Archbishop Arundel in his Constitutions.[43]

The Second Nun administers a corrective to her priest much like the rebuke that Cecilia administers to Almachius or the admonitions that Birgitta administers to erring monarchs and clerics. Through her tale, which itself might be seen as a form of public preaching or teaching to the mixed company of pilgrims, the Second Nun gives the lie to a vision of a world turned disastrously upside down by women's knowledge of, and public discussion of, religious matters in the vernacular. Chaucer's St. Cecilia amply illustrates that "mulier" is not necessarily "hominis confusio" and that female "conseil" can lead to salvation rather than damnation.[44] The first speech that Cecilia makes to her husband, Valerian, is, tellingly I think, called a "conseil"—a secret, as the note in the *Riverside Chaucer* glosses the word, but also an important piece of spiritual instruction which persuades him to embark on a chaste marriage and to convert. The Second Nun and her St. Cecilia show the value for someone outside the ranks of the clergy—and a woman at that—of possessing in-depth religious knowledge exceeding the mere basics of the faith.[45] The Second Nun's Prologue and Tale suggest not only that translation and vernacular textual production are legitimate within existing orthodoxies, but also that they can make existing orthodoxies *better* precisely by expanding opportunities for women to take on the office of teacher, talk about theology, and dare to instruct men.[46] The Second Nun, like the Lollards, as well as like such orthodox Continental holy women as St. Birgitta of Sweden, thus offers a pointed critique of powerful figures who seek to preserve the status quo for traditional religious authorities and to limit institutional reform.

Marian Devotion, Maternal Power, and Vernacular Theology: The Prioress's Prologue and Tale

Critical assessments of Chaucer's Prioress and her Tale have generally not been particularly favorable, going all the way back to John Livingston Lowes's reading of her as trapped between religion and romance.[47] Readers often call attention to what they deem to be her misplaced priorities in her concerns with dress, manners, and pets, and they comment with understandable distaste on the anti-Semitism of her tale. There is also a sort of critical minority opinion, perhaps best represented by Sister Mary Madeleva, that takes the Prioress's religion seriously.[48] Similarly, Hardy Long Frank develops a persuasive reading of "many Marian threads woven through the description of the Prioress," generally interpreting the Prioress herself, as well as her Marian miracle tale, positively in relation to the flourishing cult of the Virgin Mary in the fourteenth century.[49]

I want to take negative as well as positive assessments of the character of the Prioress and her texts into account to develop my own double-valenced interpretation. While I certainly do not want to claim that the Prioress is meant to be a Brigittine nun, and still less a Lollard (particularly given that a Marian miracle tale told by a nun seems a fairly unlikely place to look for elements suggestive of Lollardy), I want to consider the relevance of these traditions to her Prologue and Tale.[50] The ways in which the Prioress's Prologue and Tale emphasize maternal suffering as well as maternal intercessory, salvific power recall, as do the Second Nun's Prologue and Tale, innovative and distinctive dimensions of Brigittine spirituality. Similarly, the Prioress's Tale calls attention to the relationship of Latin and vernacular in ways reminiscent of later medieval debates, already discussed, about Lollard translation projects. The Prioress's Prologue and Tale are, though, even more complexly multivalent than the Second Nun's Prologue and Tale. In the Prioress's Prologue and Tale, the critiques of contemporary religious culture so central to both orthodox and heterodox emergent strands of spirituality are not only outwardly focused, as in the Second Nun's Prologue and Tale, but also redound back to the Prioress herself.

Many readers have noted the Prioress's self-infantilization in the Prologue, a process culminating with her comparison of herself to "a child of twelf month oold, or lesse" (VII 484). I would like to emphasize in contrast the importance of maternity in her Prologue. The Prologue begins with a version of Psalm 8:1–2:

> O Lord, oure Lord, thy name how merveillous
> Is in this large world ysprad—qoud she—
> For noght oonly thy laude previous
> Parfourned is by men of dignitee,
> But by the mouth of children thy bountee
> Parfourned is, for on the brest soukynge,
> Somtyme shewen they thyn heriynge.
> (VII 453–59)

This passage is frequently cited with reference to the Prioress's aforementioned infantilization, but it also provides the text for the Introit of the Mass for the Holy Innocents, a feast to which maternal suffering is as central as the infants who are slaughtered.[51] Furthermore, while I do not disagree that the Prioress does infantilize herself here and elsewhere in the Prologue and in her identification with the "litel clergeon" of her Tale, it is worth noting that this opening passage ends with an image of maternal nourishment. These lines' reference to children praising Christ while "on the brest soukynge" (VII 458) juxtaposes the maternal, feeding body with miraculously produced religious language (presumably, I would note in passing, praise performed in the children's mother tongue). The opening lines of the Prioress's Prologue thus provide a starting point to consider the ways in which the Prologue and Tale represent maternity, language, and female spiritual power, representations that are very much in harmony with Brigittine spirituality.

In the second stanza of the Prologue, the Prioress turns her attention to the Virgin Mary, stating her desire to praise and to be guided by the Virgin, "the white lylye flour" who "bar" Christ but is "a mayde alway" (VII 461–62). She thus announces her interest in the Virgin Mary specifically as a mother and highlights the process of incarnation. In a turn of phrase that recalls the Second Nun's association of tale telling with salutary busyness, the Prioress then says, "To telle a storie I wol do my labour" (VII 463). This choice of words, in the context of praising the Virgin Mary as "mooder Mayde . . . mayde Mooder free" (VII 467), suggests a conflation of vernacular textual production and maternal re-production similar to the alignment of these labors in the Second Nun's Prologue and Tale as well as in Brigittine texts.

Interestingly, the textual structure of the Prioress's Prologue mirrors the dynamics of Incarnation. It begins with the Word; the opening line "O Lord, oure Lord, thy name how merveillous" (VII 453) highlights the Holy Name *qua* name, the Name as Logos, as linguistic enunciation. Then, in the central stanza the Prioress recounts the process of the Word becoming Flesh:

> O mooder Mayde, O mayde Mooder free!
> O bussh unbrent, brennynge in Moyses sighte,
> That ravyshedest doun from the Deitee,
> Thurgh thyn humblesse, the Goost that in th'alighte,
> Of whos vertu, whan he thyn herte lighte,
> Conceyved was the Fadres sapience . . .
>
> (VII 467–72)

In the next stanza of the Prologue, the Word is fully incarnate as the Virgin's "Sone so deere" (VII 480).

The primacy and power of the Virgin Mary in the Prioress's Prologue and Tale are central features. Five of the six stanzas of the prologue are entirely concerned with the Virgin Mary, and the Marian miracle tale of course gives Mary the starring role in the account of the little clergeon's martyrdom for her sake and his miraculous subsequent performance of her praise thanks to her intervention. The tale, like Marian miracles generally, demonstrates what Benedicta Ward calls "the unpredictable workings of a limitless power held in the hands of a woman."[52] Lee Patterson considers this one of the limitations of the genre generally and the Prioress's Tale particularly. He quotes this same passage from Ward and then continues, "The genre tolerates, then, a certain spiritual carelessness, an indifference seen in the automatic, almost mechanical quality of the actions they record."[53]

Consider, though, the ways in which the Virgin Mary's primacy and limitless power feature in St. Birgitta's *vita* and revelations as evidence for a form of Marian piety similar to the Prioress's that hardly suggests "spiritual carelessness." Brigittine texts are full of scenes of Marian intercessions and intervention reminiscent of Marian miracle tales. For instance, St. Birgitta's *vita* recounts a miraculous, salvific encounter with the Virgin Mary: "Fell in one tyme þat scho was in dispaire of hir life in trauellinge of childe, and sodanli þare entirde one woman, þe faireste þat euir sho sawe, clothed in white silke, and laide hir hand on all þe parties of hir bodi, and als sone as þat woman was wente furth againe sho was deliuered withouten any perell: and sho wiste wele it was our ladi, also sho shewed vnto Bride eftirward."[54] The Brigittine tradition furthermore stresses the unity of the Virgin Mary and Jesus, highlighting Mary's extraordinary powers that accrue from this unity. In a revelation recorded in the *Liber celestis*, the Virgin Mary tells Birgitta, "I am wheene of heuen. . . . Wit þou for certain þat whoso lufes and wirshipes mi son loues and wirshipes me, for I lufed him with swilke feruour þat we ware bothe as we had bene one," a formulation of oneness of Mother and Son that parallels a Trinitarian model of unity between the Father and Son.[55]

The degree of power this unity affords to Mary is evident in the version of salvation history outlined in another revelation from the *Liber celestis*. In this brief relation, the Virgin Mary conflates the Nativity and the Passion as scenes in which she and Jesus labor together. Mary tells Birgitta:

Forsothe, he was to me as mine awne hert. Þarefore methoght, when he was born of me, as half mi hert was born and passed out of me, and when he suffird, me thought þat halfe mi hert suffird. . . . Whe he loked fro þe crosse to me and I to him, þan went þe teres oute of mi eyn as blode oute of vainnes: and when he sawe me in þat sorowe, it encresid so his sorowe þat þe sorowe of his awen woundes were noght almost felid, for þe paine he had of þe sorowe he saw in me. And þar I sai to þe plainly, þat his sorowe was mi sorowe, for his hert was mi hert.[56]

Their joint labor and pain effect joint redemption; as Mary tells St. Birgitta, "Right as Adam and Eue sald þe werld for ane appall, so mi son and I boght againe þe werld as with one hert."[57] Passion becomes compassion, and redemption becomes coredemption.

In other Brigittine texts, similar powers accrue to Birgitta's own maternal suffering; her tears and prayers have, like the Virgin Mary's, powerful intercessory capacity. In the Middle English version of St. Birgitta's life, translated from the Latin version by Archbishop Gregersson, Christ comforts Birgitta when her son Benet is ill by telling her, "Before time he was called Benet, but fro nowe hurthe sall he be blessed, and he sall be called þe son of teres and of praiere, and I sall make ends of his disese" (4). He continues, "Se what teres þan d[o]se nowe: þe son of teres wendes vnto riste and blisse (for teres are odious vnto þe fende)."[58]

In another revelation, the Virgin Mary tells St. Birgitta about the death and "doome of Sir Charles hir sone," and the salvific power of both Mary's and Birgitta's maternal suffering and labor are abundantly evident.[59] Mary compares Charles's death to a birth, indicating that she served in the capacity of a midwife who preserves a child's life. When Charles's soul "was departed from his body, I did as a woman that standith by another woman whan sche childeth, to help the chylde that it dye not of flowing of bloode ne be not slayne in that streight place were it cometh oute."[60] Birgitta then witnesses Christ's judging Charles's soul as a fiend and Mary make their respective cases for damnation or salvation. Echoing Marian miracles like that of the Prioress in which the Virgin Mary aids those who praise her, the Virgin Mary argues for mercy because "while this soule was in the body, it had grete charitee and loue un-to me, thenkyng ofte in his herte that God vouches sauf to make me his modre."[61] An angel then enters the debate on Charles's behalf, praising the work Birgitta as a mother did in aid of Charles's salvation. He says: "Whanne his modre vndirstode firste that his wille was flexible and redy to bowe to syne, anoone she socoured hym with works of mercy and longe prayers that God scholde vouche saud to haue mercy vp-on hym, that he fille not ferre from God. And by thise works of his moder he gat the drede of God, so that as often as he felle in-to synne, anone he hastid hym to schryve hym therof." Though confession and penance are necessary, it is maternal work and prayer that provide the catalyst to ensure the vital sacrament occurs. The angel then highlights the ability of maternal labor to counteract sin and to promote divine mercy. He says to the fiend, who laments the loss of his record of all of Charles's sins, "This haue wepinges and longe labour of his modre and many prayers doo; so that God, hauyng compassion of hir wailings, yaste hir sone suche grace that for eche synne that he did he gat contricion and made meke confession of godly charitee."[62] The fiend claims still to have a "sak full of writings" of Charles's sins, but when he attempts to produce them, he can find nothing, because, as the angel says, "The teres of his modre haue spoiled the and broken thy sak and distroied thy wryting, so moche hir teeres plesed God."[63] Mary and Birgitta both have, by virtue of their maternal efforts, power suggestive of Christ's power to take away sin; these mothers can give spiritual life as well as earthly life.

Maternal suffering and labor similarly exhibit salvific properties in the Prioress's Tale. In the Prioress's Tale, as many have noted, the suffering-mother/martyred-son dyad refigures Christ and Mary at the crucifixion, with the added parallel that each son's murder is effected by vilified Jews. The identification between the clergeon's mother and Mary is strengthened by the mother's calling upon Mary as she searches for her missing son. She "evere on Cristes moder meeke and kynde / . . . cride" (VII 597–98). And the account of the widowed mother, called "This newe Rachel" (VII 627), "swownynge" by her son's "beere" reminds us of not only the inconsolable biblical Rachel who typifies the bereft mothers of the children killed by Herod—another echo of the Mass of the Holy Innocents—but also the sorrowing Mary depicted in scenes of the deposition of Christ from the cross.[64] It is through the intervention of the heavenly Mother upon whom the sorrowing earthly mother calls and with whom she is so closely tied in lamenting her

son's fate that the little clergeon is able to speak and sing, even though, as
he says, "My throte is kut unto my nekke boon" (VII 649). The clergeon
explains that he "thought she leyde a greyn" upon his tongue and says:

> Wherfore I synge, and synge moot certeyn,
> In honour of that blisful Mayden free
> Til fro my tonge of taken is the greyn;
> And after that thus seyde she to me:
> "My litel child, now wol I fecche thee,
> Whan that the greyn is fro thy tonge ytake.
> Be nat agast: I wol thee nat forsake."
>
> (VII 662–69)

The Virgin Mary's placement of the "greyn" on his tongue is an act
that recalls both the maternal provision of food highlighted in the Prioress's Prologue, with its description of suckling infants, and the priestly
eucharistic provision of the life-giving body of Christ enacted by the
abbot at the "chiefe auter" before which the clergeon's "beere" rests
(VII 635–36).[65] It is through this quasi-sacramental act that the clergeon
is able to continue producing his miraculous song until the time of the
removal of the "greyn." As with Birgitta's sons Benet and Charles, maternal intervention plays a primary role in the son's fate. The fact that the
Virgin Mary performs an action reminiscent of the Eucharist not only
reminds us of anxieties about the existence of Lollard female priests who
would perform the sacraments, but also calls attention to the maternal
work of Incarnation that inescapably underpins priestly reproduction of
the body of Christ, much as, in Birgitta's revelation concerning Charles's
judgment, maternal work precedes and enables sacramental work.

In the Prologue the Prioress asks the Virgin Mary, "Gydeth my
song that I shal of yow seye" (VII 487). This prayer for heavenly inspiration connects the Prioress with the little clergeon of her tale, since
both produce language under the guidance of the Virgin Mary. When
the abbot asks the murdered child, who is miraculously still singing the
Alma redemptoris mater, how he is able to do so, the clergeon explains,
"To me she [Mary] cam, and *bad me for to synge* / This anthem verraily
in my deyynge" (VII 659–660, emphasis added). Patterson contrasts

the clergeon to the St. Cecilia of the Second Nun's Tale, another figure who continues miraculously to produce language after her throat is cut, contrasting as well the Prioress and the Second Nun. Patterson argues: "Whereas the little boy sings a song he cannot understand, Cecilia continues her work of instruction and conversion. . . . And most important, whereas the Prioress aims at a pathos that many have found sentimental, the Second Nun effaces the affective and the psychological in favor of an impassive triumphalism and doctrinal pedagogy that transcends human suffering."[66]

The connection of the Prioress and the little clergeon as figures who are bidden to speak under the guidance of the Virgin Mary may not simply suggest spiritual immaturity or powerless passivity, though. The Second Nun (who, it is worth noting, herself also produces language guided by the Virgin Mary, who, as she says, "do me endite" [VIII 32]), her St. Cecilia, the Prioress, and her clergeon with whom she identifies so strongly have more in common with each other than Patterson allows. As speakers who produce language that comes directly from a celestial source, they all occupy a subject position with a significant degree of cultural authority in the later fourteenth century, a position analogous to that of female mystics, visionaries, and prophets. Indeed, they share this position with St. Birgitta, to whom the Virgin Mary assigns the role of spokeswoman. Describing St. Birgitta as her daughter-in-law, Mary says: "For as a father and mother, growing old and resting, place the burden upon the daughter-in-law and tell her what things are to be done in the house, so God and I, Who are old in the hearts of people and cold apart from their love, want to proclaim our will to friends and the world through you."[67]

Those who serve as privileged conduits for divine messages are not purely passive, though at times they find rhetorical and political advantage in claiming passivity. In spite of such rhetorical self-fashioning, these divine messengers often offer powerful critiques of religious institutions and norms. I want to turn now to what may be just such a critique of later-fourteenth-century religious culture in the Prioress's Tale.[68] As I have discussed, Patterson has emphasized the Prioress's spiritual immaturity, and while I hope I have demonstrated that her Marian devotion and her Marian miracle tale are not necessarily just simplistic or shallow, particularly when they are read in dialogue with contemporary Brigittine Marian piety, there are key respects in which the Prioress does show lesser degrees of spiritual and intellectual so-phistication than the Second Nun, to whom Patterson unfavorably compares her. In particular, in her evident lack of Latinity, as well as in her less developed ability to participate at high levels in the discourses of vernacular theology, the Prioress is less advanced than her companion on the road to Canterbury; she is also less advanced than St. Birgitta, whose life and writings resonate so intriguingly with both her Prologue and Tale and the Second Nun's Prologue and Tale. The Prioress's Tale in a sense makes the same point the Second Nun's Tale makes in its scenes in which Cecilia instructs Tiburce in Trinitarian theology and in which she converts Almachius's pagan ministers with her "wise lore" (VIII 414). Both tales underscore, albeit in different ways, the importance of having full knowledge of one's religion, and both make clear that achieving full knowledge may well require presentation of religious tenets and texts in the vernacular.

Significantly, the clergeon is killed for singing a Latin song the literal meaning of which he does not know: "Noght wiste e what this Latin was to seye / For he so yong and tendre was of age" (VII 523–24). And, crucially, when he seeks a vernacular translation of the song from his elder schoolmate, asking him to "construe and declare" what the song means (VII 528), the elder boy cannot do so. He can only tell the clergeon:

> This song, I have herd seye,
> Was maked of our blisful Lady free,
> Hire to Salue, and eek hire for to preye
> To been oure help and socour whan we deye.
> (VII 531–34)

He continues, "I kan namoore expounde in this mateere. / I lerne song; I kan but smal grammeere" (VII 535–36). I am not suggesting that the little clergeon would not have sung the song in praise of Mary, and so would not have been killed, had he known the full meaning, and of course part of the pathos of the text resides in the fact that he sings purely because he knows the song honors Mary. I am suggesting instead that the tale presents, at least obliquely, problems connected to imperfect religious knowledge, imperfection that could be ameliorated by access to vernacular translations of religious texts.

The vital need for every individual's full knowledge of formative religious texts is, of course, precisely the Lollard rationale for vernacular translation of Scripture. A concern with women's full comprehension of Latin texts is also found in the Brigittine tradition. The fifteenth-century author of *The Myroure of Oure Ladye*, written for the nuns of Syon, highlights the importance of nuns' achieving complete understanding of their Latin divine service. In explaining how the text should he used, the author indicates that the opening words of Latin for each clause should be read so "that ye shulde redely knowe when ye haue the latyn before you what englysshe longeth to eche clause by yt self."[69] One possible lesson to take from the Prioress and her Tale is that, if a nun like the Prioress were to have access to vernacular religious texts in English (or perhaps Stratford French)—access like, for example, the Brigittine nuns of Syon had in the fifteenth century—she could achieve greater spiritual sophistication and be capable of more enlightened devotion. As the Prioress's Prologue and Tale demonstrate on several levels, dangers inhere in unknowing rehearsal of religious texts and in partially informed piety, a sentiment with which St. Birgitta and John Wycliffe alike would most probably both have agreed.

CHAPTER 2

Chaucer, the Chaucerian Tradition, and Female Monastic Readers

Much has been written about Chaucer's monastic characters in *The Canterbury Tales*, but with the exception of recent work on John Lydgate the "Monk of Bury," who has enjoyed a surge in scholarly popularity, and some work on the Austin friar Osbern Bokenham, comparatively little attention has been given to the ways in which those in religious orders read Chaucer's texts. In particular, examinations of the ways in which English nuns engaged with Chaucer's own works, as well as with works in the Chaucerian tradition by such writers as Osbern Bokenham, John Lydgate, and Thomas Hoccleve, are few and far between. Chaucer's writings, and texts by writers from the succeeding generation that attend to the figure and literary legacy of Chaucer, were, however, owned in the later medieval and early modern periods by some large, culturally influential English nunneries including Denney, Amesbury, and Syon. That nuns from these communities inscribed their names in manuscripts containing such texts suggests, furthermore, that women religious actually were reading them.

The Chaucerian material available to the nuns of Denney fits squarely within the expected parameters of later medieval and early modern monastic women's devotional reading. This community most likely owned BL Arundel 327, a complete text of Bokenham's *Legendys of Hooly Wummen*. This mid-fifteenth-century manuscript, probably

produced for Thomas Burgh to give to the nunnery, bears a scribal notation indicating it was "doon wrytyn in Canebryge by his sone Frere
Thomas Burgh, in the yere of our lord a thousand foure hundryth
seuyn and fourty, whose expence dreu thretty schyligyns, and yafe yt
on to this holy place of nunnys that þei shulde have mynd on hym and
of hys systyr dame Betrice Burgh; of þe wych soulys Jhesu have mercy.
Amen (f. 193)."[1] This hagiographical work features Chaucer prominently; Bokenham on more than one occasion invokes Chaucer as a
master of the English vernacular, as an authoritative predecessor poet.
For instance, in a classic use of the humility topos, Bokenham writes:

> But sekyr I lakke bothe eloquens
> And kunnyng swych maters to dilate,
> For I dwellyd neuyere wyth the fresh rethoryens,
> Gower, Chaucers, ner wyth lytgate.[2]

The nuns of Denney, accordingly, encounter the figure of Chaucer in
MS Arundel 327 as a great English poet in the context of religious material one would readily expect to find in a nunnery library.

My focus in this chapter is primarily on the communities of Syon
and Amesbury rather than on Denney, however, since Chaucerian texts
found in the libraries of Syon and Amesbury comprise potentially more
surprising reading material for nuns than the contents of Arundel 327.
The texts by and featuring Chaucer found in the Syon and Amesbury
libraries are not saints' lives or other conventional devotional texts (like
Lydgate's *Life of Our Lady*, which contains ample praise for Chaucer
but of which no records survive indicating possession by an English
nunnery). Rather, the Chaucerian material found in the libraries of
Syon and Amesbury concerns courtly and political subjects. What the
significances of such texts were for women religious, and how nuns engaged with these texts within and outside their monastic communities,
are what occupy me in this chapter. As I will discuss, the nuns of Syon
and Amesbury were positioned to draw upon these texts to develop
rhetorical strategies and courses of action in complex political situations, and these texts played important roles in the sophisticated de-

votional cultures of these monastic communities. As I argued in chapter 1, the Second Nun's Prologue and Tale represent Chaucer's sophisticated engagement with contemporary, and overlapping controversies concerning Continental female spirituality and heterodox English religious thought, debates addressing female religious authority, vernacular theology, and religiopolitical reforms. The female monastic communities in which manuscripts of Chaucer's work and work in the Chaucerian tradition were located were communities in which Chaucer's learned woman religious who translated the life of St. Cecilia might have felt right at home; they were communities at once committed to vibrant vernacular textual cultures, devotional and theological innovation, and political engagement. And, just as the Second Nun's St. Cecilia offers "conseil" to her husband and instruction to Tiburce, Maximinus, and Almachius, the monastic communities of Syon and Amesbury had interests in the provision of religious as well as political instruction, enterprises for which the Chaucerian works in their libraries were well suited.

CHAUCER IN THE CLOISTER

Oxford, Bodleian Library Laud misc. 416 is one manuscript filled with courtly, politically oriented Chaucerian material that was owned by the Brigittine nuns of Syon. Laud misc. 416 is a compilation that as a whole emphasizes "socio-political discourse" with a focus on the common profit.[3] One of the texts included in the compilation is John Lydgate's *Siege of Thebes*. The *Siege*, a text framed as an addition to *The Canterbury Tales* presenting the Theban backstory to the Knight's Tale, is, as Derek Pearsall's asserts, perhaps Lydgate's most political poem. Walter Schirmer reinforces this assessment, arguing that the *Siege* is, even more than the *Troy Book*, intended as a mirror for princes.[4] In reading the *Siege of Thebes*, the Syon sisters would have found praise for Chaucer expressed in terms quite similar to those that the nuns of Denney encountered in Bokenham's saints' lives. Lydgate idealizes the earlier poet's literary skill and the learning to be found in his poetry, writing:

Floure of poetes thorghout al Breteyne,
Which sothly hadde most of excellence
In rethorike and in eloquence
(Rede his making who list the trouthe fynde)
Which never shal appallen in my mynde
But alwey fressh ben in my memoryé,
To whom be give pris, honure, and gloryé
Of wel seyinge first in oure language.[5]

Though the Benedictine monk Lydgate's praise for Chaucer resembles that of the Austin friar Bokenham, the context for that praise,
both within Lydgate's own text and within the manuscript as a whole, is
quite different. Lydgate's *Siege* is preceded in Laud misc. 416 by part 2
of *Peter Idley's Instructions to His Son*, which draws upon Lydgate's
Fall of Princes as an additional source to supplement Robert Mannyng's
Handlyng Synne. Indeed, Idley takes forty-six stanzas from the *Fall of
Princes*, incorporating most with only slight changes or no changes at
all.[6] Following the *Siege* is Lydgate and Benet Burgh's *Secrets of Old
Philosophers*, a text that purports to be a letter from Aristotle to Alex-
ander the Great covering such topics as ethics, political advice, diet, hy-
giene, and astrology.[7] Laud misc. 416 additionally includes the universal
history *Cursor mundi* and an English prose translation of Vegetius's
treatise *De re militari*, a military manual afforded great authority in the
Middle Ages.[8] The final text in the manuscript is Geoffrey Chaucer's
Parliament of Fowls, an imperfect version consisting only of lines 1–142.
This portion of the *Parliament* readily fits the thematic concerns of the
other texts in the manuscript, since lines 1–142 of the *Parliament* concern themselves primarily with a synopsis of Cicero's *Somnium Scipio-
nis*, which is the final part of his *De re publica*.[9]

The Amesbury nuns, too, had opportunity to encounter Chaucer
in a manuscript context that emphasizes the courtly and the political
rather than the overtly devotional. Like Laud misc. 416, BL Add. 18632
is a mid-fifteenth-century manuscript, and it bears a sixteenth-century
Latin inscription indicating that it was presented to the prioress and
convent of Amesbury by "Richardus Wygyngton, capellanus" in 1508.[10]
Interestingly, on the flyleaves, which contain a fragment of accounts

from the household of Elizabeth de Burgh, countess of Ulster, there are records of payments made to Geoffrey Chaucer while he was a page in her household.[11] So here is Chaucer triply present in a monastic library—a manuscript containing two texts in which the figure of Chaucer appears is bound with accounts in which Chaucer also features. Also like the materials in Laud misc. 416, the contents of Add. 18632 are not as clearly applicable to the situation of female monastic readers as are female saints' lives of Arundel 327. In this manuscript, a copy of Lydgate's *Siege of Thebes* is accompanied by Thomas Hoccleve's *Regiment of Princes*, his *speculum princeps* that gives pride of place to the figure of Chaucer.

In both Laud misc. 416 and Add. 18632, Chaucer as the nuns of Syon and Amesbury encountered him is a different kind of authority figure than he is in Arundel 327, and the Chaucerian tradition is differently inflected. In Laud misc. 416 and Add. 18632, Chaucer's writings and works in the Chaucerian tradition are presented as part of a corpus of what Catherine Nall categorizes as providing political and spiritual guidance.[12] Chaucer is a figure not only of literary *auctoritas* but also of political *gravitas*; Chaucer and the Chaucerian tradition are sources of wisdom to inform good governance and right rule. The typical audience for such works, in Nall's estimation, was men engaged in "the prosecution of war and the governance of the country."[13] Indeed, the differing contextual presentations of the figure of Chaucer and the Chaucerian literary legacy in Arundel 327 versus Laud misc. 416 and Add. 18632 could be explained by the fact that, while Arundel 327 was evidently made specifically for Denney, Laud misc. 416 and Add. 18632 were most likely not custom-made for women's religious houses, though they came to reside in nunnery libraries. Rather, they were probably manuscripts that first circulated among just the sort of audience Nall describes.

Though information about the circumstances of the production of Add. 18632 is lacking, we know some significant details about Laud misc. 416's existence prior to its arrival among the Syon sisters. These details associate it with precisely the sort of readership Nall envisions for works of spiritual and political guidance. Laud misc. 416 bears a scribal notation dated October 25, 1459, indicating that it was "Scriptus ... per Iohannis Neuton."[14] M. C. Seymour identifies the scribe as Johannes

Nuton, a Benedictine monk at Battle from 1463 who later became prior of the cell at Exeter. Seymour also indicates that the manuscript may have belonged to the Tiptoft family.[15] This suggestion is plausible, since a collection of texts concerned with sociopolitical discourse and the common profit would have been a logical addition to the library of this prosperous, politically well-connected family. John Tiptoft, first Baron Tiptoft (c. 1378–1443) was speaker of the House of Commons in 1406 and participated in diplomatic activities at the Council of Constance.[16] His son John Tiptoft, first earl of Worcester (1427–70), during whose lifetime Laud misc. 416 was produced, also held important political positions. He was certainly one of those men who concerned themselves with war and governance. He served as treasurer of England from April 1452 until October 1454, and under Edward IV he held a series of high offices.[17] Though he earned a reputation as a shrewd, even merciless, politician, he was also renowned for learning and bibliophilia.[18]

How and when Laud misc. 416 came into the hands of the Brigittine nuns, in spite of John Tiptoft's love of books and in spite of the fact that the manuscript's contents suit it well for the presumed interests of members of the Tiptoft family (assuming it was a Tiptoft family book), remain unknown. However, the names of two Syon nuns (Anne Colville and Clemencia Thraseborough) are inscribed in the manuscript in the period between 1518 and 1531. In 1518, Anne Colville was a nun of Syon, and she died October 30, 1531.[19] Clemencia Thraseborough was also among the nuns who composed the community in 1518; she died March 13, 1536.[20] It thus seems safe to say that the works of spiritual and political guidance contained therein were of interest to at least some members of the Syon community as well as to men like John Tiptoft.

Given the undoubted persistence, at least to some degree, of reading habits and tastes that women religious developed in their natal families prior to professions, even as the nuns developed distinctive modes of textual engagement within their monastic communities, perhaps we should not be too surprised to find courtly and politically oriented Chaucerian material being read by nuns at Syon and Amesbury. Before the nuns became monastic readers, they were first lay women whose literate practices, interests, and tastes were shared with other women of similar social status.[21] Many of the nuns in these communities in the later fifteenth and early sixteenth centuries came from the same families that produced the very men engaged in warfare and government who were a significant audience for the sorts of works of spiritual and political guidance found in Laud misc. 416 and Add. 18632. Furthermore, as such scholars as Rebecca Krug, Claire Walker, Nicky Hallett, and others have shown, in the later medieval and early modern periods the relationship between lay literate culture and monastic culture was dynamic; each informed the other.[22]

Syon and Amesbury are, furthermore, linked by a web of familial associations during the later fifteenth and early sixteenth centuries, a web that gives us some insights into elements of the textual cultures these monasteries shared. For instance, women of the Fettyplace family were professed at both houses in the first half of the sixteenth century; Elizabeth Fettyplace was a nun at Amesbury, while Eleanor Fettyplace was a nun at Syon.[23] Eleanor Fettyplace joined Syon in the early 1520s, and her name is written in four books, so she seems to have been an active reader.[24] She recorded the obit of her sister Elizabeth, whose name appears in the pension list for Amesbury, "in her own breviary and psalter . . . in the calendar at May 21 with the date 1556 (?)."[25] In the late fifteenth century, the politically connected, pious, and learned Margaret, Lady Hungerford, also spent extended periods at both Amesbury and Syon, and her granddaughter Frideswide (daughter of her eldest son, Robert) became a nun at Syon.[26]

Even if interest in courtly and political Chaucerian materials by nuns of Syon and Amesbury owes much to their family background and the textual habitus in which the women were initially formed as readers, nuns' active engagements with such texts highlight the wide scope of their literacies in both the linguistic and cultural senses of that term. To begin to interrogate how the nuns made use of their far-ranging literacies, and to analyze the roles that Chaucerian texts concerned with courtly and political topics rather than with overtly religious content played in the textual, devotional, and political cultures of Syon and Amesbury, I want first to consider the case of a nonmonastic woman,

Margaret More Roper, who engaged with Chaucer's work in a highly fraught situation of religiopolitical conflict.

Though she did not become a nun, Margaret More Roper shared the religious and literate background of many of the later medieval and early modern women who were professed at Amesbury and Syon Abbey. Virginia Bainbridge observes that many Syon nuns came from the ranks of the intellectual elite, and their family members included "fashionable authors, cultural commentators, and influential academics."[27] By way of particular examples, Bainbridge notes: "Katherine Wey (d. 1509) was the niece of William Wey (d. 1476), the author of a pilgrimage guide to the Holy Land, a fellow of Eton College, and later of Edington priory, Wiltshire. . . . Agnes Wriothesley (d. 1529) came from a family of heralds and was the aunt of Windsor herald, Charles Wriothesley, the chronicler. Agnes Smythe (professed by 1518) was the great-niece of Bishop William Smyth of Lincoln, co-founder of Brasenose College with Syon's benefactor Sir Richard Sutton."[28] Anne Coville, whose name is inscribed in Bodleian Laud misc. 416, comes from a family of courtiers (including the diplomat Sir John Colville) whose literary tastes represented the latest fashions.[29] Margaret More Roper certainly also numbered fashionable authors, cultural commentators, and influential academics among her kin. Her father, Thomas More (both a well-known author and leading scholar whose work features in the next chapter), actually had close associations with Syon. It is likewise worth noting that women in later generations of the More family became members of highly literate English monastic communities in the Low Countries and France in the seventeenth century. In 1623, Helen More (in religion Dame Gertrude More), the great-great-granddaughter of Thomas More, was a founding member of the English Benedictine nunnery of Cambrai, and her sister, Bridget More, also joined the community. Bridget became the first prioress of Cambrai's daughter house, Our Lady of Good Hope, in Paris, which was founded in 1651.[30] Given this similarity in background, and given the mutually informing qualities of lay and monastic cultures, it is potentially enlightening to consider the reading practices of the nuns of Amesbury and Syon in relation to the interpretive habits of Margaret More Roper.

Chaucer, Religious Controversy, and the Politics of Advice

We do not have any instances of commentary on Chaucerian texts written by nuns whose names appear in manuscripts in which such texts are included. We do, however, have a letter from Margaret More Roper to her sister Alice Alington written in 1534 in which Margaret refers to Chaucer's *Troilus and Criseyde*.[31] The nature of this reference and the circumstances in which it occurs can help us posit ways in which English nuns of her era may have thought about and made use of Chaucerian material. Margaret More Roper's letter to Alice Alington recounts a conversation Margaret had with their father, Thomas More, while he was in prison for refusing to take the oaths indicating support of Henry VIII's divorce and his claim to be Supreme Head of the English Church. In reporting her conversation with her father in this letter, Margaret recounts several arguments people made outlining why her father should take the oath. She also outlines the ways in which More refuted each argument.[32] This scene of a daughter striving to provide spiritual and political advice to her father could scarcely be more filled with religious controversy. It is into this difficult conversation centered on religious and political affairs that Margaret introduces a reference to Criseyde, a reference in which Margaret identifies herself with Chaucer's character. When Margaret is pondering her father's rebuttal of all of her arguments in favor of swearing the oaths, he identifies her with Eve, aligning her with the archetypical female temptress. Margaret indicates that he says, "How now doughter Marget? What how mother Eve? Where is your mind now? Sit not musing with some serpent in your brest, upon some newe perswasion, to offer father Adam the apple againe?"[33] She continues, "'In good faith Father,' quod I, 'I can no ferther goe, but am (as I trow Cresede saith in Chauser) come to Dulcarnon, even at my wittes ende.'"[34]

The textual moment to which Margaret refers comes from book 3 of *Troilus and Criseyde*. Criseyde says to Pandarus:

But whether that ye dwelle or for hym go,
I am, til God me bettre mynde sende,
At dulcarnoun, right at my wittes ende.[35]

This moment occurs prior to Criseyde's betrayal of Troilus. Indeed, Criseyde is the victim, rather than the perpetrator, of deception here, brought to an impasse by Pandarus's wily arguments.[36] Criseyde is not, for Margaret, purely a negative figure; this Criseyde is no simple exemplar of female inconstancy. Rather, she provides an alternative model to Eve for Margaret's self-identification. Criseyde recalls Margaret's own predicament. Like Criseyde, Margaret is the daughter of a man accused of treason who can offer his daughter no protection from her enemies.[37] Margaret has obviously not judged Criseyde as harshly as Chaucer has Criseyde predict women readers will do.[38] Indeed, Margaret draws upon her knowledge of Chaucer's text as a useful resource in a difficult situation, and she puts Chaucer's text into a dialogic counterpoint with the biblical narrative of Adam and Eve invoked by her father.

For the women religious of Syon and Amesbury, as for Margaret More Roper, Chaucerian texts—even ones like *The Parliament of Fowls*, the *Siege of Thebes*, and the *Regiment of Princes* that for us might seem unusual for nuns to read—provided means of self-fashioning and identity formation as they negotiated fraught periods of political and religious turmoil, especially in the first half of the sixteenth century. Women religious from Syon and Amesbury participated in religiopolitical affairs in ways that resemble not only Margaret More Roper but also Chaucer's Second Nun (a learned woman who prizes knowledge and edifies her fellow pilgrims) and the St. Cecilia of the Second Nun's Tale (a woman who tackles theological arguments and seeks to instruct powerful political figures). In these political engagements, texts in the Chaucerian tradition offered resources upon which the Syon and Amesbury nuns could draw productively. Furthermore, just as Margaret More Roper puts *Troilus and Criseyde* into dialogue with the Bible, later medieval and early modern nuns found ways to integrate politically oriented and courtly Chaucerian material with their devotional lives.

The Chaucerian Tradition, the Lancastrian Legacy, and the Political Commitments of Syon and Amesbury

In exploring what courtly, politically inflected Chaucerian material may have meant for the nuns of Syon and Amesbury, we should consider the institutional political affiliations of the monastic communities, both historically and in the period in which the nuns of these houses were reading such texts in Laud misc. 416 and Add. 18632. Both Syon and Amesbury have, as I will discuss, histories of Lancastrian ties, and many of the works in the Chaucerian tradition contained in Laud misc. 416 and Add. 18632 have strong Lancastrian associations. The significant presence of Lydgate in the manuscripts belonging to Syon and Amesbury suggests that the collections would have harmonized well with the long-standing political sensibilities of these communities. The critical understanding of Lydgate as a pro-Lancastrian poet is well established. Richard Firth Green concisely describes Lydgate's partisan alignment, indicating that "for some years after 1425 Lydgate performed a semi-official role as apologist for the Lancastrian government."[39] Recent analyses by Lee Patterson, James Simpson, Paul Strohm, and Scott-Morgan Straker have painted a more complicated picture, arguing that Lydgate critiques Lancastrian military policies vis-á-vis France and expresses skepticism about the legitimacy of Lancastrian rule itself as well as of his own role as a spokesman for it. These complexities do not, though, fully negate Lydgate's overarching Lancastrianism, and Lydgate's *Siege* in particular, found in both Bodleian Laud misc. 416 and Bodleian Add. 18632, though a complex work and no simple piece of propaganda, is closely associated with the Lancastrian dynasty.[40]

Lydgate's *Siege* is not the only text in Laud misc. 416 and Add. 18632 with Lancastrian associations. In Laud misc. 416, Lydgate and Burgh's *Secrets of Old Philosophers* begins with a prayer for Henry VI, which reads:

> God all mighty saue & conferme our kyng
> In all vertu to the encrese of glory
> His realme and hym by poletyk levyng
> Wyth drede and love to have memory
> Wyth septur and swerd bytwene boþe to do right
> Aftyr his lawis and maner wight.[41]

Peter Idley's Instructions to His Son not only draws on Lydgate's *Fall of Princes*, but the Peter Idley identified as the author of the *Instructions* also had a long career of office holding under Henry VI. As Charlotte D'Evelyn notes, "Peter Idley's tenure of office did not continue long after the overthrow of Henry VI. He was, perhaps, no favorer or favorite of the House of York."[42] The contents of Laud misc. 416 additionally align closely with what John Bowers calls the "non-Lollard syllabus," the approved "prospectus for knightly reading" that Hoccleve (another pro-Lancastrian poet) outlines in his poem "To Sir John Oldcastle."[43] Hoccleve's recommends:

> Rede the storie of Launcelot de Lake
> Or Vegece of the aart of Chiualrie
> The seege of Troie or Thebes thee applie
> To thynge þat may to thordre of knight longe!
> To thy correccioun now haste and hie,
> For thow haast been out of ioynt al to longe.[44]

Both Vegetius and the romances of Thebes and Troy feature prominently in Laud misc. 416. In this manuscript, the figure of Chaucer and the Chaucerian tradition thus not only provide political *gravitas* for the Lancastrian dynasty and grant literary *auctoritas* to vernacular literary enterprises, another Lancastrian priority, but they also resonate with Lancastrian efforts to support orthodox religion.

It is intriguing to consider, if Laud misc. 416 really was a Tiptoft family book, that the book collector John Tiptoft might have deaccessioned it from his collection after the rise of the Yorkist dynasty—with which he was so closely affiliated—precisely because of the Lancastrian associations of several of the texts the manuscript contained.[45] The political dimensions of texts in this collection perhaps ultimately made the manuscript distasteful or embarrassing to its original owner. The same dimensions would have made it, however, an ideal fit for Syon's political orientation, and supporters of the Yorkist cause were eager to avail themselves of the spiritual and symbolic benefits of association with Syon. Indeed, Edward IV himself was so generous to Syon as to be named its "second founder."[46]

In Add. 18632, as in Laud misc. 416, Chaucer advances the causes of creating an authoritative English vernacular tradition, supporting orthodox religion, and legitimating Lancastrian succession. Hoccleve's

Regiment of Princes, which appears with Lydgate's *Siege* in Add. 18632, is a text in which Hoccleve turns his attention to Chaucer repeatedly as he offers princely instruction to the future Lancastrian monarch. In the Prologue, a reference to Chaucer follows Hoccleve's revelation of his identity to the old man (lines 1867–68). At the end of the Prologue, prior to addressing the prince, Hoccleve invokes Chaucer at the very place in which a classical writer would invoke a muse. In particular, Hoccleve laments the absence of Chaucer's "conseil and reed."[47] Furthermore, when he turns to address the prince, Hoccleve once more invokes Chaucer, lamenting again the absence of Chaucer's influence as instructor in poetry.[48] After this prologue with its address to Prince Henry, Hoccleve's *Regiment* draws upon classic works of political instruction: the *Secreta secretorum* (recall that Lydgate and Burgh's English version of this text is also in Laud misc. 416), the *De regimine principum* of Egidius Colonna (Giles of Rome), and Jacob de Cessolis's *Chessbook*.[49] In the process, Hoccleve, like Lydgate, stresses Chaucer's status as a vernacular poet, as one who brought all of the authority connected with classical literature and philosophy into English. In a representative example, Hoccleve writes:

> O maystyr dere and fadir reuerent,
> My mayster Chaucer, flour of eloquence,
> Mirrour of fructuous entendement,
> O vniversal fader in science.[50]

Hoccleve adds, though, an inflection to his praise to express his devotion (and I use this word deliberately) to his "master Chaucer." The last of his homages to Chaucer occurs in the context of a discussion of religious images, a topic under intense debate during Hoccleve's life given the perceived threat posed by the Lollard movement, against which, as we have seen, Hoccleve mobilizes Vegetius and the romances of Thebes and Troy in his poem to Sir John Oldcastle. Speaking of the dead Chaucer, Hoccleve writes in the *Regiment*:

> Al-þogh his lyfe be queynt, þe resemblaunce
> Of him haþ in me so fressh lyflynesse,

Þat, to putte othir men in remembraunce
Of his persone, I haue heere his lyknesse
Do make, to þis ende in sothfastnesse,
Þat þei þat haue of him lest þought & mynde,
By þis peynture may ageyn him fynde.[51]

Hoccleve then instructs that a portrait of Chaucer be included in the manuscripts (something that was actually done in some manuscripts of the *Regiment*). He follows his directive with a vigorous defense of religious images targeted at those who "holden oppynyoun, and sey / Þat none ymages schold I-maked be."[52] These iconoclasts "erren foule, & goon out of þe wey."[53] Religious images have, in Hoccleve's orthodox perspective, a beneficial and instructive purpose:

The ymages þat in þe chirche been,
Maken folk þenke on god & his seyntes,
Whan þe ymages þei be-holden & seen;
Were oft vnsyte of hem causith restreyntes
Of þoughtes gode: whan a þing depeynt is,
Or entailed, if men take of it heede,
Thoght of þe lyknesse, it wil in hem brede.[54]

As such scholars as Jeanne Krochalis have argued, Hoccleve not only voices the orthodox position on religious images, but by placing a homage to Chaucer in this context, he also effects a religious quasi-canonization to accompany his literary canonization of Chaucer. He puts Chaucer in the company of the saints and grants Chaucer's image beneficial qualities like those possessed by images of the saints.[55] The "holiness and power" that Hoccleve confers on the figure of Chaucer the unofficial saint, as well as on his English writings, accordingly have political benefits for both Hoccleve and the Lancastrian ruler the text is designed to advise.[56]

There is thus a good match between the long-term political alignments of Syon and Amesbury on the one hand and the contents of Laud misc. 416 and Add. 18632 on the other. From its foundation by Henry V, Syon had strong, enduring ties with the house of Lancaster.

As I have argued, Henry V's foundation of Syon had a central place in his ongoing campaign for Lancastrian legitimacy.[57] Syon's Lancastrian affiliations remained strong throughout the conflict between the houses of Lancaster and York. As we have seen, the staunchly Lancastrian supporter Margaret, Lady Hungerford, spent a good deal of time at Syon, having paid Edward IV £200 to be released from arrest and permitted to withdraw there.[58]

Though Amesbury does not have as strong a tradition of affiliation with the house of Lancaster as Syon has, there are important ties between the Benedictine nunnery and the Lancastrians. The nuns had enjoyed a close relationship with the crown during the reign of Edward III, the ancestor from whom both the Lancastrian and Yorkist monarchs fought to claim descent through much of the latter half of the fifteenth century. The community's association with the house of Lancaster was cemented when Isabel Lancaster, who would eventually become prioress, was professed at Amesbury in 1327. Isabel used her inheritance to benefit the community and secured the patronage of her father and brother for Amesbury.[59] Her father was Henry, third earl of Lancaster, who played an important role in deposing Edward II and placing Edward III on the throne. Isabel's brother, Henry of Grosmont, first duke of Lancaster, was the father of Blanche of Lancaster, whom John of Gaunt married. In 1345, this Henry granted the advowson of East Garston (Berks.) to Amesbury and procured the papal license for the house to appropriate the rectory.[60] In the 1340s the house received, furthermore, not only economic benefits but also legal preferences for which their Lancastrian connections may have been responsible.[61]

Amesbury does not seem to have been a very strongly partisan community during the fifteenth-century Wars of the Roses, though there is record of Henry VI visiting the nunnery in 1435.[62] The Lancastrian-affiliated Margaret, Lady Hungerford, who, as I mentioned previously, retired to Syon in her later years, was in residence at Amesbury between 1459 and 1463.[63] While she was at Amesbury, her son Robert fought as a garrison at the Tower of London when it was besieged by the Yorkists in July 1460.[64] His mother thereafter paid for him to go abroad in August 1460.[65] So there seem to have been at least some partisan connections between Amesbury and the Lancastrian faction during the turbulent late fifteenth century.

The somewhat old-fashioned, early fifteenth-century presentation of Chaucer as a source of symbolic support for the Lancastrian dynasty's legitimacy, as well as for the Lancastrian dynasty's commitments to religious orthodoxy, in Laud misc. 416 and Add. 18632 was not merely backward looking when the nuns of Syon and Amesbury were reading these manuscripts in the early sixteenth century. The Lancastrian dimensions of the Chaucerian materials in these manuscripts had current as well as historical political significance for these communities in the period in which their nuns were inscribing their names in these manuscripts. The quasi-saintly, religiously orthodox, and didactically oriented Chaucer of Laud misc. 416 and Add. 18632 intersects with the Syon and Amesbury nuns' engagements in contemporary political affairs in the years in which we have evidence suggesting the nuns were reading these manuscripts. The Chaucerian tradition, and all the political and religious baggage it carries, animates the contemporary moment, and perhaps informs the nuns' political activities, albeit in somewhat different ways for the two communities.

During the sixteenth century, Syon allied itself firmly with the English Catholic cause, participating in efforts to counter Henrician narratives of legitimation for an English dynastic innovation and the establishment of a church separate from Rome. Syon was committed to an account of English history in which the Lancastrian heritage was explicitly a Roman Catholic heritage, and the true Lancastrians in the sixteenth century were to be found not in England but rather in Spain, as the polemicist Robert Parsons, who had close ties with Syon, would articulate explicitly at the end of the sixteenth century in his *Conference about the Next Succession to the Crowne of Ingland*. Syon's desire to claim Lancastrian history as orthodox Catholic English history was likely intensified by the fact that Henry V, Syon's founder, had for many years featured prominently in Henry VIII's self-representational strategies. As Greg Walker observes, Henry VIII appears to have patterned his conduct on examples of kingship taken from schoolbooks and from the *speculum principis* tradition. In particular, Henry VIII took as models King Arthur, Alexander the Great, and his ancestor and namesake

Henry V.[66] Furthermore, Henry VIII commissioned the first English biography of Henry V, and during his campaign in France in 1513, he took Henry V's 1415 Agincourt campaign as a sort of playbook.[67] The orthodox Catholic, pro-Lancastrian Chaucer of Laud misc. 416 harmonizes perfectly with the dissenting Catholic interpretation of English history that Syon embraced beginning in the era of Henry VIII and crystallized in the reign of Elizabeth I.[68]

The strongly didactic dimensions of the Chaucerian texts that Syon possessed in Laud misc. 416 also assume particular significance during the years in which Syon nuns inscribed their names in Laud misc. 416. These Chaucerian texts resonate with the community's attempts to oppose Henry VIII's efforts to divorce Katherine of Aragon and his concomitant redefinitions of his roles as both king and supreme head of the church. [69] Those who resisted Henry's fight with Rome from within England drew upon rhetorics of advice and counsel to attempt to persuade the king to adopt a different course of action.[70] Not only do the Chaucerian *speculum princeps* texts in the Syon nuns' manuscripts recall an orthodox Catholic, Lancastrian version of English monarchy contrary to Henry's revisionist invocations of the Lancastrian inheritance and his Protestant model of kingship, but they also authorize a model of nontreasonous, nonheretical criticism and critique of royal behavior.

Such an instructive role vis-à-vis authority figures deemed not to be following God's will had been readily embraced by the founder of the Brigittine order. As I discuss in the previous chapter, St. Birgitta frequently addressed blunt criticisms and pointed instructions to kings, bishops, and even popes. Such a didactic role was also one taken on, fatally, by Elizabeth Barton, whom the community of Syon strongly supported (and, one might argue, also taken on fatally by the St. Cecilia of the Second Nun's Tale, martyred for her refusal to accede to the wishes of Almachius, opting instead to preach to and teach him on matters of Christian doctrine).[71] Barton declared that "God commanded her to say to the late cardinal and also to the said Archbishop of Canterbury that, if they married or furthered the King's Grace to be married to the Queen's Grace that now is [Anne Boleyn] they both should be utterly destroyed" and that "if the King's Grace married the Queen's Grace that now is, he should not be king a month after."[72]

The nuns of Amesbury participated less aggressively in royal politics than the nuns of Syon, but the community did have political roles
to play. In the early sixteenth century, just a few years before Richard
Wygyngton gave Add. 18632 to the nuns of Amesbury, the community
featured prominently in the 1501 ceremonial progress to London that
Katherine of Aragon made upon her arrival in England for her marriage to Prince Arthur. Perhaps Amesbury was chosen as a venue for
this occasion because of the nunnery's Lancastrian-aligned past as well
as its associations with the "matter of Arthur"—Amesbury being the
nunnery where Guinevere takes up residence in some versions of her
story. Both the Lancastrian and Arthurian connections may have been
useful in Henry's efforts to present for his son's bride-to-be, as well as
for the larger audience, a clear picture of the regal bona fides of his son
Arthur as inheritor of the greatness and dynastic legitimacy of his Lancastrian predecessors and of the heroic English originary figure par excellence, King Arthur.[73]

According to the account of the "Arrangements for the Reception
of Catherine of Aragon" drawn up by Henry VII's council (MS Cotton
Vespasian C xxv), an especially large and distinguished list of people
was designated to meet Katherine at Amesbury, and unlike at previous
stops at Honiton, Crewkerne, Sherborn, and Shaftesbury, formal events
were also planned. Notably, some of the key participants in this ceremony had quite strong ties to the Yorkist faction, which, not so many
years previously, had been at war with the house of Lancaster, from
which Katherine of Aragon was a descendent (she was the great-grand-
daughter and namesake of Catherine of Lancaster, daughter of John of
Gaunt and Constance of Castile). The past Yorkist commitments of
these stars of the welcoming ceremony may also help account for why
the ceremony was staged at Amesbury, since, given Katherine's Lancastrian heritage, Amesbury's Lancastrian-aligned past would have been a
useful symbolic counterweight to the Yorkist-dominated ceremonies.

The "Arrangements" specifies that the meeting and receiving were
to occur in "the maner following":

> my lord tresourer, accompanyed with the Bisshops of bathe and
> Hereford, thabbots of Abandon and Reding, my lord Dacre of the

South, my lord Zouche, Sir Robert Poyntz, Sir William Sandes, Sir John Seymor, Sir Christofer Wroughton, Sir John Brereton, and Sir John Chok, to mete her iij or iiij myles befor she come to Ambresbury. And the said duchesse of Norfolk, to receyve her after her offring in some convenient place betwix that and her loging, at which tyme William Hollybrand, which shall awaite upon her, shall in the Spanysshe tong, in the name of the said duchesse welcome the said princesse with such words as be delyvered to hym in writing.[74]

"My lord treasurer" is Thomas Howard, second duke of Norfolk, who became treasurer earlier in 1501. Together with Richard Fox, lord privy seal, and William Warham, the chancellor, he was part of Henry's "executive triumvirate."[75] Thomas Howard was an active diplomat, participating in the 1501 negotiations to arrange Katherine's marriage to Arthur.[76] He had previously served Edward IV by fighting against the house of Lancaster, and he was badly wounded at the battle of Barnet in 1471. The Howards had subsequently been strongly supportive of Richard III, to the extent that Thomas had to go to some lengths to convince Henry VII of his loyalty.[77] The duchess of Norfolk, in whose name the speech of welcome in Spanish is given, is the dowager duchess Elizabeth, widow of John Mowbray, fourth duke of Norfolk. She was a powerful political presence and remained influential in East Anglian affairs for many years.[78] She had accompanied Margaret of York to Burgundy in 1468 when Margaret married Charles the Bold, and Edward IV's second son, Richard, duke of York (who was created duke of Norfolk in February 1477) was married at age four to Elizabeth's daughter, Anne Mowbray, aged five, in 1478.[79] Henry VII famously joined the warring houses of Lancaster and York through his marriage to Elizabeth of York to form the dynasty symbolized by the red-and-white Tudor rose. Staging a ceremony featuring former Yorkist figures in leading roles against a backdrop of a community with historical Lancastrian associations suggests a similar blending of familial traditions.

Just as Amesbury is less known for Lancastrian partisanship than Syon, so too it is less renowned as a center of female monastic learning and literacy. However, if one considers Add. 18632 in relation to the (admittedly rather few) other texts that survive from Amesbury's library, it is possible to discern hints of ways in which the Amesbury nuns' engagement with the Chaucerian tradition might, as at Syon, at once have contributed to a learned, sophisticated textual culture and have intersected with nuns' participation in the realm of politics as advisors and instructors.[80] In addition to Add. 18632, a fourteenth-century manuscript from Amesbury survives that includes the Hours of the Virgin along with various other offices, services, and prayers in Latin and French (Cambridge UL Ee.6.16). This manuscript, which additionally contains hymns to St. Anne in Latin and French, hints that the nuns of Amesbury may have been among those women religious (like Chaucer's translating Second Nun) able to read Latin. It also suggests that some of the nuns could have read religious works in not just one but two vernaculars. Cambridge UL Ee.6.16 thus provides at least potential evidence for a high standard of literacy and learning in the community.[81]

An inscription in Oxford Bodleian Library Add. A 42, the only other complete surviving manuscript definitely associated with Amesbury, gives another, albeit subtle, indication of the reputation of the nuns of Amesbury for literacy and learning.[82] This fifteenth-century manuscript contains an "exhortation addressed to 'My deare systerys Mary and Anne wyth all the other devouth dyscyples of the scole of cryste in youre monastery of Amysbury, be grace and the blessyng of oure lorde euyrlastyng. Amen.'"[83] The description of a female monastic community as the "school of Christ" and the description of nuns as "disciples" in such a school are suggestive of a culture in which education and learning are priorities.[84]

Perhaps, then, the Amesbury nuns would not only have benefited themselves from the didactic and political texts in the Chaucerian tradition in Add. 18632 but might also have seen themselves, and have been seen by others, as able to impart knowledge from such texts to people other than their religious sisters; they perhaps imagined themselves, and were imagined by others, as performing a didactic role not unlike that of the old woman of the Wife of Bath's Tale who educates the miscreant knight on the virtues of age and poverty and the nature of true gentility. Though Amesbury did not operate a school, as did the Dominican nunnery of Dartford, earlier in the house's history, royal women had resided at the convent and received training there.[85] The nuns of Amesbury could readily have felt themselves appropriately placed to offer advice to someone like the young princess Katherine of Aragon, whom they helped welcome and who, it was hoped, would produce the next prince needing grooming for the throne. In this sort of task, the women religious of Amesbury could have found the advice on kingship and spiritually authoritative rule advanced by Lydgate and Hoccleve, and underwritten by the figure of Chaucer, particularly useful.

Taken together, the texts in Laud misc. 416 and Add. 18632 suggest the Syon and Amesbury nuns may well have seen themselves, and have been seen by those outside their communities, as apt and able to learn, and perhaps to impart to others in positions of political power, "knightly" lessons of good government and proper religiopolitical conduct from Chaucer's writings and from texts in the Chaucerian tradition.[86] Lessons concerning the common profit and right rule are possibly not ones we imagine nuns wanting or needing to learn in the first place. When, however, one considers the evidence available about the family backgrounds and connections of the women religious of Syon and Amesbury alongside the evidence we have about what sorts of texts these nuns were reading and when, it becomes clear that just such lessons seem to have been important to at least some later medieval and early modern English monastic women as well as to those who presented manuscripts to them.

CHAUCERIAN POETRY, AESTHETICS, AND SPIRITUAL FORMATION AT SYON

Didactic, politicized texts are not the only works by Chaucer and in the Chaucerian tradition to which the nuns of Syon had access, and lessons concerning the common profit and right rule are not the only lessons the Brigittine women religious may have drawn from the Chaucerian tradition. Another manuscript found in the Syon nuns' library is Oxford, Jesus 39. This text contains a treatise called the *Disce mori*, which also survives in the closely related manuscript Oxford, Bodleian Laud misc. 99.[87] According to Lee Patterson, both the text of the *Disce mori* and Oxford, Jesus 39 date to the middle of the fifteenth century, so this manuscript is roughly contemporaneous with Laud misc. 416.[88] To fix a terminus a quo for the compilation, Patterson points to the compiler's contemptuous reference to Englishmen "so effeminate, hert and body, as þe losyng of France and Guienne shewe at eigh," which refers to the (from the English perspective) ignominious end of the Hundred Years' War in July 1453.[89] E. A. Jones notes other textual evidence also suggesting a date for the compilation in the 1450s.[90]

In Patterson's view the *Disce mori* perhaps was compiled at Syon.[91] Jones, too, finds evidence in the *Disce mori*, as well as in the *Ignorancia Sacerdotum*, derived from it (found in Oxford, Bodleian MS Eng.th.c.57), that suggests, though not definitively, an origin at Syon (*Exhortacion*, xxvii–xxix). While Patterson argues that the *Disce mori* was written for a Brigittine nun, Jones disagrees, as does Ann Hutchison. Jones argues that the text might, though, have been written for the use of Brigittine novices.[92] Whether or not the *Disce mori* was compiled at Syon specifically for Brigittine nuns or novices, at least one Syon nun apparently read it, since her name is inscribed in it. Dorothy Slyght's name appears in a sixteenth-century hand on page iii. If the manuscript was, as Patterson believes, part of the Syon library, it also seems safe to imagine that other Syon nuns read it as well.

The *Disce mori* consists of five parts and a concluding "exhortation to the persone that hit was written to." The treatise is composed of traditional catechetical material largely drawn from a popular, influential manual of religious instruction, the thirteenth-century French text *Miroir du monde* (Jones, *Exhortacion*, x). As Jones points out, the "Exhortacion" is of particular interest, since it represents the first time the compiler specifically tailors his source material to his intended reader's religious status and female gender. It is also the part of the *Disce mori* in which the compiler departs from received models of content and structure, and so has the most scope for invention as he combines his sources to craft his argument. Finally, in the "Exhortacion," the compiler shows particular resourcefulness in selecting his sources (Jones, *Exhortacion*, xiii).

It is this resourceful selection of sources in chapter 17 of the "Exhortation" that is my primary concern. This chapter "opens by discussing obstructions that hinder the full enjoyment of the contemplative life and then turns to an account of how 'flesshly love' (*amor*) undermines 'love spiritual' (*amicitia*)."[93] The account centers on the process of discerning how to distinguish between fleshly and spiritual love, and it begins with a series of poetic quotations, including these lines:

> If no loue is, O god, what fele I so?
> And if love is, what þinge and whiche is he?
> If love be goode, from whens cometh my woo?
> If it be wykke, a wondre þenketh me,
> Sith euery turment and aduersite
> That from it cometh may me sauoury þenke,
> For ay thrust I, þe more þat I it drynke.
> (Jones, Exhortacion, 60)

This passage is taken, of course, from book 1 of Chaucer's *Troilus and Criseyde*. Chaucer takes a place here in a different kind of English canon than the one envisioned by Bokenham, Lydgate, and Hoccleve.[94] Rather than anchoring a lineage of English vernacular poets, he joins the canon of the mainstays of Middle English devotional writing, keeping company with Richard Rolle and Walter Hilton, whose works appear in excerpt along with the passage from *Troilus and Criseyde* in the *Disce mori*. The compiler finds in Chaucer's writing something of legitimate spiritual value, something worthy of inclusion in a manual of religious instruction focused on "the acquisition of self-knowledge and discernment" (Jones, *Exhortacion*, xi) in the tradition of the *Miroir du monde* and *Somme le roi*.[95] Though Thomas Elyot (kinsman of the Fettyplace women discussed above) places the Bible and *Troilus and Criseyde* in very different categories in *Pasquill the Playne* (1533), for the compiler of the *Disce mori*, and for the women religious who read it, the distinction was evidently not so stark.[96]

Patterson argues that the nuns of Syon had access to *Troilus and Criseyde* in their library, while Ann Hutchison on the contrary finds the idea of nuns reading this text in their monastery highly unlikely. Since the library at Syon contained, as we have seen, *The Parliament of Fowls* and the *Siege of Thebes*, I do not find it all that implausible that it could have contained the *Troilus* as well. Though the *Disce mori* is a different kind of didactic literature than the politically oriented, *speculum princeps*–type works found in Laud misc. 416, it is also worth noting that political engagements and fraught relationships with political authority figures may shed light on other respects in which Chaucer's *Troilus and Criseyde* may have appealed to the Syon nuns and so have been a text they wished to possess. While the Brigittine nuns probably did not identify with Criseyde as a participant in a love affair, they might have identified with her affinity for reading politically inflected texts. Chaucer portrays Criseyde as a literate woman; we are told, for instance, that she departs into her chamber "Ful pryvely this lettre for to rede" upon receiving Troilus's missive, and she remarks that it befits her status as a widow to "rede on holy seyntes lyves."[97] Not only is she literate, but she is also interested in the very sort of material that appears in Laud misc. 416 and BL Add. 18632. When Pandarus visits her in her garden, he asks her if she and her ladies are reading a book about love. She replies:

> This romaunce is of Thebes that we rede;
> And we han herd how that kyng Layus deyde
> Thorough Edippus his sone, and al that dede;
> And here we stynten at thise lettres rede—
> How the bisshop, as the book kan telle,
> Amphiorax, fil thorugh the ground to helle.[98]

Given the Brigittine Order's emphasis on female authority within the monastic community, including the subordination of the confessor general to the abbess, the Syon nuns might also have felt sympathetic toward Criseyde's reluctance to surrender the freedom from male authority she had realized as a widow, an autonomy she foregrounds when she says:

> I am myn owene womman, wel at ese—
> I thank it God—as after myn estat,
> Right yong, and stonde unteyd in lusty leese,
> Withouten jalousie or swich debat:
> Shal noon housbonde seyn to me "Chek mat!"[99]

Additionally, especially in the early sixteenth century, the Brigittine nuns might have felt an affinity with Criseyde's politically vulnerable position, as Wright suggests Margaret More Roper seems to have done. In any case, even if *Troilus and Criseyde* was not part of the Syon nuns' library apart from its presence in the *Disce mori*, by invoking Chaucer's text in the way that he does, the compiler of the *Disce mori* encourages the nuns, or nuns-to-be, to draw, in spiritually productive ways, on knowledge that they had likely already acquired before entering religion, given the literate habits of their families of origin, whether or not they continued to have ready access in religion to the text of *Troilus and Criseyde* as a whole.[100]

One might argue that *Troilus and Criseyde*'s fundamental role in the "Exhortacion" is to serve as a negative exemplar, an illustration of what to avoid. This is certainly part of the compiler's aim. As Patterson argues, the compiler reads *Troilus and Criseyde* as "an accurate (and dangerously imitable) depiction of human conduct." *Troilus and Criseyde* is for the compiler "a text to be read literally; i.e., as an exemplary text."[101] In the "Exhortacion" *Troilus and Criseyde* is not, though, simply an example of vice to stand as a foil to virtue. As Talbot Donaldson remarked long ago, *Troilus and Criseyde* resists easy summation to a *moralitee*, even though it presents what seems a relatively straightforward one.[102] Patterson, too, acknowledges that there is more than exemplarity and moralization at play in the compiler's treatment of Chaucer's text.

The Myroure of Oure Ladye, which was written for the Syon nuns, contains detailed instructions on the relationships among reading, monastic identity formation, and proper devotion. Considering what the *Myroure* tells us about what and how the Syon nuns should read helps illuminate what significances beyond exemplarity *Troilus and Criseyde* might have had for the Brigittine sisters. The *Myroure* specifies that the nuns are to read "no worldely matters ne worldely bokes namely suche as ar without reason of gostly edyfycacyon."[103] Since the *Disce mori* is at least possibly a Syon product, and since it was clearly read there, one can plausibly argue that the Brigittines placed *Troilus and Criseyde* with the works of Rolle and Hilton in the category of texts that provide "ghostly edyfycacyon" rather than in the category of worldly, and hence prohibited, books. Strikingly, though Criseyde says that it properly befits her status as a widow to "bidde and rede on holy seyntes lyves," the nuns of Syon, and whoever compiled the *Disce mori*, seem to have taken a broader view of what constituted proper ways for women religious to spend their time and what sorts of texts were appropriate for them to read.[104]

Furthermore, as Patterson observes, the compiler models a very literary and appreciative reading of Chaucer in which "moral interpretation . . . comes in the form of literary appreciation."[105] Significantly, then, in detailing the categories of books Brigittine nuns should read, *The Myroure of Oure Ladye* encourages the reading of texts that "sturre vp oure afeccyons of love and hope."[106] Appropriately, the compiler not only models a literary, appreciative reading of Chaucer but also highlights the literary and the aesthetic in the service of the text's didactic aims. One way in which the compiler foregrounds the roles for the literary and the aesthetic in advancing the text's didactic mission by "stirring up affections" is to introduce the *Disce mori* with three stanzas of original rhyme royal, the very stanza Chaucer uses in the *Troilus*. The first of the compiler's verse stanzas dedicates the work to his "best-loued sustre Dame Alice, / Whiche þat for Cristes loue haue hole forsake / þe worlde, þe flesh and þe feendes malice" (Jones, *Exhortacion*, ix). The second explicitly sets out the didactic aims of the *Disce mori*, stating:

> Hit techeth wele to lyue, and to eschewe
> Vices whiche hit declareth sufficiently
> The seuen capital; and also to sue
> Þe vertues contrarie to þe seuen.
>   (Jones, *Exhortacion*, ix)

The presentation in poetry of this description of the reader's identity (as one who for Christ's love has forsaken the world, the flesh, and the devil) and these instructions in verse for using the treatise to achieve spiritual success (by eschewing vices and pursuing virtues) emphasize the compiler's concern for the place of the aesthetic in a didactic work designed to guide the nuns toward spiritual advancement.

The scribe who annotated, corrected, and added chapter headings in Oxford, Jesus 39, evidently perceived the significance the compiler assigned to Chaucer and to aesthetic aspects of the text.[107] This scribe made an addition to the end of the section of the "Exhortacion" concerning the "viithe tokene of flesshly loue," in which the compiler earlier incorporates the stanza from *Troilus and Criseyde*. Also adopting verse as the vehicle for his didactic message, the scribe says in a rhymed couplet, "Of which poison if ye lust more to rede, / Seeþ þe storie of Troilus, Criseide & Dyomede" (Jones, *Exhortacion*, 61). The sixteenth-century politician Sir James Perrot, who donated the manuscript to Oxford in March of 1634, also apparently discerned the attention the compiler had paid to literary and aesthetic qualities, though he is admittedly somewhat dismissive in his assessment of those qualities in the *Disce mori*. In a note added on a blank leaf at the beginning of the manuscript, Perrot indicates, "The phrase, though playne according to words then in vse, yet significant inough, *and more then ordinary for the then maner of wretting*" (quoted in Jones, *Exhortacion*, ix, emphasis added).[108]

The sort of spiritual self-fashioning that Brigittine nuns or nuns-to-be undertake in reading the *Disce mori* thus involves aesthetic, affective components. Spiritual advancement occurs via the reader's sensory and sensual experiences of the text, via their emotional engagement with it. The value of *Troilus and Criseyde* for the compiler of the *Disce mori* thus rests not simply in the story that Chaucer tells, but rather also in the ways in which Chaucer tells that story, in the poetry and the affective components thereof. *Troilus and Criseyde* thus is a particularly fitting companion in the *Disce mori* to the works of Richard Rolle, since Rolle places considerable spiritual importance on affect and the senses. Rolle, for instance, presents saying or reading the psalms as a glorious, multi-sensual experience. In the opening passage of his *English Psalter* he writes: "Grete habundance of gastli cumforth and ioy in God cummes into þe hertes of þame þat saies or synges deuouteli þe psalms of þe sauter in louing of Ihesu Crist. Þay drop swettnes in mans saule and helles delite into þaire thoghtes and kindilles þaire wylles with fyre of louf, makand þaim hote and brynand within and faire and luffli to Cristes eghen. And þay þat lastes in þaire deuoucioune þai raise þaim in contemplatif lyffue and oft sithes [in] sonne and mirth of heuen."[109]

The positive valence granted to aesthetic dimensions of textuality in the *Disce mori* aligns, furthermore, with distinctive aspects of Brigittine textual culture, a culture shaped by the Brigittine Order's privileging of desire for texts and by a Brigittine emphasis on the importance of the materiality of texts. Roger Ellis, commenting on the Brigittine Rule's provisions for allowing the nuns extensive access to books for learning and study, points out, "Religious, indeed, are to have these books not as they need, but rather as they want, them."[110] In the Latin version of the Brigittine Rule, the place of desire in Brigittine textual culture is even clearer than in the Middle English *Rewyll of Seynt Sauioure*. The Latin reads, "Illos vero libros habeant, quotquot voluerint" (they should have as many books as they wish).[111] The legitimate desire for texts emphasized by the Brigittine Rule translated in the later fifteenth and sixteenth centuries into a sense of strong spiritual value attached to books as material objects. Over the course of the fifteenth century the central importance of the material book to the Syon nuns, both before and after entering religion, intensified significantly.[112] By the beginning of the sixteenth century "readers at Syon had come to consider their books, and not just the words in the books, as intermediaries between themselves and God."[113] In other words, for the Brigittine nuns of Syon, in reading, form matters and the material matters. It is thus not surprising that the aesthetic and the literary, the sensory and the sensual aspects of texts, would also matter and would be taken seriously as components of devotional practice and spiritual formation.

One suspects the Brigittine nuns and the compiler of the *Disce mori* (quite possibly a Syon brother, and thus a sort of nuns' priest himself) of feeling a sense of affinity with the sentiments expressed by Chaucer's Nun's Priest at the end of his tale: "For Seint Paul seith that al that written is, / To oure doctrine it is ywrite, ywis; / Taketh the fruyt, and lat the chaf be stille" (VII 3441–43).[114] For the compiler and for the Syon nuns, what one might expect to be chaff in *Troilus and Criseyde*—including its explicitly literary qualities—may actually be fruit after all. In the treatment of *Troilus and Criseyde* in the *Disce mori* one glimpses an expression of an understanding that sensory, even sensual, delight in the literary qualities of a text is part of the way in which the text teaches lessons that may be at once of use in this world and the next.

CHAPTER 3

Competing Chaucers

The Development of Religious Traditions of Reception

The late 1520s and early 1530s were, it is an understatement to say, a pivotal and uncertain time in English religious and political history. They were also pivotal years for the development of the Chaucer canon and the establishment of religiously inflected traditions of Chaucerian reception. This chapter first considers the emergence in the late 1520s and early 1530s of two strands of Chaucer reception that compete with each other through subsequent centuries. In this period, we find the origins of the proto-Protestant Chaucer as a "right Wicclevian" (the Chaucer who would largely dominate the English early modern era), promoted in the later sixteenth century by John Foxe, as well as Chaucer the orthodox Catholic poet, an interpretation embraced, as I discuss in the next chapter, by Dryden and by Catholic controversialists in the middle to late seventeenth century. Because the early modern reception of the proto-Protestant Chaucer is so well known, after presenting the contours of the emergence of this tradition alongside the emergence of the Catholic tradition of reception in the first part of this chapter, I will concentrate in the latter part on texts from the 1550s through the 1580s in which the Catholic strand of Chaucer reception develops. Representing this Catholic tradition are St. Thomas More's *Dialogue concerning Heresies*, William Forrest's *History of Grisild the Second* (1558), and other religious writings that Forrest produced in a manuscript (BL Harley 1703) on which he worked possibly into the early 1580s.[1] In these texts, questions concerning gender, religious and political legitimacy, and proper devotional practices—questions that, as we have seen, inform English monastic women's engagements with Chaucer and the Chaucer tradition—remain prominent. A nexus of overlapping debates about literary canon formation, the nature of the true English church, and representations of English dynastic histories that are central to the seventeenth- and eighteenth-century texts treated in the final two chapters of this book also emerge perceptibly in Forrest's engagements with Chaucer and the Chaucer tradition in the second half of the sixteenth century.

Thynne's 1532 Chaucer and the English Reformation

1532 was a very important year for both the history of Chaucer reception and the history of the English Protestant Reformation. In 1532, Henry VIII promulgated the Act for Submission of the Clergy, establishing his authority over the English ecclesiastical establishment.[2] In the same year, William Thynne published his edition of Chaucer's works, which added significantly to the Chaucer canon as it had been printed by Pynson in 1526. Given this convergence, and given that Thynne's edition was dedicated to Henry VIII, it is not surprising that, as Greg Walker observes, the 1532 edition is frequently associated with Henry VIII's reformation politics.[3] The dominant version of this reading has been to associate Thynne's Chaucer with advancing ecclesiastical reform, particularly reform focused on clerical abuses of power.[4] In this view, Thynne's edition meets a need for the presentation of Chaucer as a magisterial figure not afraid to take on ecclesiastical, and especially papal, authority.[5] In those first years of the 1530s, the idea of a Wycliffite Chaucer, of Chaucer as the Reformation proto-Protestant hero, was clearly beginning to take shape, even if it was not as fully developed at this point in the sixteenth century as some have argued. Lollardy would, as Foxe's appellation for Chaucer demonstrates, eventually come to be strongly associated with Chaucer and the Chaucer tradition in early modern reception. Though the Lollard Plowman's Tale was not included in Thynne's 1532 edition (it was added in the 1542 edition), it was first printed separately sometime between 1532 and 1536 by Thomas Godfrey. Furthermore, the early 1530s saw the publication of numerous Lollard texts, including William Thorpe's account of his heresy trial, John Oldcastle's *Testament*, and *The Praier and Complaynte of the Plowman unto Christe*.[6] Henry VIII and others interested in ecclesiastical reform were also attracted to Lollardy and Wycliffite thought in the early 1530s. Henry wrote on August 2, 1530, to the convocation of the University of Oxford asking for Wycliffe's articles that resulted in his condemnation as well as the judgments pronounced by the Council of Constance upholding the condemnation.[7]

Though Walker ultimately argues for a less direct relationship between the 1532 Chaucer and Henry VIII's Reformation propaganda efforts, he concedes that there is some truth to the idea that Thynne's presentation of Chaucer did contribute to royal representational projects and also supported England's attempts to create the concept of an English empire separate, in both religious and secular terms, from that of Rome.[8] Walker's more nuanced argument, however, is that Thynne, and Brian Tuke, who wrote the preface to the 1532 edition and who likely had a significant collaborative role in the production of the edition, did not primarily intend to present Chaucer as a Lollard sympathizer or proto-Protestant. Rather, they had a more moderate agenda, aiming to provide guidance on the proper uses of literature in politically and religiously uncertain times.[9] Thynne's reputation as a radical reformer largely stems from the biographical sketch his son, Francis Thynne, wrote of his father—a sketch written many years after the 1532 edition about a father who died when Francis was two years old.[10] Significantly, Tuke and Thynne included among Chaucer's works texts like the "Ballad of Commendation of Our Lady" (actually a conflation of two poems probably written by Lydgate) that suggest they evidently had no problems accepting Chaucer as a conventional Catholic.[11] Walker argues that the way in which Thynne and Tuke frame Chaucer's works with poems by Chaucer and others shapes a particular vision of the figure of Chaucer to guide Henry VIII toward a specific reading of Chaucer and the Chaucer tradition. Much as Chaucer was a didactic and politicized figure for the later medieval and early modern monastic readers discussed in the previous chapter, in Thynne and Tuke's presentation, too, Chaucer is both a political and moral authority who serves to guide princes needing advice.[12]

This more moderate view of the role of the 1532 edition of Chaucer also harmonizes with the fact that, in spite of his interest in Wycliffe, Henry VIII would come to want to dissociate himself from Lollardy. Significantly, he would invoke Chaucer as part of that process of dissociation. To help to differentiate his theology from Lollardy, Henry VIII promulgated the "Acte for thadvancement of the true Religion and for thabolishment of the contrarie" of 1543.[13] This act prohibits publication of works written in English prior to 1540 except authorized editions of the Bible, "Canterburye tales, Chaucers bokes, Gowers bokes and stories of mennes lieues."[14] So the figure of Chaucer who becomes for John Foxe a "right Wicclevian," while visibly emergent in the 1530s, has at the important moment of canon formation in the 1530s and 1540s more subtle dimensions.

St. Thomas More's *Dialogue concerning Heresies*: Chaucerian Strategies and the Catholic Response to the Henrician Reformation

1532 saw another major event involving a figure with a key role in the development of religiously inflected literary adoptions of Chaucer. On May 16 of that year, Thomas More resigned his chancellorship. As we saw in chapter 2, Thomas More's daughter Margaret More Roper drew upon *Troilus and Criseyde* in a discussion with her father about signing the Act of Allegiance, modeling the religiopolitical engagements with Chaucer that characterized those of English women religious in the fifteenth and sixteenth centuries. A few years prior to 1532, in an early contribution to the religious polemical writing that would come to occupy him through much of the rest of his life, Thomas More himself turned to Chaucer in the context of politico-religious debate. In 1529, More published the *Dialogue concerning Heresies* (which appeared in a second edition in 1531), a text in which Chaucer features importantly. This text provides an early instance of the sixteenth-century presentation of Chaucer as a representative of English Catholic orthodoxy, a presentation that crystallizes in Forrest's texts and is taken up by Dryden as well as by Catholic controversialists in the seventeenth century. As with the reform-minded but moderate Chaucer of Thynne and Tuke's 1532 edition, though, the Catholic Chaucer as presented in much of More's 1529 text is a somewhat more complex, ambiguous figure than he would later become. Indeed, the *Dialogue* in some respects bears witness to the transition, since the Chaucerian strategies More employs shift by the end of the work.

In 1528, Cuthbert Tunstal, bishop of London, licensed More to read German books translated into English that were deemed heretical so that More could write a response "for the 'simple and unlearned' ('simplicibus et idiotis hominibus')."[15] This response to the ideas of Martin Luther and William Tyndale is the *Dialogue concerning Heresies*, which, in spite of Tunstal's directive, is itself neither simple nor unlearned. With the publication of the *Dialogue*, More transitioned from advising the king on theology to occupying the role of "public defender of the faith."[16] Though not explicitly a didactic text in the same way that William Forrest's *History*, discussed below, is, the *Dialogue* is, as the title indicates, structured around scenes of conversation, and these conversations have distinctly pedagogical, didactic imperatives. The premise for the work is that More is visited by a university student, sent to him by an old friend in order to receive counsel and advice about matters of theological controversy in which the student has become interested. The young man, called the Messenger, comes to More's house for a series of six conversations that take place over the space of four days. In these conversations, More seeks to disabuse the Messenger of his enthusiasm for evangelical ideas, striving to refute the views of Luther and Tyndale while making the case for orthodox Catholic faith and practices. Central to More's methods are the incorporation of Chaucerian allusions and references and, even more importantly, the adoption of Chaucerian narrative strategies and personae.

More and members of his circle knew Chaucer well. More's extended family included several devoted Chaucerians. His brother-in-law John Rastell printed the *Parliament of Foules* in 1525. More's personal secretary, Walter Smyth, wrote *The Twelve Merry Jests of the Widow Edith*, featuring a main character much in the vein of the Wife of Bath; Smyth also bequeathed a volume of Chaucer to Thomas More's son, John More. Additionally, John Heywood, son-in-law to More's sister, wrote an interlude entitled *The Pardoner and the Frere*, which includes word for word several speeches from the Pardoner's Tale.[17] More's own familiarity with Chaucer seems to have been quite deep. Alistair Fox argues compellingly that More does not, in incorporating Chaucer's writings, rely on a commonplace book but instead draws upon the experience actually of reading of *The Canterbury Tales*.[18] More makes numerous allusions to Chaucer in the *Dialogue* and includes some direct references. For instance, he twice mentions the Pardoner and his false relics, specifically the Pardoner's "bone of some holy Jewes shepe."[19] His use of *The Canterbury Tales* is largely consistent with interpretive trends of the sixteenth century in that he finds Chaucer to be a source of proverbial, sentential wisdom; More often develops Chaucerian references into proverbial sentiments.[20]

More does not, though, simply incorporate allusions and references to Chaucer into the *Dialogue*. He also employs what Fox terms Chaucer's "representational mode."[21] It is toward More's less direct, but highly suggestive, mobilization of Chaucer in the *Dialogue* that I wish to turn now. In the *Dialogue*, More strives to craft persuasive arguments to convince the Messenger and his readers of the truth of the Catholic side of the raging religious controversy of the late 1520s, and his rhetorical strategies rely on his adoption of Chaucerian personae and the use of Chaucerian techniques. Anne Lake Prescott has noted how different the *Dialogue* is from More's previous entry into polemical debate, the *Responsio ad Lutherum*. The *Dialogue* exhibits more joviality and includes quite a few entertaining stories.[22] Indeed, More's reliance on "merry tales" to make his points in the *Dialogue* contributes importantly to the Chaucerian qualities of the text. At the end of the *Dialogue*, however, when More moves away from comparatively tolerant positions to argue for the necessity of executing heretics, he adopts a different sort of Chaucerian strategy.

The character More develops for himself throughout most of the *Dialogue* to serve as an interlocutor with the Messenger resembles the self-effacing, humorous Chaucer character who appears in *The Canterbury Tales*, *The House of Fame*, and the prologue to *The Legend of*

Good Women. Like the character Chaucer creates for himself, More's self-representation as "Mayster Chauncellour" provides a protective fiction as he ventures into controversial territory.[23] Also like Chaucer's persona, More's character is self-deprecating, willing to make jokes about himself and so perhaps deflect criticism. For example, in chapter 31 of part 1, as part of a discussion of the proper means of interpreting Scripture, the Messenger says to More, "I haue another tale to tell you that all thys gere graunted / tournyth vs yet in to as moche vncertaynte as we were in before" (185). More replies with a Chaucerian jest, invoking Pandarus as he says, "Ye . . . than haue we well walked after the balade, The further I go the more behynde" (185).

Furthermore, More as presented in the *Dialogue* enjoys, and tells, many "merry tales," tales that resonate both with Chaucerian fabliaux and with Chaucerian clerical satire.[24] More gestures toward Chaucerian bawdiness reminiscent of the Wife of Bath's Prologue in a conversation with the Messenger about how the Messenger knows the truth of Scripture. More asks, "But how be ye sure that ye matter of the boke is trewe?" (180). The Messenger, somewhat shocked, replies, "Mary . . . for I am" (180). More responds, "That is . . . the reason that a mayde layeth for her owne knowledge of her maydenhed. But she coulde tell another howe she knoweth she hath hit / sauying that she is lothe to come so nere as to be a knower that she coulde tell howe she myght lese it. But here is no suche fere" (180). Similarly, in a discussion of the possibility that witnesses to miracles may be false, the Messenger tells a story of a poor man who finds his wife in a compromising position with a priest and is then forced to deny what he saw in an act of public penance for having told others what he witnessed. The *Dialogue* here channels the end of the Merchant's Tale, when Januarie and May debate whether Januarie did or did not see May copulating in a pear tree with Damian. The Messenger's poor man is forced to say in church, "Mouth thou lyest," to which he adds, "but eyen . . . by the masse ye lye not a whytte" (69). More's eponymous character reacts heartily to this story, saying, "A mery tale . . . commyth neuer amysse to me" (69).

The Chaucerian (false) dichotomies of earnest and game, as well as of experience and authority, also operate significantly in More's development of a Chaucerian persona and his adoption of Chaucerian strategies. More's reliance on merry tales in the *Dialogue* suggests the sort of slippage of categories between earnest and game so characteristic of much of *The Canterbury Tales*, in which jokes and humor are serious business indeed and in which, as in the Friar's Tale, intent makes all the difference. Much as at the end of the Nun's Priest's Tale, when what counts as fruit and what counts as chaff remain an open question, for More in the *Dialogue* what is "earnest" and what is "game" cannot be readily separated or even easily distinguished. What More says in the *Apology* applies equally to the *Dialogue*: one "may sometimes say full truth in jest."[25]

Similarly, in refuting the Messenger's argument that the study of Scripture and grammar are all that are necessary, in combatting evangelists' doctrine of *sola Scriptura et sola fides*, More advances a position combining authority (Scripture as well as Catholic doctrine) and experience (in the form of reason and "good mother wyt" [132]) that resonates with Chaucer's dual reliance on experience and authority outlined in the Prologue to *The Legend of Good Women*, where the narrator acknowledges the importance of what is experienced personally but also argues for the importance of giving credence to "olde appreved stories" and "olde bokes."[26] More's position also resembles that of the Wife of Bath in her Prologue, in which she masterfully turns textual authorities to her purpose even while attesting the authority of her own experience. For example, in rebutting the Messenger's argument that reason is the "enemy" of faith in reading Scripture, More evokes the earthy, embodied logic of the Wife of Bath to argue for the importance of bringing human experience in the form of reason to bear on the authority of the text: "Nowe in the study of scripture, in deuysynge vpon the sentence / in considerynge what ye rede / in pondering the purpose of diuers commentes / in comparynge togyder dyuers textes that seme contrary and be not / albeit I denye not but that grace & goddes especyall help is the great thynge therin / yet vseth he for an instrument mannes reason therto. God helpeth vs to ete, but yet not without our mouth" (131–32). Reason, like the mouth, is an instrument given to humans by God to be employed with God's grace to help to sustain the soul and strengthen faith, not undermine it—just as employing the mouth to eat allows the nourishing and strengthening of the body.

Likewise, employing reason in studying Scripture and in studying the liberal arts enables humans to improve and strengthen that instrument, just as practice improves the performance of the hands and exercise strengthens the body. Much as the Wife of Bath argues for using the organs God has given us for their proper purposes (as well as, she implies, for pleasure), so More argues for using the capabilities God has given us for their fit purposes, since doing so can augment, rather than undermine, faith.[27]

For all his Chaucerian geniality, for all his pragmatism, his balancing of earnest with game and experience with authority, More undeniably and unambiguously turns at the end of the *Dialogue* to argue forcefully for the necessity of executing heretics. He states, for example:

> And surely as the prynces be bounden yt they shall not suffer theyr people by infydels to be inuaded / so be they as deeply bounden that they shall not suffer theyr people to be Seduced and corrupted by heretykes / syth the parell shall in shorte whyle growe to as grete / bothe with mennes soules withdraen from god / and theyr goodes lost / and theyr Bodyes destroyed by comen sedycyon / insurreccyon / and open warre / within ye bowelles of theyr owne lande. All whiche maye in the begynnynge be right easely auoydded / by punysshment of thosre fewe tht be the fyrste. Whiche fewe well repressed / or yf need so require vtterly pulled vp / there shall farre the fewer haue lust to folowe. (415–16)

And it is worth remembering that in his years as chancellor (1529–32), six evangelicals were burned as heretics.[28]

In the end, More adopts another Chaucerian strategy—that of the retraction. More abandons the form of dialogue; as James Simpson notes, the *Dialogue concerning Heresies* is More's last use of the form for religious polemic, and he does not return to it until he is defeated and imprisoned in the Tower of London. More also turns away from merry tales. Like Chaucer in the retraction, who rejects those writings "that sownen into synne" and turns his back on "many a song and many a leccherous lay," More abandons "fiction, or what his enemies called 'poetry.'"[29] Poetry is something More had previously defended with eloquence in the *Dialogue*, saying, "Albeit poetes ben with many men taken but for paynted words / yet do thei moche helpe the iudgement," furnishing the all-important "good mother wyt" without which "all lernynge is halfe lame" (132). The Chaucer that More channels by the end of the *Dialogue* though is no longer a figure who can engage in bawdy or humorous banter for serious ends. Rather, this Chaucer whose strategies More emulates is the orthodox Catholic who produced "the translacion of Boece de Consolacione, and othere books of legends of seintes, and omelies, and moralitee, and devocioun." This is the Chaucer who ends *The Canterbury Tales* contemplating the fate of his soul and incorporating an orthodox Catholic prayer seeking grace from "Lord Jhesu Crist and his blisful Mooder and alle the seintes of hevyne. . . . *Qui cum Patre et Spiritu Sancto vivit et regnat Deus per omnia secula. Amen.*"[30] Indeed, the *Dialogue*, too, ends with a vision of the last judgment and a prayer that Christ

> shall make all folke one flocke vnder hym selfe the shepeherde / and shall delyuer a glorious kyngdome to his father of all the saued people from our foremare father Adam to ye last day / from thens forth to reygne in heuyn in ioy & blysse incogytable one euerlastyng day with his father hym selfe & the holy goost / which sende these dedycyous sects the grace to ceace / & the fauourers of those faccyons to amende / & vs the grace yt stoppynge our eres from the false enchauntementes of all these heretykes / we may by the very faith of Crystes catholyke chyrche so walke with charyte in the way of good warkes in this wretched worlde / that we may be parteners of the hevenly blysse / whiche the blood of goddess owne sonne hath bought vs vnto. (435)

More's character then remarks, "And this prayer quod I seruynge vs for grace / let vs nowe syt downe to dyner. Which we dyd" (435). And that brings us to the end of the text, which closes, "And after dyner departed he home towarde you / and I to the courte" (435). Just as Chaucer's pondering of his own final judgment and the writing of the prayer that concludes the retraction put an end to his tale telling, so for More this apocalyptic prayer for the destruction of heretics and the salvation of the faithful ends dialogue, conversation, and the telling of merry tales. The Chaucer More channels at the end of book 4 of the *Dialogue* has transformed from a jovial provider of merry tales and sentential wisdom to the resolutely orthodox Catholic poet of William Forrest, as well as of John Dryden and of the Catholic controversialists involved in the "Stillingfleet Controversy" whom I discuss in the next chapter.

WILLIAM FORREST'S CHAUCER: CATHOLIC FEMALE VIRTUE AND THE MAINTENANCE OF THE PUBLIC GOOD

In chapter 1, I argue that Chaucer's nuns and their tales provided an opportunity for him to participate in contemporary debates about women's religious speech and their roles as didactic figures in politico-religious affairs. In chapter 2, I explore ways in which actual later medieval and early modern monastic women engage with texts by Chaucer and in the Chaucer tradition dealing with such topics as good government and right rule. I consider that perhaps these women saw themselves, and were seen by those presenting them with manuscripts, as positioned to offer advice to those in positions of political power. In my analysis of William Forrest's writings in this chapter, I want to examine a different configuration of the intersection of gendered political authority, Chaucer's writings, and the provision of royal advice.

William Forrest was a royal chaplain to Queen Mary, and he presented the *History of Grisild the Second* to her in 1558.[31] Prior to this royal service, he had been at Oxford in 1530, when Henry VIII sent to the university to procure a judgment in favor of his proposal to divorce Katherine of Aragon. Additionally, Forrest was also present at Katherine of Aragon's funeral at Peterborough in 1536, so he was an eyewitness to arguments and events he brings into his reworking of the Griselda story. Forrest also, earlier in his career, wrote for the Protestant Edmund, duke of Somerset, dedicating to him the *Pleasant Poesye of Princelie Practise* and some psalm paraphrases. Though some have argued that this choice of patron indicates Forrest was willing to change his religion to accommodate that of the ruler, in fact sections of the *Pleasant Poesye* resonate quite strikingly with Forrest's *History* and his other, later writings, suggesting significant consistence and continuity in his views. [32] Furthermore, after Mary's death, Forrest dedicated his *History of Joseph* to the Catholic Thomas Howard, duke of Norfolk, who received the work shortly before his execution. Forrest's name also appears, along with the dates 1572 and 1581 (perhaps—the latter date could also be 1561, and his death date is unknown but is given by Peter Holmes in the *Oxford Dictionary of National Biography* as 1576 or shortly thereafter), in MS Harley 1703, a collection of Catholic devotional treatises and verse focusing on the Virgin Mary on which Forrest evidently worked for many years while living under the rule of the Protestant Elizabeth. [33]

Forrest spent much of his life in an age of female rule, also an age in which Catholicism was strongly associated with transgressive femininity by Protestant reformers and polemicists. As Forrest ponders questions of royal and religious authority and considers how rulers should be advised, he turns to a different part of the Chaucerian corpus than those which occupied the female monastic readers of Amesbury and Syon whom I consider in the previous chapter. While the nuns read *The Parliament of Fowls* and excerpts from *Troilus and Criseyde*, along with Lydgate's *Siege of Thebes* and Hoccleve's *Regiment of Princes*, in the context of works that model proper behavior and position them potentially to provide political advice, Forrest turns instead to the Clerk's Tale, retelling the story of Griselda and Walter with the starring roles played by Katherine of Aragon and Henry VIII. His retelling also associates Chaucer with a type of Marian piety and forms of female devotion in some ways quite different from those found among the nuns who engaged with Chaucerian texts or in Chaucer's own work.

Chaucer's Clerk's Tale helps Forrest to reanimate a Catholic, medieval past that was an age of female virtue and Catholic religious devotion. In earlier work, I argue that later medieval and early modern writers often adopted a strategy of "cloistering" such politically engaged women writers as Christine de Pizan and such politically active women as Isabel of Castile, mother of Katherine of Aragon.[34] In many respects, Forrest's *History of Grisild the Second* represents another iteration of this strategy, one that draws upon the authority of Chaucer to advocate a feminine, Catholic, nonthreatening mode of queenship. Thomas Betteridge contrasts Forrest's vision of Queen Mary with that of John Heywood in *The Spider and the Fly*, saying that while Heywood's Mary jettisons the past and restores order in the present, Forrest's Mary is instead returned to the past.[35] I would add, she is returned by Forrest to a particular version of the past—the medieval, Catholic past envisioned as an age of "cloistered" women who are chaste, passive, silent on matters of religious controversy and political conflict, obedient to male authority figures, and occupied with traditional devotional practices of prayer, contemplation, and good works. That Catholic, medieval past continued to live in Katherine of Aragon embodied as Griselda in the *History*, and Forrest means by his presentation of her exemplary life to ensure that this past is revived in Mary and perpetuated in the lives of the offspring he hopes she will have.

Because of the strong support it expresses for Katharine of Aragon, Forrest's *History of Grisild the Second* might initially seem to be an instance of imitation of what Amanda Holton describes as Chaucer's sympathy for women, especially wronged women.[36] I would argue, however, that instead this text written for one queen about another seeks carefully to restrict women's political agency though the imposition of a model of female conduct predicated on an idealized interpretation of medieval, female Catholic devotion. Forrest's prescriptions for female virtue and ideal queenship minimize possibilities for women's activities in the religiopolitical spheres, particularly the sorts of didactic, autonomous activity represented by the Second Nun and her St. Cecilia, or by the Wife of Bath, or by the nuns of Syon and Amesbury. In the *History of Grisild the Second*, and elsewhere in Forrest's writings, the preservation of English religious orthodoxy, which is Roman Catholic orthodoxy, and the assurance of the proper government of the realm depend on the maintenance of these modes of female conduct and female devotion. As he will do for Dryden and the Catholic controversialists whom I discuss in the following chapter, "Father Chaucer" proves quite useful in Forrest's efforts to mobilize yet manage medieval legacies and to assert fairly narrowly constrained roles for women in religious and political affairs. As I argue in the final chapter, though, the active, vocal, didactic women of the Chaucerian tradition like the Second Nun and the Wife of Bath do not disappear from the scene, and will come to have a role of their own to play in the writings of the New England poet Anne Bradstreet, who participated in the political and religious controversies of her day.

Forrest's choice to adapt the Clerk's Tale is rather odd in some regards. Forrest makes his association of Katherine with Griselda and Walter with Henry VIII quite explicit; he is not writing an allegory or merely suggesting similarity. However, there is significant variance between the plot points of the Walter and Griselda story and the life history of Katherine of Aragon. While the Griselda of the Clerk's Tale is "povreliche yfostred up,"[37] Katherine of Aragon comes from Spanish royalty, a background that Forrest assigns to his Griselda—her father being, as he says, "one *Ferdynande*, / Kynge of *Spayne* and *Cicilye* also" (26)[38] rather than poor Janicula. Walter's rejection of Griselda in the Clerk's Tale is temporary, and he never actually intends to take a new queen, but of course Henry VIII's rejection of Katherine of Aragon is permanent, and he does in fact take Anne Boleyn as a new queen. And much of the real pathos of Griselda's story in the Clerk's Tale resides in her acquiescence to what she believes to be the death of her children— children who are in fact safe and with whom she is reunited. Katherine of Aragon's first child does actually die (a death that Forrest treats at length), and Forrest presents no forward-looking, joyful reunion of Katherine and Mary. Once mother and daughter are separated, they are not reunited until Katherine is on her deathbed. So, while the Clerk's Tale gives us, however problematically, a happily ever after ending (an ending admittedly complicated by the Clerk's own glossing of the tale, by his introduction of the figure of the Wife of Bath into that gloss, and by the "Envoy de Chaucer" that follows), Katherine's life and Forrest's text offer no such options for happily ever after.

Griselda's attraction as a model of female virtue outweighs these problems, though, and indeed Forrest makes a virtue of necessity, capitalizing on the divergences to argue that Katherine is actually an even better embodiment of virtue than Chaucer's Griselda. He indicates that "the *Seconde Grysilde*" is "of more authorytee" because "she was a *Christian*, the other an *Ethnyke*, she a noble woman of byrthe and delicatlye brought upp . . . thother farre base[r] broght upp in penury and hardenes" (21). Furthermore, drawing upon very Chaucerian terminology, Forrest continues: "Somuche as is betweene *earnest* and *game*, so was the unkyndenes done to this *Seconde Grisilde* of more ympor-taunce then to the *Firste*, for she, relinquysched, was received agayne, *so* did her *Walter* but dissemble withe her. But this *Seconde Grysilde*, deposed of her honour, was neaver thearto reeaved agayne, so was she cruellye used and dallied witheall" (21). Forrest's use of the evocative pairing of "earnest and game," categories so important in More's adop-tion of Chaucerian strategies, is one of the reasons I am persuaded For-rest is working with Chaucer's Clerk's Tale, which, although other ver-sions of the story were certainly available in the 1550s, was likely the most familiar version of the Griselda story to readers of his era.[39] In-deed, the Clerk himself gestures toward the juxtaposition of earnest and game that appears so frequently in *The Canterbury Tales* with the closing couplet of his tale that precedes the "Lenvoy de Chaucer": "And lat us stynte of ernestful matere. / Herkneth my song that seith in this manere."[40] Though Forrest does not mention Chaucer by name in the *History of Grisild the Second*, there are significant dimensions of his presentation of his Griselda/Katherine that evoke other parts of Chaucer's work, adding to the Chaucerian atmosphere of the text.[41] Be-fore launching into his verse *History*, Forrest includes a lengthy "table directing to the chief and principall poyntes of this Booke by ordre of Chapiters" (7). Offering a detailed, itemized summary of the key points of each chapter, the "table" suggests Forrest's strong desire to guide readers' interpretation, to highlight what aspects of the *History* are wor-thy of particular consideration. The synopsis of chapter 2 in the "table" evokes another passive, patient Chaucerian woman to shape readers' perceptions of Griselda/Katherine—that is, Custance of the Man of Law's Tale. As readers of the Man of Law's Tale will recall, the sultan of Syria falls in love with Custance and decides to marry her on the basis of accounts brought to him by merchants of "hir goodnesse" and "beau-tee."[42] In his discussion of how Griselda/Katherine came from Spain to England, Forrest writes, "The worthie fame of this noble Grysilde blowne into great *Britaine*, was, by the kinge theare (called the Sec-onde *Saloman*) procured in marriage to his eldest sunne," a formulation he repeats in chapter 2 itself, when he writes that her "passing wor-thynes was blowne by fame / Vnto the noble cowntrey of Brytayne"

(30). Both Custance and Forrest's Griselda/Katherine are thus married as a result of powerful men's hearing stories of their virtue, and both are exchanged between men without any account of their desires, consent, or agency.

As an object of exchange among men, Griselda/Katherine as Forrest presents her also resembles Emelye of the Knight's Tale. His description of Griselda/Katherine's marriage to Arthur occupies two stanzas, including the crucial detail that "the marryed togeathers not slepte, / For the saide Prynce was but tender and yonge" (31). In the very next stanza, Forrest indicates, "This noble Prynce this life departed hee" (32). Griselda/Katherine laments, but is resolved to "take (as God sendthe) this worldys varyetee," although, much as Emelye would have preferred to remain a chaste Amazon rather than marrying anyone at all, Griselda/Katherine would prefer "no more of worldely greeif taste" (32). Having already been handed from Theseus to Arcite as the prize for his tournament victory, Emelye is handed by Arcite on his deathbed to his cousin Palamon, who will be her "housbonde and . . . lord."[43] Similarly, in the *History*, Henry VII determines after Arthur's death "that it myght bee conuenyently done, / To haue her marrye with his oother soone" (37), and so Griselda/Katherine is transferred from one prince to the other.

At the end of his Tale, Chaucer's Clerk claims to reject Griselda as a figure to be emulated by wives, saying:

> This storie is seyd nat for that wyves sholde
> Folwen Grisilde as in humylitee
> For it were inportable, though they wolde.[44]

Rather, he claims the tale is more generally to be interpreted as providing an example of how "every wight, in his degree, / Sholde be constant in adversitee."[45] The Clerk, though, for all his protestations, clearly still does hold on to some desire for wives to follow Griselda's example, since he laments that "It were ful hard to fynde now-a-dayes / In al a toun Grisildis thre or two."[46] Furthermore, the figure of Griselda was, in the later medieval and early modern periods, often held up as an exemplary one for women. In fact, Juan Luis Vives used the Griselda story in this way in a treatise he wrote for Katherine of Aragon in 1523 to guide the education of her daughter who would become Queen Mary.[47]

Forrest very much shares Chaucer's Clerk's, and Juan Luis Vives's, interest Griselda as an exemplary figure. Included ahead of the "Table" in the *History* is additional prefatory material designed to guide interpretation, specifically a verse "Prologe to the Queenis Maiestee." This verse dedication, like the "Table," strongly establishes a paradigm of exemplarity. Forrest intends Mary herself and other readers to learn from and emulate the accounts of Griselda's/Katherine of Aragon's life, which is given the status of a *forma vitae*. Forrest opens the verse prologue with a discussion of how and why children should follow examples of good behavior provided by their parents while the "parentys euyll example the chylde ought tauoyde" (21). Tactfully not pointing directly to Henry VIII as an example of behavior to be avoided (though Walter/Henry certainly features as such in the *History* itself), Forrest apostrophizes to Mary:

> Howe muche (O noble excellent Queene!)
> Maye then delyte youre domination
> Youre Mothers meek life of youe to bee seene,
> Or reduced to commemoration,
> That was of moste worthy commendation,
> Perfectly knowne to hundreadys that yeat bee,
> As moste especyall to youre maiestee. (3)

Because Griselda/Katherine was "so special notable," the printed marginal commentary to the verse prologue indicates, "Her life may be as a rule others lyves in virtue to direct" (3). Using monastically inflected language suggestive of the cloister, Forrest says that her life can serve "As rule to induce to all godlynes" (3). In presenting Griselda's/Katherine's life as both exemplary and regulatory, Forrest posits that it is especially useful for effecting spiritual and religious reform:

> I thought it goode for reformation,
> By her examples vertues to increase.
> Wheare restethe gohostely inclination.
> (3)

Forrest then makes the case for the exemplarity of Griselda's/Katherine's life even more emphatically in chapter 1 itself, when he indicates that his purpose is to write of the "godly talentis" of "a noble woman" in order "an exemplar in some maner sute, / Other of virtue to take thearby frute" (25).

The "Table" also foregrounds ways in which Griselda/Katherine serves as an instructive model of ideal female conduct, highlighting "her education and wonderful towardnes yn her youthe to all godlynes and virtue." Forrest notes "Howe (voydinge idlenes) she oftetymes wolde practice with the nedyll, and other handye business, to ladies necessarye," calling attention to Griselda's/Katherine's engagement in the traditionally female work of sewing. He also discourses extensively about her devotional practices, which resonate with medieval affective piety and a Catholic emphasis on good works. He says that "Euery moarnynge, and at nyght, twoe howres (at the leaste) vpon her kneeis in her chamber or closet occupying herselfe in godlye prayer" (7), and he indicates that she always shows "benynge cheare" to rich and poor alike, constantly "endeavoringe the glorye of God, detesting (as deathe) all worldly praise and vaine glorye" (8).

Forrest's descriptions of Griselda's/Katherine's devotional practices contribute strongly to the creation of a cloistered identity for herself that Mary is to emulate. Evoking the affective devotion to the passion so associated with medieval feminine piety, while at the same time getting in a blow against Protestant iconoclasts, Forrest says, "For the devotion she specially had to the Passion of Christe, shee let make an Image representing the same, of wondrefull woorkemanshippe, a little from London" (10). Forrest elaborates further on the orthodoxy of Griselda's/Katherine's intent in having a devotional image of the Passion made, saying it was done "Not to any ydolatryall entent / (As miserable men manye dothe holde) / But to the beholders to represent / Of Christe towards man the mercyes manyfolde" (47). Forrest furthermore aligns her devotional activities with monastic practices. He says that she "Oftentyme wolde . . . rise at myddnyght, and serue God in prayer (as the Religious dyd)" (10). His treatment of her nocturnal devotions further associates her with the monastic virtues of chastity and poverty. Noting her practice of sleeping separately from the king and emphasizing the simplicity of her clothing, Forrest places her in the company of actual professed religious:

> This godlye maner ofte wolde shee frequent
> At Greenewiche, she lyinge alone from the Kynge;
> The Fryers at matins with hartye entent
> She woulde bee theare, in devotion kneeling,
> A mantyll aboute her which was no riche thynge,
> Theare in prayer and contemplation
> Renderinge to God Sweete commendation.
>
> (47)

Finally, Forrest's Griselda/Katherine expresses directly her desire to withdraw from political affairs entirely so that she and her daughter Mary might embrace lives of claustration and prayer:

> I cowlde bee content, and shee (I dare saye),
> (If *Walters* goode will wolde graunte to the same)
> To lyue togeathers yn some pooare Nunraye,
> Praysinges to render to Goddys holye name,
> The quieter to lyue, oute of this worldys blame;
> For fye on this worldys highe Domynation
> Commytte (in this sorte) with tribulation!
>
> (86)

Forrest devotes two chapters to Griselda's/Katherine's good death, and these chapters concentrate on Griselda's/Katherine's devotional practices and on providing instruction in proper female conduct to Mary. Forrest takes pains to emphasize that, in correct Catholic fashion, "She humbly besought, with hartys compunction / To haue (as was dwe) the *Extreme Vnction*" (113) so that she could die "in true Christian Sorte" (114). Forrest imagines a wholly invented set of prayers that Griselda/Katherine offers, and he provides a pathos-filled account of "Grisildys most pytefull takynge her leave at Marye her Doughter" (107). In Griselda's/Katherine's extended deathbed address to Mary, she tells Mary to continue to practice good works, especially aiding the poor, saying, "The pooare (to the poure) releaaue and susteyne" (110). She additionally reiterates the importance of meekness and humility for royal women:

> Bee meeke and lowlye in harte and in looke,
> Beare thee not bolde of thy nobylitee;
> Busye thy selfe in Goddys dyuyne Booke,
> Whiche teachethe the rulys of pure humylitee;
> Bewares the ways of false fragilitee,
> Vse fastynge and praying for best remeadye;
> So shalte thoue trulye withe all facylitee
> *Purchesse of* God *His fauour and mercye.*
>
> (110)

Griselda's/Katherine's parting words to Mary recall the language of devotion to the Virgin Mary, which for Forrest, as we shall see in his devotional writings, is the medieval religious Catholic practice par excellence. Griselda/Katherine addresses her daughter, "O *Mary* mayden, by lyneall descent / Springe of the fresche and sweete Rose rubycounde" (108). The description of Mary as "maiden" and the association of her with the rose (which also of course reminds readers of her Lancastrian lineage) connect the earthly princess with the heavenly queen.

After Griselda's/Katherine's death, Forrest transforms her from a cloistered queen to a quasi-saint with intercessory powers. He writes, "*Grysilde*, joyinge the heauynly felycitee (as we fully truste), dothe praye for us theare is no mysdoubtys" (22). He suggests that she deserves a place in the ranks of the martyrs, declaring:

> If wrongefull entreatinge and trobled harte
> For stedfastely standynge in rightuousnes
> Bee a Martyrdome, by cowrse of panges smarte,
> Thorowe Goddys woorkinge meryte to encresse,
> Then, as holye *Hierom* dothe expresse
> Of *Paula* that clearly this worlde did forsake,
> This *Grisild* maye in the number bee take.
>
> (147)

Though he does qualify this assertion by stating "it sittethe [*sic*] not our facultee / Suche honor to anye as to impute" (147), since "Onlye the Highest asignethe that sute" (147), Forrest still performs an act of textual canonization reminiscent of the one that Hoccleve enacts for Chaucer in the *Regiment of Princes*, as I discuss in chapter 2.[48] Describing her apotheosis, Forrest places Griselda/Katherine in the company of the Virgin Mary and other saints in heaven, including John the Baptist, John the Evangelist, St. Paul, "the holy martyrs *Laurence* and *Vincent, / Stephen* and *Dyonyse*" (117–18). Griselda/Katherine occupies her rightful place in the heavenly hierarchy, "set in place (as well we maye suppose) / Of heauynly blysse, moste gloriously shynynge" (116). Incorporating praise for the "moste excellent *Virgyn Marye*," whose "seate" in "the celestiall sanctuarye . . . transcendethe all cretures certaine" (117), Forrest concludes, "Then is this *Grysilde* in place situat" (119).

Forrest's Virgin Mary in heaven is a reigning queen due all the honor accorded to her in orthodox Catholic devotion. Queens on earth, including the earthly Mary, ought, however, to emulate the meekness embodied by the Virgin Mary during her earthly lifetime, or that embodied by Griselda/Katherine. Forrest strongly connects this model of meek, humble queenship and Catholic female virtue with the maintenance of political order. It is particularly significant, in considering how Forrest's model of ideal womanhood applies to Mary as a royal reader, to note the extent to which Forrest strongly stresses Griselda's/Katherine's meekness and humility. In his opening apostrophe to Mary in the verse prologue, the first description he attaches to Griselda's/Katherine's exemplary life is meekness ("Youre Mothers *meek life* of youe to bee seene" [3, emphasis added]). In chapter 1, rather than extolling patience—the virtue with which Griselda is typically associated— Forrest says that Griselda/Katherine is unsurpassed in "meekenes in aduersytee" in all "historyes of Gentyles or Jues" (26). He also specifies that his chief aim in writing the *History* is for readers to profit from, and presumably thus practice, meekess. In indicating "to what ende writers endeauorethe their paynes" he says that "this historye of *Grisilde the Seconde* wryten to this ende, other (of meekenes) to take thearby fruyte" (7). As Betteridge observes, "It is impossible to imagine Katherine's daughter as depicted in *Grisild* as being able, or indeed wanting, to rule."

Indeed, Forrest would seem to share the interpretation of queenship and female virtue espoused by that earlier adopter of the Griselda story, and "cloisterer" par excellence, Juan Luis Vives, who in the 1523 *Instruction of a Christian Woman* deplores women who (to quote the English translation of Richard Hyrd, made shortly after the Spanish version was published) "wyll medle with comen matters of realms and cites / and wene to gouerne peoples and nacions."[49] This is a significant departure from Chaucer's Griselda, who, while clearly a paragon of patience, actually does govern, and quite successfully, in Walter's absence. Chaucer writes that Griselda "whan that the cas required it, / The commune profit koude she redresse" (IV 430–31). He continues:

> Though that hire housbonde absent were anon,
> If gentil men or other of hir contree
> Were wrothe, she wolde bryngen hem aton;
> So wise and rype words hadde she,
> And juggementz of so greet equitee,
> That she from hevene sent was, as men wende,
> Peple to save and every wrong t'amende.
>   (IV 436–41)

In contrast, for Forrest, when queens are engaged not in governing but rather in prayer, traditional devotion, and good works, when princesses are trained in "all kynde of virtue . . . / To Goddys dwe honour most speciallye" (44), then peace, prosperity, and good order hold sway in the realm. Forrest directly connects the time of Griselda's/ Katherine's "upp trading her goodly princes, of her singular towardnes in all virtue" (9) with an age of good government and prosperity. He says, "In *Britayne* that season was muche quyetnes and plenty of all goodde thingis, the honour of God flourischeinge, the riche merciful, the pooare nurisched" (9). He enlarges on this golden age in which female virtue and traditional devotion held sway, saying:

> In Brytayne that tyme was muche tranquyllytee,
> Plentye of althyngis in computation
> That serued (of neade) to mannys sustentation.

The honour of God duelye florischinge,
His seruyce mayntayned euerye wheare.
(45)

Forrest even has Griselda/Katherine herself connect female virtue, particularly chastity, with the public good. Once Walter/Henry has finally been "presented with Thunyversiteis Seale" and moves definitively "goode sealye *Grysilde* for to put downe, / And in her steade his nwe mynyon to crowne" (82), Forrest includes a long section in which Griselda/Katherine puts forth her case that her marriage to Walter/Henry is legitimate and that accordingly she will not consent to resigning her crown. Not surprisingly, given Henry VIII's subsequent history as well as the arguments he advanced in attempting to procure a divorce, Griselda's/Katherine's speech features adultery quite prominently. Griselda/Katherine insists that she has not engaged in that sin. Adultery, she says, is something "Of whiche all the worlde coulde her not accuse" (83). More strikingly, though, she argues that her nonadulterous behavior and the legitimacy of their marriage have ensured the success of Walter/Henry's reign. Using language that resonates with Elizabeth Barton's prophecies, discussed in chapter 2, of the downfall that will occur if Henry takes Anne Boleyn as his queen, Griselda/Katherine says:

For in Adultery whoe so ioynethe,
Hee maye bee sure to bee infortunat;
No luckye successe God hym assignethe,
But is with myscheeifes manye intricate;
So hathe not (*throughe her*) happened hym euyl fate,
But tryumphauntly, in pryncelye degree,
Florischinge in wealthe and felycitee.
(84, emphasis added)

Because for Forrest public order and prosperity, true religion and good government depend on the maintenance of medievally inflected, Catholic female virtue, the arrival on the scene of Anne Boleyn not surprisingly ushers in an age of decline, disorder, and heresy. Forrest marks

Anne Boleyn from her entry into the text with the shadow of the end she will eventually meet, executed for alleged adultery. He calls Anne Boleyn "this new Queene *Anne* / Whoe, as she was, declared at the laste, / Whome God vanysched with muche sodayne blaste" (80). Walter/Henry's rejection of Griselda/Katherine in favor of Anne Boleyn results in a state of affairs that Forrest laments at considerable length. He stresses repeatedly in this lament the detrimental aspects of innovation and novelty, highlighting again his attachment to the past, especially the medieval, Catholic past. For one thing, though he does not explain the causal relationship, Forrest says that Anne's arrival causes unprecedented economic woes. "Upon this induction," Forrest says, "suche innouation" occurred as "Raysinge of Rentes in wondreful fashion" and "cawsynge of dearthe in utayl and warys" (80). Forrest says that "All goode orders weare cleane set oute of use" (79), and continues by depicting Anne as the opposite of the meek Griselda/Katherine. Recalling what could readily be a negative interpretation of Alison of Bath, who always desires to be first in making her offering in church and who advocates female sovereignty and mastery, Forrest writes of Anne:

> Then was true Meekenes ouercome with Pryde,
> Then to perdition all Goodenes faste hyde,
> Then was Selfe wyll chief Ruler ouer all,
> Then might, in right, none for Aduocat call.
>
> (79)

Furthermore, the entirety of religious observance collapses when Anne displaces Griselda/Katherine as queen:

> Then of the Churche began thaffliction,
> Then entred Heresies cursed and nought,
> Then increased Goddys malediction,
> Then His due honour in great decaye brought,
> Then the goode not regarded as they ought,
> But euery Ribaulde myght them checke and chace;
> The Goode depryued, the Badde in their place.
>
> (79)

Fasting and prayer are "made but iestinge" (81), iconoclasm flourishes (81), and "Goddys seruantes" are "Dysmembred (like beastes) in thopen highe waye" (81). Most tellingly, the replacement of Griselda/Katherine by Anne Boleyn results in perversions of devotion for holy virgins and the Virgin Mary:

> In earthe they cowlde not their malice extende,
> But vnto heuen shewed indignation;
> The holy Saynctys theare they dyd discommende
> By too muche abomination,
> Sclaunderinge certayne vndre this faschion,
> Howe holye Virgyns, of no lyttle some,
> Weare Concubynes to the Busshoppe of Rome.
> The glorious perpetuall Virgyn *Marye*
> No better esteamed then an other woman.
>
> (80)

And, in what Forrest treats as his ultimate example of the horrors that "came by exchaunge of good *Grisildis*" (81), of the "myscheifes, with hundredefolde moe" that "began / At the incummynge" (80) of Anne Boleyn, he exclaims, "Churches and Monasteries downe they wente, / To haue the treasure speciallye thearfor, / Althoughe they feyned for other entent" (81). The dismantling of the cloisters and the desecration of cloistered women corresponds with the downfall of the embodiment of cloistered female virtue, and all of society suffers as a consequence.

Language of Marian devotion and a marked concern with the maintenance of proper hierarchy similarly characterize Forrest's writings in BL MS Harley 1703, a collection of devotional writings which as a whole politicizes female virtue much as the *History* does. MS Harley 1703 includes a collection of didactic poems, about half of which concern the Virgin Mary.[50] The datings of the compositions and that of the manuscript itself are uncertain. The date 1571 appears on folio 15v and again on folio 66r, and the date "27 Octubris 1572" appears on folio 153v. Another date, which could either be 1561 or 1581, appears on folio 95r. In any case, it appears that Forrest, who names himself as the author on more than one occasion in the manuscript (see, for example, fol. 40r), worked on this collection for some time during Elizabeth I's reign.

In poems in this collection, and especially in the first item, which is a long verse treatise on the salutation of the Virgin Mary, Forrest pleads for the resumption of Marian devotion in England.[51] Forrest frequently in his Marian writings connects the use of orthodox Catholic devotional practices with the state of individuals' personal affairs and the affairs of state. In the process, he considers many of the same political events discussed in the *History of Grisild the Second*.

In the Marian treatise that opens Harley 1703, Forrest's sometimes curious choices of emphasis and example highlight the ways in which he associates English political affairs with Marian devotion. Forrest takes pains to stress that Mary and Joseph are "Immedyatelye" after the Annunciation united in "true matrymonye" (fol. 1r) because, as he says, "Els, hauinge Childe, myghtist have borne yis blame: / To haue offended: in Adulterye" (fol. 1r)—a topic obviously central to much religiopolitical controversy throughout the reign of Henry VIII. Forrest additionally spends considerable time making the case for the Immaculate Conception, demonstrating a particular inflection of his interest in female sexual purity. Another emphasis of his Marian devotional writing in this treatise is to argue for the legitimacy of the Virgin Mary's claim to the title "lady," much as in the *History* he argues that Griselda/Katharine deserves the title of queen. In developing these claims in the treatise, Forrest turns frequently to language of hierarchical dynastic relations, suggesting another link between Marian devotion and contemporary English political debates about royal legitimacy. For example, Forrest writes:

> If they weare Crownys / of Immortall glorye,
> surmounting the Crownys / of kings here terrayne:
> (sithe their Crownys here, but transytorye:)
> then dare I saye / and neaver Aught fayne
> the virgyne marye / hathe Crowne soueraigne,
> Above all Creatures, so farre more passinge:
> as she is in virtue: before them florischinge,
> As crowned so nexte her soueraigne Soone:

so prove we shall Queene: by good Authoryte;
And after so, suffycyentlye done:
that she is mater misericordiae,
If Queene / then ladye, of sett necessyte,
for, as to knighthood, ladye isyued is:
so Queene, to kinge: we certainlye knowe this.

(fol. 1r–fol. 1v)

Similarly, in a formulation that recalls Walter's choice of Griselda from a humble background to be his wife in the Clerk's Tale, and that also echoes Forrest's support for Katherine of Aragon's status as queen throughout her lifetime, Forrest writes:

What kinge thus pleasethe: of his benynge grace,
A mayden to Marrye, of the Countreye:
Come she of progenye / neaver so base:
for Queene is she take: tyll her dyinge deye,
ffor, of the husband (by lawe) we doo saye,
the womans fame of honour to Aryse:
then, whie not the virgin marye lykewyse,
Sythe here / her life: was mere spyrytuall,
the Carnall / in her Abolysched quyte:
her Spowse onelye, the kinge celestyall:
in whome specyallye he dyd delyte:
why not, for Queene then: her name to recite.

(fol. 15r)

As he does in the *History*, Forrest again in the opening treatise of MS Harley 1703 connects Anne Boleyn's appearance on the scene with social and religious decline, and particularly with destruction of devotion to the Virgin Mary. After putting forward his case for the truth of the Immaculate Conception and his arguments about why Mary has legitimate claim to the title "lady," Forrest turns his attention to "Theis fortye yeares togethers (excepte A fewe betweene)" in which "hathe theis Blaspheamyes bene vsed Against the gloryour virgin marye" (fol. 26v). This section of the treatise consists of anecdotes that are inversions of Marian miracle tales like that of the Prioress's Tale. In Forrest's glee-fully related negative exempla, the Virgin Mary does not intervene to aid someone who praises her or prays to her. Rather, those who neglect to give the Virgin Mary proper devotion, or those who slander her, are duly punished. Forrest's first unlucky victim is a priest, who, Forrest makes sure to add, is married, but not legitimately, since under "goddes lawe" he has no wife but rather a "concubine" (fol. 27r). This priest scurrilously denies the Immaculate Conception and perpetual purity of Mary, comparing her to "A safforne Bagge" which, while it contains saffron, is "sweete and saverye," but when it is empty is merely an or-dinary bag. Likewise, he continues, while the Virgin Mary is pregnant with Christ, she is free "from syn." However, after Christ's birth (and presumably before she becomes pregnant), she is just another female. He says, "Christe departed owte of her wombe, than: / She was no bet-ter: then other women" (fol. 27r). The priest's sorry fate is to become so intoxicated that "hee (through drynkynge) had neare hym beepyste" (fol. 27r), and upon exiting the tavern, "he fel downe dead" immedi-ately. At once "All his mowthe, with fflyes was over blowne" because with "that cursed mowthe" he uttered "Suche Blaspheamye" (fol. 27r).

In this list of those who sin by neglecting Marian devotion and so receive retribution, Forrest includes the case of a female "malignor . . . of meane estate boarne" who "yeat dyd excel" (fol. 27v). Though not named, this woman can only be Anne Boleyn. Forrest describes her "most carnall" living, her "not favouringe lyef spyrytuall," and says that her lack of virtue leads others astray. He writes:

Her lyef, fro all virtue: seavered cleane,
so weare Almoste all: to her that dyd leane,
muche dissolute lyef, entering by her:
continued also: in wicked maner,
And, vnto this deye, nodeale dothe decrease.
(fol. 27v).

Much as in the *History*, in this treatise in MS Harley 1703, slander of holy virgins and in particular the Virgin Mary is paradigmatic of the decline of the realm. In the treatise, Forrest equates Anne Boleyn's lack of Marian devotion with her own, as well as society's, downfall. He says:

> Owre ladye, that Chryste into this worlde brought:
> was owte of Regarde in her deade / and thought,
> She was all Iolye, in this worldes pleasaunce:
> witheout respecte: to her sowlles governaunce,
> with hereasyes, she afflowed such wyse,
> and thorowe her meanys, here cawsed taryse:
> As, neaver the lyke, to goddess dyshonour:
> and yeat contynuethe: vnto this howre,
> As so she was vnprofytable fownde,
> and with suche errours, seene for to Abownde:
> The Chief, vnto whome / she made moste offense:
> shortyned her tyme: by dyvyne sentence.
>
> (fol. 27v–28r).

Specifically, "for she cowlde not: the Aue Marye / saye, in goode parte . . . / she had overthrowe: for her wicked syn," a fate that will, Forrest predicts, be shared by "All thaye: / the Aue marya: that lyste not to saye" (fol. 28r).

For Forrest, both in the treatise in Harley 1703 and in the *History*, all of the Henrician Protestant Reformation is recast as a fall narrative in which sin enters with Anne Boleyn as a daughter of Eve, and in which Walter/Henry rejects virtue as embodied in Griselda/Katherine (who is the inverse of Anne, just as the Virgin hailed by the salutation *Ave Maria* is the inverse of *Eva*).[52] With Henry's choice, all of the civic and religious institutions that at once simultaneously depend on and maintain "cloistered" modes of female devotion and conduct crumble. Forrest declares that once Griselda/Katherine dies, the "dwe awe of God is seene neglected" (115), and problematic novelties proliferate, taking England further from medieval forms of religion: "Newe vpon Newe theare followed nonaye, / As neauer the like in so little space" (115). All can be redeemed only by the return of female virtue and correctly practiced Catholic female devotion as embodied in Queen Mary.

She, Forrest hopes, will enable the maintenance of order and the public good by embracing the meek, humble, cloistered identity presented to her as exemplary by the *History*—and she will reestablish actual cloisters in England to boot.

Strikingly, Forrest draws upon the figure of Chaucer and the Chaucer tradition to authorize his religiopolitical vision of a Catholic future that reanimates the medieval past. Though he does not do so in the opening treatise in Harley 1703, Forrest does in a text later in the manuscript bring Chaucer to bear in making a case for the return to Marian devotion. Forrest includes a continuation of an earlier devotional poem to the Virgin Mary. In the heading to this poem, Forrest writes:

> This salutation, most eloquentlye,
> a devoute Scotte: of love most entire,
> longe time sithen: dyd yt edyfye,
> and throwe like spirite (which can Inspire) me,
> of like devotion, so well as I maye
> I shall continue: In this poore qwyre,
> to saye with the scotte: Salue Maria.
>
> (fol. 79v)

The "devoute Scotte" is the Scottish Chaucerian William Dunbar. Chaucer stands in the background, occupying tacitly his familiar position as authorizing English poet in a line running from him to Dunbar to Forrest. Much as for the community of Syon in the sixteenth century, for which Chaucer represents medieval Catholic orthodoxy and the Catholic Lancastrian tradition, in this case Chaucer serves Forrest as a figure underwriting Catholic devotion to the Virgin Mary as practiced in the Middle Ages and the all of the attendant social and political good that obtained in England when it was ruled by Catholic monarchs. Just as for More the devout, orthodox Chaucer of the retraction models the way to achieve spiritual salvation within the community of the Roman Catholic Church, for Forrest, Chaucer and the era he represents point the way to social and political salvation for England as a Roman Catholic realm.

CHAPTER 4

"Let Chaucer Also Look to Himself"

Gender, Religion, and the Politics of Canon Formation
in Seventeenth-Century England

This chapter brings together some prominent canonical English writers not typically today found to keep each other's company outside the pages of a British literature anthology or the syllabus of an undergraduate survey class: Julian of Norwich, John Dryden, and Geoffrey Chaucer. However, in the seventeenth century these writers did keep each other's company, particularly in textual exchanges among debating Catholic and Protestant factions. Both Julian of Norwich and Chaucer were reintroduced to late seventeenth-century audiences by Catholic writers—respectively by Serenus Cressy and John Dryden. Additionally, Cressy and Dryden also shared an opponent in textual expressions of confessional controversy: Edward Stillingfleet, bishop of Worcester. Because the Middle English of the sixteenth-century editions of Chaucer by Thynne, Stow, and Speght was by Dryden's day difficult for many readers, Dryden included what he called translations of selections from *The Canterbury Tales* in his *Fables Ancient and Modern* (1699), which he wrote after his conversion to Roman Catholicism. Julian of Norwich's text came to light for early modern readers in 1670 when Cressy published his edition of her revelations. This publication sparked a set of textual exchanges often called the "Stillingfleet Controversy," because in 1671, in response to Cressy's edition of Julian of Norwich, Stillingfleet, a well-known preacher, theologian, and apologist for the

Church of England, published *A Discourse concerning the Idolatry Practised in the Church of Rome and the Danger of Salvation in the Communion of It.* Various Catholic responses and Protestant counterresponses ensued. Stillingfleet and Dryden also had their own exchange of textual salvos on the subject of religion and politics. When James II published the so-called strongbox papers concerning Charles II's conversion to Roman Catholicism, along with an account of the conversion of his first wife, Anne Hyde, Duchess of York, Dryden defended the papers against the attacks of Anglican pamphlet writers and debated with Stillingfleet over "Protestants' lack of insight into the virtue of humility."[1] Stillingfleet attacked Dryden in "A Vindication of the Answer to Some Late Papers," and Dryden responded in kind, targeting Stillingfleet in his 1687 work *The Hind and the Panther.*

The early modern intersection of Julian of Norwich, John Dryden, and Geoffrey Chaucer sheds light on competing Catholic and Protestant processes of canon formation. These processes began, as we have seen in the previous chapter, in the sixteenth century, and they have broad political implications on both sides of the Atlantic through the seventeenth century and into the eighteenth century, as I consider in this chapter and the next. Though the dominant reception of Chaucer in the early modern period was as a proto-Protestant hero, Catholic writers like Cressy, the anonymous author of *The Roman Church's Devotions Vindicated from Doctor Stillingfleet's Mis-Representation* (1672) (which is one of the "Stillingfleet Controversy" contributions that respond to Stillingfleet's *Discourse*), and Dryden found in Chaucer, as in Julian of Norwich, a means of accessing the past textually in order to reanimate England as a Catholic realm and Roman Catholic devotion as the authentically English faith in the late seventeenth-century Protestant present.[2] They share with William Forrest an interest in bringing the medieval Catholic past, which has complicated gendered dimensions, into the present, and they, like Forrest, turn to Chaucer as a valuable resource for using and managing the medieval.

The gendered elements of the medieval Catholic past and the need to manage the medieval take on particularly urgent significance as gendered discourses of rationality emerge in the later seventeenth and early eighteenth centuries. These discourses reinforce established associations of Catholicism with the feminine, the fleshly, and the irrational. The urgency and complexity of the task of mobilizing while controlling medieval material are further intensified for the Catholic writers considered in this chapter, because the modes of textual encounter theorized by these writers are also predicated on intricately gendered imbrications of bodies and words. The Catholic literary and political histories that these writers shape through their engagements with medieval texts depend on interlocking sets of generative, genealogical relationships in which words cause bodies—as well as the legacies associated with those bodies—to have presence and be present. Chaucer becomes for the early modern Catholic writers in whom I am interested a stabilizing figure, a figure who masculinizes and rationalizes the English Catholic Middle Ages. Chaucer enables Catholic writers to access aspects of the past necessary for their literary and religiopolitical aims, as well as to include female figures in the genealogies they craft to envision alternative versions of English history, without having those aims and histories undermined by the negative associations of the feminine, the "mother tongue," and the Catholic.

"MOTHER" JULIAN AND "FATHER" CHAUCER: GENDER, RELIGION, AND THE STILLINGFLEET CONTROVERSY

Serenus Cressy published his edition of Julian's revelations accompanied by a dedication "To his most Honoured Lady, the Lady Mary Blount of Sodington" and by an epistle "To the Reader." In these prefatory materials, Cressy makes clear his religiopolitical aim of framing the edition as what Jennifer Summit calls "an exile's return."[3] He also conveys his related commitment to a mode of textual encounter that I have, in other work on Julian of Norwich, described as incarnational textuality, a mode that is fundamentally concerned with recursivity and reanimation. Summit observes that Cressy encourages Lady Mary to think of Julian of Norwich as her contemporary.[4] I would actually go further to say that Cressy encourages Lady Mary in some sense to *be* Julian, to reembody, by means of reading her text, Julian's experience.[5] In the dedicatory letter, Cressy emphasizes the similarities between

Lady Mary and Julian, despite the historical gap separating them, stating, "The Author of it, is a Person of Your Sex, who lived about Three Hundred Years since" (Watson and Jenkins, *Writings*, 449). He continues by noting, "[Julian] intended it for *You*, and for such Readers as yourself" (449). Cressy also underlines the corporeal, affective, experiential aspects attached to Lady Mary's reading of Julian's text, framing the textual encounter in terms of visual perception and bodily sensation. He says to Lady Mary, "[You] will enjoy her Saint-like Conversation, attending to her, whilst with Humility and Joy, She recounts to you the Wonders of our *Lords* Love to *Her*, and of his *Grace* in *Her*. And being thus employed, I make no doubt but you will be sensible of many Beams of her Lights, and much warmth of her Charity, by reflection darted into your own Soul" (450).[6]

It is significant, too, that the experiential scene of reading is framed as "saint-like conversation," and that Cressy writes of Julian "recounting to you" her experience. Such a person-to-person understanding of textual encounter places a special importance on the words as Julian's own words. The words of Julian's revelations do not merely describe Julian's experiences of divine love and her thoughts about those experiences, but rather they seem to embody Julian herself, making her present to, and her experience alive in, Lady Mary. The crucial role the words themselves play helps make sense of Cressy's desire not to modernize Julian's language to make it more comprehensible for seventeenth-century readers, but rather to provide glosses. Cressy writes in the epistle to the devout reader, "*I conceived it would have been a prejudice to the agreeable simplicity of the* Stile, *to have changed the Dress of it into our* Modern Language, *as some advised. Yet certain more out of Fashion,* Words *or* Phrases, *I thought meet to explain in the Margine*" (Watson and Jenkins, *Writings*, 450). As Nicholas Watson and Jacqueline Jenkins note, much was at stake for Cressy and his Catholic contemporaries in defending the Middle English language of the fourteenth-century religious writers to whom they were devoted (449). Middle English matters so much to Cressy at least in part because of the nature of his understanding of reading. To translate the words (to carry them across from one language into another) would inhibit the ability of those words to allow access to the past, to translate the past by bearing it across the historical gulf from Julian's body to the body of the reader.

In the *Discourse concerning the Idolatry Practised in the Church of Rome*, Stillingfleet's central aim is to shift onto Catholicism allegations that Protestant churches encouraged "fanaticism." In the 1670s, the term "fanaticism" was strongly linked with such dissident Protestant groups as Quakers and Ranters. Protestants defensively argued in contrast that Catholic toleration of visions, miracles, and mysticism made Catholics the true fanatics (Watson and Jenkins, *Writings*, 449). Stillingfleet also objects strongly to Julian's Middle English idiom as a language marked by strangeness (449).[7] In other words, the distinctively personal elements, the affectively and sensually resonant dimensions of her text, and Julian's Middle English language that Cressy thought so important to preserve rather than to modernize, are all problematic for Stillingfleet. Strikingly, the personal and affective elements and the Middle English language were troubling to Stillingfleet largely because of their associations with the feminine. Stillingfleet's attack on Cressy's edition of Julian's text thus contains, not surprisingly, strongly gendered aspects.

Indeed, Stillingfleet adopts a strategy widespread in anti-Catholic polemic of the second half of the seventeenth century: he uses major female mystics and visionaries of the Middle Ages (very frequently St. Birgitta of Sweden and St. Catherine of Siena) to emblematize Catholicism's falsity, superstition, and fanaticism. Catholicism is, in short, a feminine faith, irrevocably tainted by the sorts of female carnality and weakness both intellectual and spiritual demonstrated by the lives of such women as Birgitta and Catherine. In an illustrative passage that brings together all the negative associations of the medieval, the feminine, and the Catholic, Stillingfleet writes:

> *Blosius* in his works hath one Book called *Monile Spirituale*, which consists of nothing but the new and strange revelations which were made to four Women Saints St. *Gertrude*, St. *Mathilde*, St. *Bridgett*, and St. *Catharine*; and in his Preface saith, *it is a sign of a carnal mind to despise such revelations as these are: for the Church of God is wonderfully enlightened by them. What*, saith he, *did not the Prophets and Apostles receive truth from Heaven by Revelations?*

As though the case were the very same in these melancholy Women and in the holy *Prophets* and *Apostles*: and we had just as much reason to believe the effects of *hysterical vapours* and the *divine spirit*.[8]

For comparison, note that William Guild's *Anti-Christ Pointed and Painted Out . . .* (1655) describes the cross speaking to St. Birgitta in Rome as an example of a false popish miracle, and Walter Pope's satirical "The Catholick Ballad: or an Invitation to Popery . . ." (1674) also includes a mocking reference to St. Birgitta.[9] Pope writes:

O the Catholic cause! Now assist me my Muse,
How earnestly do I desire thee!
Neither will I pray to St. Bridget to day,
But only to thee to inspire me.[10]

Significantly, the nature of textual encounter, the very questions of what one should read and in what language that are so important to Cressy, provide the starting point for Stillingfleet's blow-by-blow effort to debunk passages from Birgitta's *Revelations*. Again pairing Julian with St. Birgitta of Sweden—that standby figure for those wishing to undermine contemporary Catholicism by associating it with feminine irrationality—Stillingfleet points to both women's "Fantastical Revelations" and lampoons Gonsalvus Durantus and Serenus Cressy for publishing the work of these medieval mystics. Stillingfleet continues, "We have, we thank God, other ways of imploying our devout retirements, than by reading such fopperies as those are. Excellent men! That debar the people reading the *Scriptures* in their own tongue, and instead of them put them off with such Folleries, which deserve no other name at the best than the *efforts of Religious madness*" (Watson and Jenkins, *Writings*, 452). The vernacular Middle English of medieval Catholic texts, texts that are strongly and pejoratively feminized by Stillingfleet, problematically replaces for contemporary Catholics the vernacular Scriptures embraced by early modern Protestants.[11]

Stillingfleet again juxtaposes the feminine texts of medieval mystics with the masculine Word of Scripture in *An Answer to Several Late*

Treatises, Occasiond by a Book Entitled "A Discourse concerning the Idolatry Practices in the Church of Rome, and the Hazard of Salvation in the Communion of It" (1673), a reaction to, among other publications, O. N.'s work discussed below. Stillingfleet writes, "But I would fain know of these men, whether they do in earnest make no difference between the writings of such as Mother *Iuliana* and the Books of *Scripture*; between the Revelations of *S. Brigitt*, S. *Catharine* &c and those of the *Prophets.*"[12] Similarly, in another section of *An Answer*, Stillingfleet writes that the Catholic faction is guilty of "*paralleling the expressions and practices of S.* Brigitt, and *Mother* Juliana (than which scarce any thing was ever Printed more ridiculous in the way of *Revelations) with those of the holy Prophets and Apostles.*"[13] Catholic texts and the Middle English in which they are written thus represent the "mother tongue" in a debased, feminine form, while the vernacular Scripture represents the masculine divine Word. Importantly in this regard, Stillingfleet repeatedly and mockingly calls Julian of Norwich "mother Juliana." For example, in the *Discourse* he asks, "Have we any mother *Juliana*'s among us?," and he describes "*the sixteen Revelations of Divine Love shewed to a devout servant of our Lord* (and Lady too) *called Mother* Juliana" (Watson and Jenkins, *Writings*, 452). As Vickie Larsen has pointed out, Cressy probably assigned Julian the title "mother" (which features prominently on the title page of his edition) as a way to give Julian authority for Catholic readers both monastic and lay.[14] As we have seen, maternity and vernacularity alike have quite positive dimensions in the tales of Chaucer's female monastic pilgrims and in the writings of St. Birgitta of Sweden. As Larsen further points out, however, Julian's critics pick up the title and give it a pejorative thrust, mocking Julian by associating her status as mother with poor, uneducated women who trade in "old wives' tales and superstition."[15]

In presenting his case for Julian of Norwich's fanaticism, Stillingfleet zeroes in on a set of Middle English words that are complexly multivalent and multilayered in their meaning in Julian's text: "substance," "sensuality," "kindness," "one-ing." In illustrating her language that "we befool our selves to think . . . *sense*" (Watson and Jenkins, *Writings*, 452), Stillingfleet writes in the *Discourse*:

Did ever H. M. Jacob *Behmer*, or the highest Enthusiasts, talk at a more extravagant rate than this *Juliana* doth? As when she speaks of *our being beclosed in the mid-head of God, and in his meek-head, and in his benignity, and in his buxomness, though we* feel in us *wrath, debate, and strife; Of being substantially united to God, and that, God is that goodness which may not be wrath, for God is not but goodness; and between God and our soul is neither wrath nor forgiveness in his sight, for our soul is so fulsomely oned to God of his own goodness, that between God and our soul may be right naught.* (Watson and Jenkins, *Writings*, 452)

Such terms and phrases have a great deal to do with incarnation and epistemology, with bodies and words (both human and divine) and the ways in which the interactions among them produce knowledge.

Tellingly, Stillingfleet also focuses on Julian's Trinitarian theology, showing particular concern with the role she assigns to motherhood. In the *Discourse* he writes, "Afterwards she discourseth *of three proper-ties in the Holy Trinity, of the Fatherhead, of the Motherhood, and of the Lordship, and she further saw that the second person which is our Mother substantially, the same dear worthy person is not become our Mother sensual; for we be double of God's making, substantial and sensual*" (Watson and Jenkins, *Writings*, 453). This passage in which the femi-nine, the affective, and the strangeness of Julian's Middle English lan-guage converge powerfully seems the last straw for Stillingfleet, since it provokes him to pronounce judgment as follows: "We may justly ad-mire what esteem *Mr. Cressy* had of that *Lady* to whose devout retire-ments he So gravely commends the blasphemous and senseless tittle tattle of this *Hysterical* Gossip. It were endless to repeat the Canting and Enthusiastik expressions, which signifie nothing in Mother *Ju-liana*'s Revelations" (453). In *An Answer to Several Late Treatises*, Still-ingfleet's response to Cressy's contribution in a volume entitled *A Col-lection of Several Treatises against Doct. Stillingfleet*, the bishop goes so far as to depict Julian's "hysteria" as contagious, perhaps transmitted by her very language to infect Cressy, so feminizing him, diminishing his reason, and distorting his language. Stillingfleet writes of Cressy,

"By this we may guess what Ecclesiastical History we are to expect from him, who writes so at random about the matters of our own times. But the man is to be pitied: he was under one of Mother *Juliana's* fits, he writ with a good mind, but he knew not what. Some vent must be given to a violent fermentation, else the vessel might burst asunder."[16]

Cressy responds to Stillingfleet's objections to his publication of Julian of Norwich in *Fanaticism Fanatically Imputed* (1672), and his answer to Stillingfleet both defends Julian's Middle English idiom and highlights the affective, embodied nature of what Cressy deems proper reading practices. Of Julian of Norwich's Middle English Cressy says, "It is true, her language to the ears of this age, seems exotick: But it is such as was spoken in her time: therefore she may be excused."[17] Cressy also emphasizes in this work the important qualities of Julian's own language in enabling a reader to experience Julian's text, recalling his dedicatory epistle to Lady Mary Blount. Cressy notes the special ability of Julian's language to cause affective responses and to effect the bodily incorporation of the text, saying, "Her expressions touching Gods favours to her are homely but that surely is no sin. For affections to *God* are set down with great simplicity indeed, but they are withall cordiall and fervent, and apt to imprint themselves in the heart of an unpreiudiced *Reader.*"[18] Emphasizing the embodied nature of the experience Julian conveys in her text, Cressy commends the "sense and tast she shews to have had of *Gods speciall love.*"[19] Cressy argues that Stillingfleet reads improperly, precisely because his method of reading does not involve affective and embodied experiences. Stillingfleet therefore misapprehends Julian's text and so falsely attributes fanaticism to it. Cressy writes of Stillingfleet: "And what account does he give his *Readers* of the *Spirituall* Benefit reaped by him from his laborious reading? He it seems is not able out of them all to suggest any point of Instruction in *Christian Doctrin*, not one good affection to *God*, not the least encouragement to a vertuous holy life. All of these things are vanished out of his memory, and evaporated out of his brain, having never affected his heart."[20]

The Roman Church's Devotions Vindicated represents another Catholic response to Stillingfleet's arguments. The title page attributes the text to "O. N. a Catholick," and I want now to examine O. N.'s strategies in countering Stillingfleet's arguments, linking those strategies with other seventeenth-century Catholic engagements with the English medieval past and its texts. O. N. tackles the negative association of the Catholic with the feminine so prominent in early modern Protestant polemic and upon which Stillingfleet draws so heavily with a multipronged strategy. Not surprisingly, O. N. works in a mention of Scriptural endorsement of female visionary experiences: "in the last dayes God's powring out his Spirit Vpon all flesh, so that their sons, and daughters too shall Prophesy"; the writer notes Acts 2:17 in the margin for good measure.[21] He also turns the affective capacities so frequently associated with women, qualities that Cressy finds valuable but Stillingfleet finds so troubling, back into assets, including in his argument a defense (albeit one somewhat backhanded by modern sensibilities) of women's spiritual capabilities. O. N. states: "Simple people, who are less nimble and subtle in their notions, and women, who are commonly stronger, and more tender in their Passions, by this way, which they can chiefly take, arrive many times to a greater degree of the Love of, and Vnion with, God, then persons of greater learning or witt, because, these are more apt to take the former way of speculation, and to vse their brain more, then the heart."[22] Furthermore, the lives of medieval female mystics that Stillingfleet uses to reveal what he sees as the fanaticism and impossible contradictions of Catholicism are for O. N. evidence of the rigorous strictness with which the Catholic Church examines claims of "supernatural favours and extraordinary celestiall communications."[23] To illustrate this point, he chooses the example of St. Theresa, saying, "I much recommend . . . the perusal of the life of S. *Teresa*," in which one can observe "the great diligence that Was vsed, for severall years in the Triall of the Spirit of that most Holy Virgin." He continues by noting that the "33 Observations made by a Confessor of her in Approbation thereof" provide evidence of that her "works" are "approved by the most eminent persons for learning & Sanctity that were in her Age."[24]

Catholicism is for Stillingfleet a feminized inheritance, a corrupt bequest carried from the ignorant past into the deluded present through a female line, transmitted in debased vernacular by such women as "mother" Juliana. O. N. transforms that inheritance and its means of transmission, regendering Catholicism and the language of its medieval texts as predominantly masculine. He positions holy women as well as their texts in a safely contained, carefully controlled position—a strategy not unlike the "cloistering" enacted by William Forrest in the *History of Grisild the Second* and his Marian devotional writings. The maternal and feminine are made acceptable by the dominant presence of the paternal and masculine, as O. N. introduces a long list of church fathers and male English saintly ancestors into the picture. Much as the lives of female mystics are vouchsafed by the close supervision and approbation of male ecclesiastical authorities—as O. N. illustrates with reference to the case of St. Theresa—so too, mystical experience itself as a form of devotion becomes safe because it is portrayed not purely as an activity of potentially hysterical women, but rather as a spiritual practice securely grounded in "more ancient and Primitive times."[25] This legacy is then passed from those times to the English Middle Ages, and then to the English seventeenth-century present, by a saintly male visionary genealogy. O. N. writes, "Whereof he who doubts may read the relation S. *Dionysus Areopage* makes of St. *Carpus*: The life of S. *Antony* written by S. *Athanasius*, the reading of which was partly a cause of the conversion of *S. Austin.*" He continues by calling the reader's attention to the lives of "S. *Benedict* by S. *Gregory*: of our *English* Saints by S. *Bede*; not long after the general conversion of *England*: Of S. *Malachias* by S. *Bernard*, his intimate acquaintance: and again of *S. Bernard*, by some *Abbots*, his familiar Friends: of *S. Francis* by S. *Bonaventure*, who lived immediately after his time. I descend no further to later times, because, possibly, they may have with Protestants lesse credit."[26] Similarly, when discussing "supernaturall and extraordinary Grace," O. N. takes fifteen pages to "sett down some passages I have met with in the Fathers" on this topic.[27]

Notably, Cressy defends St. Birgitta and St. Catherine of Siena from Stillingfleet's aspersions also by associating them with male clerical figures and minimizing female prophetic authority, and in his response to Stillingfleet he enacts a strategy of masculinizing mystical experience similar to the one O. N. employs. One of Stillingfleet's charges against the legitimate sanctity of St. Birgitta and St. Catherine is that they had contradictory revelations concerning the Immaculate Conception.

Cressy observes that while St. Birgitta's and St. Catherine's revelations "may in generall be useful to stirr up devotion in *Readers* minds," they are not "infallible." He continues by noting that in examinations of miracles in canonization processes, "The testimony of women will not be received." Then he indicates that to resolve the contradiction between the revelations of the two female saints "it will suffise therefore to set down here what two illustrious *Catholic Writers* have declared touching this point."[28] These two Catholic writers, whose pronouncements are given more weight than the revelations of St. Birgitta and St. Catherine, are the male figures "*S. Antoninus*" (68) and "Cardinal Baronius."[29]

Defending mystical language that attempts to convey the ineffable experience of divine union from Stillingfleet's charge of being "unintelligible Canting," Cressy describes the "wonderfull *Extasy*" of a "certain *Holy Man*" who "found himself present in Paradise."[30] Cressy continues:

> Now what soever it was that he saw and heard, he was, no doubt, willing to have communicated it to his brethren, but he had not the power to doe it. No human language could afford words to express matters so elevated and Divine. For if it could, I am assured he, who was the greatest *master of language* that perhaps ever was, had not failed to do it. Nay more, which still increases the wonder, though he professes that he really saw and heard these inexplicable glorious things, yet he could not determin whether all the while his corporall senses, externall or interall, were employed in this *Divine visitation.*[31]

Cressy then tips his hand, revealing that this visionary holy man, this "greatest *Fanatick* that ever was, yea the *father of all Fanaticks*," is the Scriptural authority par excellence: "S. Paul."[32]

While Stillingfleet criticizes Catholics for depriving readers of vernacular Scripture, instead attempting to satisfy them with the Middle English writings of such women as Julian of Norwich, O. N. reunites the language of vernacular mystical texts with the language of the Scriptures. Countering the gendered dimensions of the problems of Julian's language that Stillingfleet raises, O. N. observes, "If then the language of our Mysticall Divines savours of Fanaticism, I see not how severall passages in the Scripture do not run the same risk."[33] Then, significantly, he proceeds to give a long list of Scriptural passages, a list in which I find close correspondence thematically and linguistically with the very list of passages from Julian of Norwich's revelations that Stillingfleet incorporates as evidence of her fanaticism. For example, as we have seen, Stillingfleet has particular contempt for Julian's account of union with God as "one-ing." In what seems to be a direct gesture toward this criticism of Stillingfleet's, O. N. begins his discussion of Scriptural passages that might run "the same risk" of fanaticism, if indeed the language of the mystics "savours of Fanaticism," with biblical verses devoted to union with God, to enclosing and being enclosed in the divine. In other words, he foregrounds verses describing what Julian calls "one-ing." He writes, "Such are (to name some of them) S. *Paul's not living*, but Christ living in him; Not his acting, but grace with him. His being in travel with the Galatians, till Christ was formed in them: our inward, and outward: our old, and our new Man—We dead, and our life hid in Christ."[34]

Similarly, Stillingfleet objects to Julian's claim that, as he reports it, *"we may never come to the full knowing of God till we know first clearly our own soul; for into the time that it is in the full mights, we may not be all holy; and that is, that our sensuality by the virtue of Christs passion be brought up into the substance, with all the profits of our tribulation, that our Lord shall make us to get by mercy and grace. I had in party touching, and it is grounded in kind; that is to say, our reason is grounded in God which is substantially kindness"* (452–53). O. N. seems to have this objection of Stillingfleet's in mind when he chooses the following passages from Scripture to add to his list: "Attaining a knowledge of the love of Christ that passeth knowledge, but our being rooted in charity, so as to be able to comprehend the breadth, length, depth, and height thereof; Filled with all the fullness of God according to the power that worketh in vs, above all that we, can desire or vnderstand; He that is joined to the Lord is one Spirit: The Kingdome of God not coming with observation from abroad, but within vs."[35] The result is that for O. N., Julian of Norwich's Middle English is not a debased, strange mother tongue conveying fanatical, hysterical content but rather is language aligned with the masculine divine Word of Scripture.[36]

I turn now to O. N.'s invocation of Chaucer as the culmination of his effort to legitimate Middle English devotional texts and the Catholic devotional practices such writings carry into the seventeenth century. As we have seen, O. N. masculinizes and Anglicizes visionary experience, and he brings mystical texts and Scripture together. Finally, in response to Stillingfleet's claim that if the "sixteen Revelations of Mother Juliana . . . be not *new* and *Strange*, I think none ever ought to be accounted so," O. N. argues, in what is very nearly his last word (only a page of the book remains), that if the *Revelations* are new and strange, if they contain anything that "will amount to Heresy," if Julian's "Old English . . . be Fanaticism," then "let Chaucer also look to himself."[37] I hope by now this invocation of Chaucer by an early modern writer might not seem such an unusual one, even given the strong identification of Chaucer as a figure who provided significant symbolic resources for Protestant propagandists following the break with Rome as they sought to create a legacy for the reformed, non-Roman church as the authentically English true church. For O. N., however, an orthodox Catholic Chaucer serves, as for William Forrest, as an illustrious male progenitor who guarantees the inheritance of a "pre-lapsarian" (that is, pre-Protestant) idealized medieval England of Catholic devotion and Catholic writers. The past is not the realm of the feminine or the irrational; rather it offers an orthodox legacy that authorizes the Catholic present. Furthermore, Chaucer serves to combat the negative Protestant associations of the Catholic and the Middle English with the feminine that Stillingfleet employs to delegitimize Julian of Norwich's writings and to align Catholic devotion with fanaticism. Through Chaucer, Middle English becomes not a strange, heretical mother tongue but instead the orthodox, authoritative paternal idiom of the figure that Dryden, to whom I turn now, calls the Father of English poetry.

THE (CATHOLIC) FATHER OF ENGLISH POETRY: THE FIGURE OF CHAUCER IN DRYDEN'S *FABLES ANCIENT AND MODERN*

What O. N. does with Chaucer is not unlike what John Dryden does, albeit considerably more extensively, with Chaucer in his *Fables An-*

cient and Modern, his major work first published in 1699 not so long after the "Stillingfleet Controversy" and following Dryden's conversion to Roman Catholicism. Chaucer is a central figure in Dryden's *Fables Ancient and Modern*. Not only does Dryden include translations of three of Chaucer's *Canterbury Tales* (the Knight's Tale, the Nuns' Priest's Tale, and the Wife of Bath's Tale), but Chaucer also features prominently in the Prologue as well as in the poem dedicated to the duchess of Ormond that precedes the translation of the Knight's Tale. Additionally, Chaucer's character of the Parson inspires Dryden's poem "On the Good Parson," one of the two poems that close the *Fables*. Chaucer serves for Dryden as a crucial resource to create versions of religiopolitical and literary history that provide alternatives to the dominant models current in the England of William III. Furthermore, Dryden found himself forced to contend after his conversion with the same negative Protestant associations of the Catholic and the feminine that O. N. had to combat, since Dryden's opponents frequently drew on such associations as they invoked Dryden's conversion to feminize him in satirical writings.[38] Accordingly, a nexus of religion, lineage, and gendered modes of production/reproduction coalesces around Chaucer in the *Fables*, as Chaucer helps Dryden not only to reimagine English political and literary history but also to negotiate authorial identity and cultural authority.

In some regards Dryden's engagement with Chaucer is very much in line with early modern trends in reception. His choice of the particular tales to include in the *Fables* is revealing. Given Dryden's interest in defining what constitutes legitimate English kingship, his choice to open the *Fables* with the magisterial Knight's Tale, with its long history of interpretation as a model of wise kingship, is not surprising. Similarly, given Dryden's didactic proclivities, his choice of the Wife of Bath's Tale, that popular font of sentential wisdom, makes sense. His choice of the Nun's Priest's Tale is perhaps more unusual, but that tale harmonizes well with the satirist's interest in "merry tales" as vehicles for serious thought, a quality he shares with his Catholic predecessor St. Thomas More as well as with Chaucer himself. The tales Dryden chooses also gesture toward the gendered aspects of early modern Catholic reception of Chaucer that we have seen develop in the work of William Forrest

and the Catholic controversialists of the "Stillingfleet Controversy."
Both the Knight's Tale and the Nun's Priest's Tale minimize female
agency while bolstering male religious and political authority. Furthermore, by presenting the Wife of Bath's Tale without her Prologue,
Dryden recalls somewhat the cloistering move of silencing female religious and political speech found in Forrest's *History*. Such gendered
strategies are, as I will discuss, additionally borne out in the ways in
which Dryden guides readers of his *Fables* with prefatory materials,
much as Forrest does in the *History*.

Religion, politics, and the creation of an English literary canon appear to be strongly linked in Dryden's thoughts about the process of
writing the *Fables*. In his letters Dryden often juxtaposes references to
writing the *Fables* with discussions of religious and political affairs. In
a characteristic example, writing to Mrs. Seward on November 7, 1699,
Dryden sets out one of his clearest and most sincere expressions of his
Catholic faith even as he situates that faith in the fraught political environment of the end of the seventeenth century: "I can neither take the
Oaths, nor forsake my Religion, because I know not what Church to
go to, if I leave the Catholique; they are all so divided amongst them
selves in matters of faith, necessary to Salvation: & yet all Assuming the
name of Protestants. May God be pleasd to open your Eyes, as he has
opend mine: Truth is but one; and they who have once heard of it, can
plead no Excuse; if they do not embrace it."[39] He then claims to turn
his attention away from religion and politics to the subject of poetry,
continuing, "But these are things too serious, for a trifling Letter. If
you desire to heare any thing more of my Affairs, the Earl of Dorsett,
and your Cousin Montague have both seen the two Poems, to the
Duchess of Ormond, and my worthy Cousin Driden: And are of the
opinion that I never writ better."[40] The poems that he mentions are "To
Her Grace the Duchess of Ormond" and "To My Honour'd Kinsman,
John Driden, of Chesterton in the County of Huntingdon, Esquire."
The claim that a consideration of these poems represents a shift away
from religion and politics to lighter fare is somewhat misleading,
though, since in fact these poems occupy themselves quite seriously
and centrally with religious and political material, as I discuss below in
the analysis of "To Her Grace the Duchess of Ormond."

Furthermore, for Dryden in the *Fables* the domain of the literary is itself highly politicized, as it is in much of Dryden's writing. Literary considerations and debates serve to advance religious and political positions, providing the ground upon which such topics are negotiated. The religious and the literary converge strongly in the preface. Dryden first defends the literary and linguistic merits of his project using religious language. He defies those who deem it "little less than Profanation and Sacrilege to alter" Chaucer's language in any way.[41] For Dryden, unlike for Cressy, who resists modernization of Julian of Norwich's Middle English, what is essential in Chaucer's text does not reside in Chaucer's language itself. Whereas Cressy sees the reader's engagement with the actual words produced by Julian as the means of effecting a connection between past and present, of reembodying the past in the present, for Dryden that work of forging a connection is something he as a poet performs. Dryden himself makes Chaucer's essential qualities, and the valuable inheritance of Chaucer's medieval, Catholic England, available and accessible in his present. As I will discuss below, this interpretation of the poet's role is an aspect of Dryden's association of literary activity and priestly work. Dryden then asserts his own poetic orthodoxy by proclaiming his fidelity to Chaucer, proclaiming that "no Man ever had, or can have, a greater Veneration for Chaucer, than my self" (42).

That Dryden claims to "venerate" Chaucer not only signals Dryden's literary faithfulness and devotion to Chaucer but also suggests Chaucer's quasi-saintly status, a status not unlike the one Hoccleve advances for Chaucer in the *Regiment of Princes*, as I discuss in chapter 2. Hoccleve was faced with Wycliffite iconoclasts who objected to religious images and whose commitment to vernacular scripture cast shadows on vernacular writing more generally, and his saintly Chaucer helps counter those threats to orthodox Catholic religion and an English literary canon. Dryden has to resist the proto-Protestant Chaucer he inherits from the sixteenth century and re-Catholicize him in order to venerate him and to found an alternative, Catholic literary canon.

Dryden was clearly well aware of the dominant understanding of Chaucer's religion in early modern reception; for instance, a proto-Protestant identity for Chaucer is central to Speght's edition of Chaucer's *Works*, from which Dryden included material in the *Fables*. Dryden acknowledges but minimizes Chaucer's association with Wycliffism. In the preface to the *Fables*, Dryden writes of Chaucer's supposed Lollard proclivities, stating, "As for the Religion of our Poet, he seems to have some little Byas toward the Opinions of Wickliff" (35). Dryden, though, excuses this tendency by attributing it in part to Chaucer's loyalty to his patron, John of Gaunt, who was considered to have had Wycliffite sympathies. Dryden then also reframes Chaucer not as a proto-Protestant but rather as an orthodox Catholic writer who, like Dryden himself, engaged in socially and spiritually beneficial satire to stamp out clerical corruption. Dryden states, "Yet I cannot blame him for inveighing so sharply against the Vices of the Clergy in his Age. . . . For the Scandal which is given by particular Priests, reflects not on the Sacred Function. . . . A Satyrical Poet is the Check of the Laymen, on bad Priests" (35). As Sean Walsh observes, in this passage Chaucer is situated perfectly as a figure who embraces loyalty and superpolitical affiliations; he holds a position of moral authority with "only a shade of Lollard radicalism in the background."[42]

Enlarging upon the rights of satirists to criticize corrupt individuals without impugning the legitimacy of entire institutions or undermining the authority of particular offices, Dryden further advances an orthodox, Catholic, and even saintly identity for Chaucer. Much as Cressy suggests in his letter to Lady Mary Blount that she can reembody Julian's experiences by reading Julian's revelations, Dryden, too, relies on a paradigm of equivalency and reembodiment, a logic to which he resorts frequently in the *Fables*. Dryden invokes the case of Henry II and St. Thomas à Becket, stating:

> But they will tell us, that all kind of Satire, though never so well deserv'd by particular Priests, yet brings the whole Order into Contempt. . . . If the Faults of Men in Orders are only to be judg'd among themselves, they are all in some sort Parties: For since they say the Honour of their Order is concern'd in every Member of it, how can we be sure, that they will be impartial Judges? How far I may be allow'd to speak my Opinion in this Case, I know not: But I am sure a Dispute of this Nature caus'd Mischief in abundance

betwixt a King of *England* and an Archbishop of *Canterbury*; one
standing up for the Laws of his Land and the other for the Honour
(as he call'd it) of God's Church; which ended in the Murther of
the Prelate, and in the whipping of his Majesty from Post to Pillar
for his Penance. (36)

Dryden refers here to Henry II's taking of murderous revenge on his
clerical opponent St. Thomas à Becket for the saint's excommunication
of the bishops who crowned Henry in breach of Becket's own
archiepiscopal privilege of coronation. Dryden continues by suggesting that Chaucer occupies a position like that of St. Thomas à Becket,
strikingly calling Chaucer a "holy man" (36) who, like the archbishop
of Canterbury, does not refrain from rebuking clerics who overstep
their bounds. Dryden thus also aligns his own critiques of the clergy
with those advanced by Chaucer, writing, "Yet my Resentment has not
wrought so far, but that I have follow'd *Chaucer* in his Character of a
Holy Man, and have enlarg'd on that Subject [that is, the recrimination
of clerical corruption] with some Pleasure, reserving to myself the
Right, if I shall think fit hereafter, to describe another sort of Priests,
such as are more easily to be found than the Good Parson" (36–37). In
other words, Chaucer and Dryden, like the saint to whose shrine
Chaucer's pilgrims traveled, speak truth to power, upholding legitimate
ecclesiastical authority and calling corrective attention to clerical ex-
cesses and misconduct like those of the rogue bishops who crowned
Henry II. Chaucer the "holy man" stands as a reembodiment of the
saintly archbishop of Canterbury, and Dryden in turn becomes a reembodiment of Chaucer as an orthodox Catholic poet, right-thinking ecclesiastical critic, and satirist.

Dryden's multivalenced canonization of Chaucer continues in the
poem "To Her Grace the Duchess of Ormond." In the opening lines of
this poem, Dryden gives Chaucer's English poetry a tradition of literary authority equal, or even superior, to those of Greece and Rome; he
has canonized the poet as Catholic quasi-saint in the preface, and now
he canonizes the saintly Catholic English writer as an *auctor* equal to
the classical greats:

The Bard who first adorn'd our Native Tongue
Tun'd to his British Lyre this ancient Song:
Which Homer might without a Blush reherse,
And leaves a doubtful Palm in Virgil's Verse:
He matched their Beauties, where they most excel;
Of Love sung better, and of Arms as well.

                                        (1–6)

This passage not only posits the value of Chaucer's English verse but also demonstrates how complexly fluid the relationship between past and present can be in the *Fables*. As James Winn points out, Dryden plays remarkably with verb tenses in the poem's opening lines; "the blurring of tenses and the trope of rivalry make all those poets (and Dryden) simultaneously present in the mind of the reader."[43] The temporal malleability also calls to mind the oscillation between the fourteenth and the seventeenth centuries that characterizes Cressy's model of reading outlined in his prefatory epistles in his edition of Julian's revelations.

The process of setting up literary genealogies in which Chaucer occupies an originary role as "Father of *English* Poetry" (33) offers another paradigm for linking past and present in the *Fables*. Genealogies are indeed central to Dryden's project in the preface; in fact, genealogies and lineages dominate not just the preface but the *Fables* as a whole. As Anne Cotterill indicates, in the works that Dryden wrote in his last decade, he turns insistently to complex paradigms of lineage to defend his Jacobite opinions and his poetic successes.[44] Dryden's interest in lineage signals as well his concerns with gendered processes of production and reproduction (biological, textual, and symbolic) in his navigation of relationships among past moments and the present. Correspondingly, Dryden's engagement with Chaucer in religiopolitical as well as literary terms is shaped by complicated negotiations of the masculine and the feminine.

As is well known, Dryden writes in the preface, "We have our Lineal Descents and Clans, as well as other Families: *Spencer* more than once insinuates, that the Soul of *Chaucer* was transfus'd Into his Body; and that he was begotten by him Two hundred years after his Decease.

Milton has acknowledg'd to me, that *Spencer* was his Original" (25). Spenser reembodies Chaucer, and Milton in turn reembodies Spenser in a patrilineal (womanless) reproductive process: Chaucer's soul is trans-fused into Spenser's body and begets the later poet, and then Spenser more or less clones himself as Milton. A clear parallel exists between Dryden's mystically linked line of male authors and apostolic succession.[45] Dryden further crafts a strong association between the mascu-line and the Catholic by "re-Catholicizing" the adamantly Protestant Spenser and Milton, since the soul that passes from Chaucer to Spenser (whom Dryden positions as the original of Milton) is a soul whose eternal salvation had, from Dryden's and presumably Chaucer's own perspective, been ensured by Roman Catholic sacraments.

In "To Her Grace the Duchess of Ormond," the poem that fol-lows the preface and precedes Dryden's translation of the Knight's Tale, Dryden creates a set of reembodiments similar to the paradigm he establishes with Chaucer, Spenser, and Milton in the preface. In this poem, however, the picture is somewhat complicated by the presence of a woman. The Duchess of Ormond doubles the "fairest Nymph . . . Plantagenet" (134), and Dryden doubles Chaucer. Vinton Dearing, the editor of the *Works of John Dryden*, identifies "Plantagenet" as Joan, countess of Kent and princess of Wales, and for many years this has been the received scholarly opinion for the identification of the figure. Joan is "Plantagenet" through her marriage to the Black Prince, who was Edward III's eldest son and Richard II's father. The Duchess of Ormond is related to Joan of Kent, and so herself "Plantagenet," because her father, Henry Somerset, first duke of Beaufort, descended from Charles Somerset, Earl of Worcester, the illegitimate son of Henry Beaufort, third Duke of Somerset, who in turn descended from John of Gaunt, duke of Lancaster, fourth son of Edward III.[46] In other words, if the "Plantagenet" in question is Joan of Kent, then the two women are linked because the Duchess of Ormond descended from Joan of Kent's husband's younger brother. Recently, however, Cedric D. Reverand II has made a persuasive case for identifying the Plantagenet woman in question as Blanche, duchess of Lancaster, re-viving an identification first made by Walter Scott in his 1808 edition of Dryden.[47]

Whichever medieval woman Dryden intends, he posits that, since as a poet he knows another poet's mind, he can infer that "Plantagenet" inspired Chaucer to create Emily of the Knight's Tale. Dryden writes:

> If Chaucer by the best Idea wrought
> And Poets can divine each others Thought
> The fairest Nymph before his Eyes he set;
> And then the fairest was Plantagenet.
>
> (11–14)

He further suggests that the duchess of Ormond is, in effect, the reincarnation of her medieval Plantagenet kinswoman. Using the idea of the Platonic year to indicate a recursive cycle, he says, "Thus after length of Ages, she returns, / Restor'd in you and the same Place adorns" (26–27). He hails the duchess of Ormond as "*true Plantagenet*, O Race divine" (30), and repeatedly emphasizes the genealogical connection between the two women by using the name Plantagenet for both, highlighting their descent from Edward III. Dryden also posits that, even as he is inspired to write poetry by the duchess of Ormond's beauty, so too Chaucer would have been likewise inspired: "Had *Chaucer* liv'd that Angel-Face to view, / Sure he had drawn his *Emily* from You" (32–33).

Much as the language of religious devotion infuses literary justifications, authorial lineages, and paradigms of reembodiment set forth in the preface, so too there is a religious dimension to the genealogies and equivalencies set out in "To Her Grace the Duchess of Ormond." In his praise for the duchess of Ormond, Dryden emphasizes the presence of something holy in her, as when he praises her "divine" Plantagenet race as well as her "Angel-Face." Similarly, Dryden says that her face is "Paradise, but fenc'd from Sin: / For God in either Eye has plac'd a Cherubim" (155–56). This praise is couched in conventional poetic terms, but the conventions have particularly weighted significance here. That which is holy within the duchess may well signal the Roman Catholic legacy passed from the Middle Ages to Dryden's day, existing as a living, sacred presence of the past.[48]

In Dryden's imagining of the duchess's second voyage to Ireland, his representation of the interplay of gender and a Roman Catholic legacy is especially daring. Dryden casts the duchess as a Christlike messianic figure, writing:

> When at Your second Coming You appear,
> (For I foretell that Millenary Year)
> The sharpen'd Share shall vex the Soil no more,
> But Earth unbidden shall produce her Store:
> The Land shall laugh, the circling Ocean smile,
> And Heav'ns Indulgence bless the Holy Isle.
>
> (80–85)

The tone is playful, but the conceit of the duchess's arrival as a "second coming" has serious implications. The duchess—the true Plantagenet and the reincarnation of her medieval kinswoman—not only has holy qualities but also has the capacity for resurrection. She can make the holy, medieval, Catholic past live again. Embodied in the duchess of Ormond is the utopian world of the fourteenth century, which her second coming will cause to live again, so enabling Ireland to become once more a blessed paradise, a "Holy Isle" as it was before nonconformist Irish and Protestant English forces battled with Irish Catholics.

Dryden's letter to the duchess of Ormond from the winter of 1698 also focuses on her voyage to Ireland. In this letter, too, Dryden explicitly addresses the duchess as "Plantagenet," and, in lamenting her absenting herself from England, casts her trip to Ireland as a repetition of religiopolitical actions of her medieval ancestors. Dryden describes her voyage as reenacting either crusading voyages or campaigns in the Hundred Years' War, writing:

> But you Plantagenets, never think of these mean Concernments; the whole race of you have been given to make voyages into ye Holy Land to Conquer Infidells or at least to Subdue France without caring what becomes of your natural subjects ye poor English. I think we must remonstrate to you yt we can no longer live without you: For so our Ancestours have done to some of yr Family when they have been too long abroad And besides who knows but God who can do all things which seem impossible to us may raise

up another beauty in *your* Absence who may dispute *your* Kingdome with you for thus also has *your* Predecessour Richard Coeur
de Leon been servd when his Br John whose christened name I
bear while he was taking Jerusalem from ye Turks was likely to
have Usurpd Eng*land* from him.[49]

Note that here too Dryden subtly suggests a place for a version of himself in the earlier historical period, noting the shared name with Richard I's brother John. With his evocation of the second coming of the
"true Plantagenet," Dryden envisions a return to a pre-Protestant,
idealized medieval world of orthodox faith, Catholic monarchs, and
Catholic poets that serves as a point of origin for an alternative historical narrative leading to a vision of a future Britain quite different from
the one ruled by William III.

In the preface, as we have seen, Dryden creates an all-male literary
lineage and casts himself and Chaucer as holy men, suggesting that poetic production is a quasi-priestly (and thus strictly male) endeavor. In
the poem to the duchess of Ormond, Dryden not only has to contend
with the fact that he is writing for a powerful female patron, but he also
has to account for and legitimate women's presence in dynastic lines.
The feminine is for Dryden necessary as a conduit to the past, as it is for
Cressy. However, as does O. N., Dryden needs to find a safe, contained
method of making use of the feminine while eliminating the negative associations of the feminine, the Catholic, and the medieval that Protestant critics found so irresistible—a task similar to that facing William
Forrest in the later sixteenth century. Dryden also needs to determine
methods of protecting a masculine subject position as a Catholic poet as
well as of maintaining an exclusively masculine poetic/priestly lineage
in which he has a privileged place. This latter genealogical need seems
particularly urgent in Dryden's poem to the duchess of Ormond, since
in this poem the feminine seems even to invade the apostolic succession
(recalling the quasi-clerical roles enacted by St. Cecelia in the Second
Nun's Tale and the Virgin Mary in the Prioress's Tale). Dryden not only
posits the duchess's Christlike capabilities in forecasting her second
coming, but he also acknowledges what appear to be female iterations of
priestly power and succession when he writes of the duchess of Ormond

and her medieval Plantagenet kinswoman, "You perform her Office in the Sphere / Born of her Blood" (28–29).

What, then, is Dryden to do, faced with the competitive dynamics between male and female, between the living and the dead, that he has created, given his interest in maintaining privilege for patrilineal relations as well as for masculine modes of literary and cultural production like those defined in the preface?[50] Dryden's solution is to carve out a legitimate, but relatively disempowered, role for women. He crafts a necessary but subordinate role like that constructed in *The Roman Church's Devotions Vindicated* for simple women and medieval female mystics safely under male clerical authority; his treatment of the duchess also recalls the cloistered mode of queenship and the restrained model of traditional female virtue embraced by Forrest.[51] In his representation of the duchess, Dryden reorients the focus to her female body, depicting it as pure but also frail and weak. Recounting the duchess's illness, Dryden compares her to porcelain which "by being Pure, is apt to break" (121). The poem continues to dwell at some length on the duchess's physical infirmity, then turns to rejoicing at her recovery, which has "restor'd / The Hopes of lost Succession to Your Lord" (146–47), highlighting the biological reproductive imperative to which the duchess is subject.

Dryden speaks of the duchess's illness in terms of humoral disorder, saying, "That Heav'n alone, who mix'd the Mass, could tell / Which of the Four Ingredients could rebel" (116–17). "Mass" here literally means, of course, the material corpus of her body, formed by God. However, the word "mass" coupled with the reference to heaven, and used to describe the creation of a body, recalls the Catholic Mass and the priestly work of consecrating the Host to produce the body of Christ. Furthermore, though Dryden says heaven alone can tell the cause of the duchess's illness, in effect he is assuming the authority to do so, to make a diagnostic judgment, telling the condition of the duchess's body by writing a poem about it. The lines suggest the proper assignment of sacramental reproduction and poetic, quasi-sacerdotal labor to those divinely ordained to be part of a male apostolic succession descended from the heavenly High Priest, even as the passage highlights the corporeality—and weakness—of the female body, which excludes women from that succession, delegating them to the work of biological reproduction.

By the end of the poem, Dryden has shifted the duchess from what might be interpreted as a Christlike priestly role as one who performs divine offices, or a Christlike messianic role, into what is an unambiguously female, maternal role recalling the Virgin Mary. He emphasizes the duchess's chaste purity—he calls her "a Chast Penelope" (158)—and looks forward to her producing a male heir who will "fill in future Times his Father's place, / And wear the Garter of his Mother's Race" (167–68). Unable to rely either on the mystical transmigration of souls from one male figure to another or on the process of male cloning imagined in the preface to transmit the Plantagenet, medieval, Catholic legacy to a male heir, Dryden treats this legacy like the divine Logos that passed through the chaste and clean body of the Virgin Mary to take on human form.[52] The legacy, in Dryden's formulation, moves from its incarnation in the Catholic rulers of the medieval past through the pure, noble body of the duchess to be embodied in a future male heir.

Gender and Ambiguity:
The 1713 Frontispiece of the *Fables*

I want to turn now to the textual history of the *Fables* to explore the ways in which Dryden's negotiations of past and present, masculine and feminine, resonate as the text performs the cultural work of suggesting particular versions of literary and political history. Though the poem to the duchess of Ormond seeks in some respects clearly to delineate a hierarchy of masculine and feminine roles in the process of bringing the legacies of the past through the present and into the future, the relationships between the categories of masculine and feminine, as well as past and present, remain fraught—as they were for Dryden himself. Those complications become more pronounced, and indeed take on lives of their own, as Dryden's text and his own legacy themselves pass out of his hands into the next generation. In 1713, Jacob Tonson put out a second issue of the first edition of Dryden's *Fables Ancient and Modern*. This second issue included a frontispiece depicting a scene of poetic inspiration (fig. 1).[53]

FIGURE I. Frontispiece to Dryden's *Fables Ancient and Modern* (Harry Ransom Center, University of Texas at Austin shelfmark PR 3418 F3 1713; used by permission; photograph by Aaron Pratt)

At the top of the image, putti hold volumes labeled "Chaucer" and "Ovid." From these volumes beams of light shine onto a mirror held by another putto to illuminate the central figure, who wears a laurel wreath and holds a quill pen in one hand and a volume marked "Dryden's Fables" in the other hand. At the central figure's feet are two other putti, one of whom leans on a stack of books (the bottom of which bears the inscription "Homer" on the spine) holding a theatrical mask in one hand and a volume marked "Boccace" in the other.

On the one hand, this is an unsurprising, stylized neoclassical image. On the other hand, some details of the image are somewhat unexpected. Interestingly, this image ideally captures the intricate interplay of gender, lineage, and modes of production/reproduction present in "To Her Grace the Duchess of Ormond." It would initially seem that the central figure must be the poet Dryden, given that the scene represents the writing of a volume labeled as Dryden's *Fables*. The laurel wreath also suggests that the central figure ought to be identified as Dryden. He was appointed poet laureate in 1668, although by the time he wrote the *Fables* the Catholic poet no longer officially held the position, since he had been stripped of the title when William III and Mary came into power in 1688. Other aspects of the central figure's appearance give a different impression. In particular, in spite of the heavily muscled arms and legs, the figure has attributes suggestive of femininity. For instance, the figure has a bare torso and what seem to be enlarged breasts, and from beneath the laurel wreath a curled lock of hair cascades over the figure's right shoulder in a style suggestive of feminine sensuality—a hairstyle reminiscent of the coiffure worn by Eliza Haywood in the portrait satirized by Pope in the *Dunciad*, which Janine Barchas describes as "unfastened locks of hair arranged suggestively."[54] Perhaps, then, the figure is not meant to be Dryden, but rather a muse, and literary production is being represented as a feminine, generative process.

Still other elements of the image make this feminine reading of the figure difficult to sustain, though. The light passing between the volumes of Chaucer and Ovid in the heavens and the mirror onto which the central figure gazes does not seem to reflect from the mirror onto the figure's head, hand, or heart, as one might expect; nor does it fall onto the open volume of Dryden's *Fables*. Indeed, no beam of light seems to come off the mirror at all in the engraving. The light evidently travels back and forth between the mirror and the heavens—perhaps heavenly inspiration descends from Chaucer and Ovid, and clarifying light is cast upward by Dryden's work, which reveals the truth of the originals in his translations. However, the composition of the image draws the eye down the beam from the mirror to a spot directly between the central figure's legs, where a downward pointing fold in the drapery strongly suggests the shape of male genitalia. So even as the image attaches suggestions of female fecundity to the figure, it also contains strong suggestions of male virility.

Focusing on the connections created through the image's composition, one can read it as depicting the patrilineal transmission of masculine literary *auctoritas*. Dryden is both the current possessor of such *auctoritas*, the son and heir of Chaucer the "Father of English Poetry," and a future transmitter of such *auctoritas*—the genitor of the next great English poet.[55] The image thus recalls both the lineage set out in the preface and the poetic pedigree outlined in the patent granting the position of poet laureate to Dryden. This patent construes Chaucer as the first poet laureate (granting him knighthood in the process) and then outlines an exclusively male succession of writers reaching from Chaucer down through Dryden's predecessor as laureate, William Davenant, to Dryden himself. The king grants to Dryden "All and singular the rights privileges benefits and advantages thereunto belonging as fully and amply as Sir Geoffrey Chaucer knight Sir Iohn Gower knight Iohn Leland Esquire William Camden Esquire Beniamin Iohnson Esquire Iames Howell Esquire Sir William Davenant knight or any other person or persons having or exerciseing the place Or employment of Poet Laureat or historiographer or either of them in the time of any of Our Royall progenitors."[56]

I wonder, though, whether we have to choose whether the central figure is a female muse or a male poet. Perhaps, in fact, we are *supposed* to read the figure as both masculine and feminine, as a poet who was, historically, a male human being but who at times performed roles and identities marked as feminine, both by himself and by others. Indeed, for all his emphasis on patrilineal literary affiliations and male sacramental/sacerdotal work both priestly and poetic, Dryden did, as Cotterill has demonstrated, engage in strategic self-feminization in some of his writings. She observes that after the revolution, Dryden strategically takes on a subordinate, feminine identity and feminine discursive modes of subordination and digression.[57] The complexly gendered iconography of this frontispiece evokes, significantly, a complexly gendered history, specifically a medieval Catholic history, that has great relevance for understanding Dryden's engagement as a Catholic writer with England's past and his efforts to shape a particular vision of England's literary and political cultures at the end of the seventeenth century.

The frontispiece image, like the poem to the duchess of Ormond, is centrally concerned with incarnation. In the frontispiece image, incarnation is represented in overlapping, quasi-Trinitarian configurations, configurations that, like Julian of Norwich's account of the Trinity, include both masculine and feminine properties, maternal and paternal roles. The image recalls medieval Annunciation scenes in which the Logos descends from Heaven (often represented by the dove of the Holy Spirit) along a beam of light, instantly impregnating the Virgin Mary as she is hailed by the angel Gabriel, often positioned to the viewer's left, like the putto holding the mirror in the frontispiece image.

Figures 2 and 3 provide fifteenth-century examples, while figure 4 provides a seventeenth-century Rubens Annunciation for something a bit closer temporally to Dryden, to show the continuation of the artistic conventions I think the frontispiece echoes. In such Annunciation images, the Virgin is frequently pictured with an open book, as the central figure here is. She reads the word of God as it is made incarnate in her by the angel's salutation. In the frontispiece, the divine poetic word proceeds from Father Chaucer (and perhaps also from Ovid in the guise of the Holy Spirit) in the heavens to become incarnate in Dryden, who occupies the position of the Virgin Mary. Dryden as translator is a maternal figure, "bearing" the word of earlier poets, giving it new life in the mother tongue of his day as inscribed in the book open before him. Indeed, the conceit of the Virgin Mary as a translator, as one whose maternal body renders the divine Logos into the human, material form that enables human interaction with it is not uncommon in medieval religious writing; we have seen, for instance, how it features in the Second Nun's Prologue and in Brigittine writings.

FIGURE 2. Workshop of Robert Campin, Mérode Altarpiece (The Metropolitan Museum of Art, New York; image and permission courtesy of Art Resource)

FIGURE 3. Roger van der Weyden, Annunciation Triptych Central Panel
(The Louvre, Paris; image and permission courtesy of Art Resource)

FIGURE 4. Peter Paul Rubens, *Annunciation* (Kunsthistorisches Museum, Vienna; image and permission courtesy of Art Resource)

Dryden in the frontispiece image is, though, not just a Marian figure but also simultaneously a Christlike figure. He is the incarnate, male representation of the English poetic Logos made flesh in a Trinitarian composition with Chaucer and Ovid. The seemingly paradoxical doubling of Christ and Mary, including the association of feminine, maternal qualities with Christ, itself has a medieval, Catholic history. In addition to the attribution of maternal properties to the second person of the Trinity in Julian of Norwich's revelations, we find in medieval understandings of the Incarnation an association of Christ's flesh with female flesh, because his human body came solely from the female flesh of his mother, Mary. As Caroline Walker Bynum has so persuasively argued, in later medieval devotional culture, Christ's body is associated with the maternal body in that Christ's body "bleeds and feeds," shedding blood in the crucifixion to give new life, to give birth to Ecclesia the church, and to provide eucharistic food.[58] Similarly, Christ's suffering on the cross is frequently aligned with the pain of a woman in labor, and though the Virgin Mary was believed to have experienced a painless childbirth, the suffering she underwent at the crucifixion—her compassion, literally her suffering with Christ—was understood to be the replacement for the labor pains she did not endure.

Furthermore, in addition to situating Dryden in the place of Christ in a literary Trinity, the image also positions him in a priestly role as a vicar (placeholder) of the divine figure of Chaucer, who first made the English poetic word incarnate. As in the preface, literary lineage becomes a version of apostolic succession, and Dryden the poet/translator performs a masculine, quasi-sacramental act in making Chaucer's writings (re)incarnate in the *Fables*. The creation of this priestly role for the poet recalls the emphasis Dryden places, in the preface, on the validity of priests' sacred function ("For the Scandal which is given by particular priests, reflects not on the Sacred Function" [35]). The intermediary role of the priest—or the poet—to enable access to the divine is real and vital. Only the priest can make the body of Christ accessible; similarly, Dryden positions Chaucer as divine but accessible only through Dryden's mediation. Significantly, Greg Clingham aligns Dryden's procedure as a translator with the Catholic doctrine of transubstantiation, writing that the Catholic emphasis on the real presence in the Eucharist resonates with the spirit and letter of the ways in which Dryden approaches the translation process.[59] Because Dryden can "divine" the thoughts of Chaucer (as he says, "And Poets can divine each others Thought"), the divinity of Chaucer lives again, is present again, and present in authentic, orthodox form, in the *Fables*.

The frontispiece image thus positions Dryden simultaneously as a Marian translator of the divine word, a Christlike embodiment of that word, and a priestly (re)incarnator of that word. His textual production is both maternal incarnational work and paternal reproductive work that is at once genealogical and sacramental. The suggestion that the frontispiece depicts Dryden as a poet and translator performing roles at once Marian, Christlike, and priestly might seem my twenty-first-century feminist/historicist critical fantasy. However, the 1713 frontispiece image is not the only place where this combination of roles and identities is associated with Dryden not many years after the end of his life. It appears again in a poem in a collection of verses by poets both named and unnamed marking Dryden's death, a volume entitled *Luctus Britannici*. An unnamed poet writes, at the close of the final poem in the collection, "And *Chaucer* shall again with Joy be Read, / Whose Language with its Master lay for Dead, / Till *Dryden*, striving His Remains to save, / Sunk in His *Tomb*, who *brought* him from his *Grave*."[60] Invoking the belief that Dryden was actually buried in Chaucer's tomb, this poet casts Dryden's translation of Chaucer as an act of salvific self-sacrifice on Dryden's part.[61] The passage evokes birth, death, and rebirth. Dryden's "striving" recalls the labor of childbirth, a striving that, like the Virgin Mary's act of giving birth, enables salvation, while the final two lines also suggest both burial followed by Paschal resurrection and the life-giving eucharistic confection of Christ's body. Dryden brings the medieval past back to life through both masculine, Christlike, priestly productive and female, Marian, reproductive processes, even after his own death.

CHAPTER 5

"Flying from the Depravities of Europe, to the American Strand"

Chaucer and the Chaucerian Tradition in Early America

In the "General Introduction" to the *Magnalia Christi Americana*, Cotton Mather describes the English women and men who journeyed to settle in America as "Flying from the Depravities of *Europe*, to the *American Strand*."[1] This chapter is concerned with something— something perhaps unexpected—that these English women and men brought with them on their journey across the Atlantic: a constellation of texts, tropes, and figures associated with Chaucer and the Chaucerian tradition, including texts like the Plowman's Tale attributed to Chaucer in the early modern period, though not actually by Chaucer.[2] Though Mather represents those coming to America as leaving behind European corruption and religious conflicts, in fact the colonialists carried with them to the New World early modern religious controversies, both those involving Catholics and Protestants and those involving Protestants of rival stripes. The figure of Chaucer, Chaucer's works, and works in the Chaucerian tradition feature significantly in colonialists' involvements in and negotiations of such religiopolitical conflicts in Old England and New England alike during the mid-seventeenth century.[3]

This chapter focuses on three colonial American writers—Cotton Mather, Anne Bradstreet, and Nathaniel Ward—who had personal and textual connections to each other. Anne Bradstreet, author of *The Tenth Muse Lately Sprung Up in America*, was the daughter of Thomas Dudley, one of the governors of Massachusetts whose life Mather recounts in his *Magnalia Christi Americana*. Mather also praises Bradstreet's poetry in the *Magnalia*, recommending her "Poems, divers times printed" (2:17). Connections between the Cotton family and the Dudley family existed in England as well. Around 1625, prior to their departure for New England, Thomas and Dorothy Dudley, along with their daughter Anne, moved to Boston to join the congregation of John Cotton (Cotton Mather's maternal grandfather), with whom Nathaniel Ward also had close ties. By this time Anne would have met her future husband, Simon Bradstreet, the son of Simon Bradstreet, who was a nonconformist Puritan vicar from Lincolnshire.[4] The print editions of Bradstreet's poems feature an extensive paratextual apparatus, including a series of commendatory poems. One of these poems is by Nathaniel Ward, who was Bradstreet's neighbor in Ipswich, Massachusetts, and who is perhaps best known as the author of the *Simple Cobler of Aggavvam in America*.

Mather, Bradstreet, and Ward engage with Chaucer and the Chaucerian tradition to negotiate relationships of past and present, old and new, as they establish textual, political, and spiritual authority. Chaucer and texts associated with him play key roles in these writers' processes of creating distinctively colonial religio-political visions and developing forms of New English identity distinct from those of Old England. As these colonial writers work to promote their faith and enact political as well as cultural transformations rooted in their faith, Chaucer and the Chaucerian tradition ensure the reformed legitimacy of the religion practiced in the churches of New England as well as the English authenticity of reformed Protestant religion.

"OLD CHAUCER" AND NEW ENGLAND: COTTON MATHER'S *MAGNALIA CHRISTI AMERICANA*

To begin exploring the textual and cultural significance of "Old Chaucer" and New England, it is worth considering how Chaucer's writings were, and were not, available in colonial America. Part of the reason that little attention has been paid to the place of Chaucer in early American textual culture undoubtedly has to do with the fact that in the seventeenth and early eighteenth centuries, appreciation of and readership for Chaucer's texts were at an especially low ebb. As Candace Barrington points out, American editions of Chaucer were not published until the nineteenth century, so in colonial America, Chaucer reception relied on British editions, including, in the period in which I am interested in this essay, Thynne's, Stow's, and Speght's.[5] The evidence we have from wills and catalogues for estate book sales reveals that the earliest known instance of a colonialist owning an edition of Chaucer's work dates to the last quarter of the seventeenth-century. The 1679 will of Daniel Russell of Charlestown records the bequest of a library including two folio editions of Chaucer, likely Thynne's.[6] The available evidence suggests that ownership of Chaucerian texts was not terribly widespread in the pre–Revolutionary War period, though by the time of the American Revolution, Thomas Jefferson believed Chaucer to be an essential part of a gentleman's library; he included Chaucer in the library catalogue he drew up for Robert Skipworth.[7] As will become clear, however, the figure of Chaucer, along with his works and works in the Chaucerian tradition, was by no means unknown to colonialists in the first half of the seventeenth century, even though evidence of ownership from wills, estate catalogues, and libraries catalogues is sparse.

Given the evident rarity of colonial ownership of Chaucerian texts, it is understandable that the few scholars who have devoted time to thinking about the place of Chaucer in early America would generally conclude, as Candace Barrington does, that Chaucer was simply not to the taste of the devout Protestants who fled England for the sake of their faith. Barrington argues, "These colonialists had little room on their shelves for books that did not edify, and they concurred with John Foxe, who saw the printing press as part of the providential design." She continues, "Because Chaucer was generally associated on both sides of the Atlantic with secular entertainment rather than religious truth, he was not found in the large libraries of colonial intellectuals such as John Winthrop or Cotton Mather."[8]

Interestingly, the claim that Chaucer was too strongly associated with the secular to appeal to the likes of Cotton Mather, whose views of the press and Providence were influenced by John Foxe, is undermined by none other than Cotton Mather and John Foxe themselves. Famously, as I mention in the introduction, in the *Acts and Monuments*, Foxe writes of Chaucer that he "saw in Religion as much almost, as even we do now, and vttereth in his workes no lesse, and semeth to bee a right Wicclevian, or els was never any."[9] And indeed, Foxe strongly associates Chaucer *with* religious truth, writing, "I am partlye informed of certaine, which knew the parties, which to them reported, that by reading Chausers workes, they were brought to the true knowledge of Religion. And not unlike to be true" (7:965). For Foxe, Chaucer was a proto-Protestant, a voice of true reformed religion speaking to the present from the Catholic, medieval past and effecting religious reform in Foxe's contemporary time by bringing people to "the true knowledge of Religion." While volumes of Chaucer may not have been present in Mather's library, Mather clearly knew of Chaucer, and of this proto-Protestant, spiritually efficacious Chaucer, through Foxe, if not also through more direct textual encounters—and I think some sort of direct encounter is a likely possibility, as I discuss below. Foxe was one of Mather's favorite authors; the *Acts and Monuments* was an important model for, and frequently cited source in, the *Magnalia*. For example, in framing his project in his "General Introduction," Mather mentions Foxe early on, writing, "There were many of the *Reformers*, who joined with the Reverend John Fox, in the *Complaints* which he then entered in his *Martyrology*, about the *Baits of Popery* yet left in the Church" ("General Introduction," n.p.). Foxe was also a key influence on Mather's approaches to writing biography and history.[10]

Book 2 of the *Magnalia Christi Americana*, titled "Shields of the Church," admirably illustrates Mather's biographical methodology. It includes the lives of eighteen colonial governors, giving extended accounts in separate chapters of those of William Bradford (1590–1657) of Plymouth, John Winthrop (1588–1649) of Massachusetts Bay, Edward Hopkins (1600–1657) of Connecticut, Theophilus Eaton (1590?–1658) of New Haven, and John Winthrop Jr. (1606–76) of Connecticut and New Haven. This collection of biographies is preceded by an introduction meditating on the topic of good governance, particularly on the wisdom of learning from past examples of good governance. Mather states his theme:

> *The Father* of Themisocles *disswading him from Government, show'd him the* Old Oars *which the Mariners had now thrown away upon the* Sea-shores *with Neglect and Contempt; and said,* That People would certainly treat their Old Rulers with the same Contempt. *But, Reader, let us now take up our* Old Oars *with all possible Respect, and see whether we can't still make use of them to serve our little Vessel.* . . . THE WORD Government, properly signifies the *Guidance of a Ship.* . . . New-England is *a little Ship, which hath Weathered many a Terrible Storm.* (2:1)

Mather closes the introduction to book 2 with a further reiteration of the idea that present, as well as future, generations should learn from past models and with a reference to the exemplary "Old Chaucer." The final sentence of the introduction, which suggests some direct knowledge of the content of Chaucer's writing, reads, *"And I please my self with hopes, that there will yet be found among the Sons of* New-England, *those Young Gentleman by whom the Copies given in this History will be written after; and that saying of* Old Chaucer *be remembered,* To do the Genteel Deeds, that makes the Gentleman" (2:1).

Mather's citation comes from what might seem to us today an especially surprising part of the Chaucerian corpus, the tale told by the famously lusty and much-married Wife of Bath. In the tale, an old hag forces a young knight into marriage in exchange for providing him with the answer to the question, "What thing is it that women most desiren," a question he must, by the terms of the queen's sentence, answer to avoid being put to death for committing rape.[11] On their wedding night, the old hag lectures the young knight on the virtues of age and poverty as well as on the nature of true gentility. She says:

> But, for ye speken of swich gentillesse
> As is descended out of old richesse,
> That therefore sholden ye be gentil men,

Swich arrogance is nat worth an hen.
Looke who that is moost virtuous alway,
Pryvee and apert, and moost entendeth ay
To do the gentil dedes that he kan;
Taak hym for the grettest gentil man.

(III 1109–16)

As mirth-making as it might seem to a twenty-first-century reader
to imagine the staunch Puritan Cotton Mather encountering the bawdy
Wife of Bath, it is entirely possible that he did not think about her character as developed in *The Canterbury Tales* at all. Rather, as I mention
in the introduction, he may have known the Wife of Bath's Tale as a font
of providential wisdom, as so many early modern readers did. Thus,
Mather may have encountered this part of Chaucer's corpus as textual
material largely disassociated from the personality of the teller. As we
have seen, Dryden certainly presented the Wife of Bath's Tale in such a
manner in his *Fables*, where he includes a translation of the tale but omits
entirely the Prologue that establishes the teller's identity so memorably.

The figure of the Wife of Bath also had, however, a seventeenth- and
eighteenth-century existence of her own largely separate from her tale,
as I also discuss in the introduction. Versions of the ballad "The Wanton Wife of Bath" were circulating in print well before Mather's time
and continued to circulate on both sides of the Atlantic through the
eighteenth century, so it is also possible that he *did* know of the Wife as
a vocal, pleasure-seeking, religiously transgressive figure from the ballad if not from, or if not also from, *The Canterbury Tales* itself.

So, Mather may have been aware of the Wife as a distinctive character rather than simply knowing her Tale as sentential material. In any
case, the figure of the Wife of Bath summoned by Mather's quotation
is, as I shall discuss in detail below, in fact a figure with much to offer to
colonial writers striving to negotiate spiritual and political modes of
identity vis-à-vis Old England.

Pride of place in the concatenation of biographies in book 2 intro-
duced by Mather's reference to the Wife of Bath's Tale is given to
William Bradford, governor of Plymouth Colony. As one considers
the ways in which Mather frames Bradford's life in chapter 1 of book 2,

layers of significance accrete to the Chaucer reference that ends the introduction. "The Life of William Bradford" does not actually begin with the birth of William Bradford or with another conventionally accepted place to begin a biography, Bradford's religious conversion, though Mather does eventually touch on both of these events. Rather it begins, seemingly incongruously, with a punning account of a fairly obscure Protestant martyred by Queen Mary. Chapter 1 opens: "It has been a Matter of some Observation, that although *Yorkshire* be one of the largest Shires in *England*, yet, for all the *Fires* of Martyrdom which were kindled in the Days of Queen *Mary*, it afforded no more *Fuel* than one poor *Leaf*; namely, *John Leaf*, an Apprentice" (2:2). As quickly becomes clear, John Leaf is not significant simply for his own suffering. Instead, he is important to Mather because he "suffered for the *Doctrine* of the *Reformation* at the same Time and Stake with the Famous *John Bradford*" (2:2).

John Bradford, who was martyred at Smithfield on July 1, 1555, never married and had no children, so William Bradford cannot be a direct descendant of the Marian martyr.[12] A familial bond between the two men is not the connection that concerns Mather, however. Instead, as is his typical *modus operandi*, Mather sets up a typological relationship between the martyr John Bradford and the Plymouth governor William Bradford, capitalizing on the shared last name and mobilizing a figuralism that, as Sacvan Bercovitch observes, "appears in every substantial way—intellectual, stylistic, exegetical—to follow the teachings of Foxe and his successors."[13] Mather so begins a process of crafting a reiterative dynamic, a system of equivalencies of past and present not unlike that employed by Dryden in the *Fables*.

Mather shifts immediately from Marian martyrdoms, still not to William Bradford's own life, but instead to Queen Elizabeth's persecutions of Separatist congregations in Yorkshire. He says, "But when the Reign of Queen *Elizabeth* would not admit the *Reformation* of *Worship* to proceed unto those Degrees, which were proposed and pursued by no small number of the Faithful in those Days, *Yorkshire* was not the least of the Shires in *England* that afforded Suffering *Witnesses* thereunto" (2:2). Some of these persecuted Separatists attempted to flee to the Low Countries, and Mather turns, *still* not to William Bradford, but rather to the misadventures and providential survival of "Divers of this People" who "Hired a *Dutchman* then lying at *Hull*, to carry them over to *Holland*" (2:2). Mather's account of this voyage recalls the emphasis, in the introduction, on governance as guiding a ship, as he outlines how the ship, eventually escaping the pursuivants, encounters "*an horrible Tempest*, which held them for Fourteen Days together" (2:2). Thanks to the passengers' prayers and the divine favor shown to them, "the Lord accordingly brought them at last safe unto their *Desired Haven*" (2:3).

In a transition that seems deliberately obfuscatory, Mather only now introduces William Bradford into the narrative, saying, "Among those Devout People was our *William Bradford*" (2:3). Bradford was, however, not on the ship at all. Indeed, we know from Bradford's own account of this ship's voyage in the *History of Plymouth Plantation* that he was not on the ship, and Mather knew it too, because he used Bradford's *History* as a source for the *Magnalia Christi Americana*.[14] For Mather, though, there is a typological truth to the claim that William Bradford was "among those Devout People." Just as William Bradford is in effect a reincarnation of the Marian martyrs John Leaf and John Bradford, so too is he one of the faithful, providentially favored Separatists in his own day. Indeed, as the introduction suggests, Plymouth is another iteration of the Separatists' miraculously preserved ship, just as it is another version of the ship of state guided by wise leaders of the past. Similarly, in the opening pages of book 2 of the *Magnalia*, the Catholic Mary and the Protestant Elizabeth merge into iterations of a single persecuting queen; rather than being, as Elizabeth famously is said to have claimed, Richard II, for Mather, Elizabeth is Mary.[15] The Marian martyrs Leaf and Bradford, the miraculously preserved company of Separatists, and the governor of Plymouth plantation also all become one, all iterations of a type.

Mather's Chaucer who closes the introduction to book 2 serves as a catalyst, transforming the Catholic, English medieval past into the age of true religious reform, a source of true English Protestant identity. In a move that resembles the strategies of both Catholic and Protestant propagandists in the sixteenth century, figures who strove to claim primitive Christianity as their own to ground their faith's legitimacy as the true church, Mather claims the medieval past embodied in Chaucer as a point of origin. For Mather, Chaucer stands at the head of the lineage of types that opens chapter 1 of book 2, giving the Marian martyr John Bradford, the ship of Separatists, and William Bradford an ancestor, a spiritual forefather who establishes and speaks for an authentic English tradition of religious reform. Whereas for Dryden, Cressy, and the Catholic participants in the "Stillingfleet Controversy," Chaucer anchors a Catholic textual tradition that links the English Catholic Middle Ages with an alternative Catholic mode of English identity in the late seventeenth-century Protestant present, for Mather Chaucer provides an alternative model of the past in which the Middle Ages is an era of English religious reform that serves as a foundation and source of legitimation for *New* England's religiopolitical project. Rather than the *translatio imperii* that so famously enables England to identify itself, via the travels of Aeneas and his descendant Brutus, as New Troy in medieval texts, in the *Magnalia Christi Americana* Mather enacts what might be termed *"translatio reformati"* from Old England to New, from "Old Chaucer" through the Marian martyrs, the Elizabethan Separatists, and finally across the Atlantic with John Bradford.

Another invocation of Chaucer in the *Magnalia* strengthens the case that Chaucer is for Mather a figure who grounds (as we shall see, in this case quite literally) a lineage of English religious reform through a concatenation of holy men who embody reformed religion, a lineage stretching back from seventeenth-century New England to fourteenth-century Old England. Chaucer appears again in book 7 of the *Magnalia*, which is entitled "Ecclesiarum Praelia, or The Book of the Wars of the Lord." As Mather describes it, this book relates "The Afflictive Disturbances which the *Churches of New-England* have Suffered from their Various Adversaries and The Wonderful Methods and Mercies whereby the Churches have been Delivered out of their Difficulties" (title page, book 7). In article 15 of this book, Mather recounts *"The Martyrdom* of Mr. Shubael Dummer, *with the fate of* York" (7:77). The narrative relates a Native American attack on January 25, 1691, on the town of York in which Dummer, "The Pastor of the *little Flock*," was killed along with approximately fifty other townspeople, while a hundred or so more were taken into captivity. Mather describes Dummer as a "Gentleman," repeating the theme sounded in his earlier Chaucerian allusion, further noting that he is "*Well*-Descended, *Well*-Tempered, *Well*-Educated." Though Dummer had opportunity to leave York for a safer post, "he chose rather with a paternal Affection to stay amongst those who had been so many of them Converted and Edified by his Ministry" (7:77).

Mather then conventionally highlights the savagery of the Native Americans by describing them in animalistic terms, calling them "Wolves" (7:78), "Salvage Hounds" (7:78), "Blood-Hounds" (7:77), and "Tygres" (7:77). Somewhat more surprisingly, though, and more significantly for our purposes, he also calls them "Popish *Indians*," and he explicitly associates their attack on the minister Dummer with Catholic hostility. He says that the Native Americans were "set on by some *Romish Missionaries*" and that they "had long been wishing, that they might Embue their Hands in the Blood of some *New-English* MINISTER; and in this Action they had their Diabolical Satisfaction" (7:77). So, just as Catholic Queen Mary and Protestant Queen Elizabeth collapse into each other as persecutors of reformed religion, so too the Native Americans and the Old World Catholics merge as forces of evil arrayed, in Mather's eyes, against righteous reform, reform begun in England in "Old Chaucer's" time when Wycliffites first took on "popery."

Article 15 ends with a verse epitaph for Dummer, followed by this assertion: "To compleat the *Epitaph* of this Good Man there now needs no more than the famous old *Chaucer's* Motto, *More mini aerumnarum Requies*" (7:78). Mather's reintroduction of Chaucer illuminates the link between Old World and New, the correspondences among Lollards burned at the stake, Marian martyrs, persecuted Separatists in the Elizabethan era, and a colonial minister attacked by Native Americans. This motto, which translates "My death is a rest from cares," comes not from any of Chaucer's works, but rather from the inscription on his tomb in Westminster Abbey. The phrase actually comes from Sallust (*The War with Catiline* 51.20). Until Urry published his 1721 edition of Chaucer, it did not appear in any Chaucer editions. Mather probably knew the motto from the description of Chaucer's tomb present in William Camden's *Reges, reginae, nobiles, at alij in ecclesia collegiata B. Petri Westmonasterij sepulti*.[16] The tomb of a medieval poet who was buried with Catholic rites becomes for Mather the tomb of something like a Protestant saint, providing the appropriate last words to memorialize the New World saint Shubael Dummer. Chaucer here again is at the head of a chain of the sacred, reformed dead—as he is at the head of the series of John Leaf, John Bradford, and William Bradford. "Old Chaucer," whose tomb provides a fitting memorial for a New England minister, underwrites Mather's claims for New England, for the colonies, as the true locus of English-speaking reformed religion and of proper governance. America is, somewhat paradoxically, for Mather more authentically "English" than the England of his day, and the churches of the colonialists represent the truest exemplars of the English reformation.

PIERS PLOWMAN, THE CHAUCERIAN TRADITION, AND ANNE BRADSTREET'S *THE TENTH MUSE*

Just as Chaucer is for Mather not a Catholic poet but a proto-Protestant quasi-saint, so too Chaucer's fourteenth century is the originary era not only of reformed religion but also of political reforms that revise established social hierarchies. The encapsulation of such social revisionism in words attributed to "Old Chaucer"—"To do the Genteel Deeds, that makes the Gentleman"—comes, as I mentioned, from the Wife of Bath's Tale. The revisionist tenor of this version of gentility accords with the Wife of Bath's rebellious and, in her time perhaps even heterodox, behavior.[17] The claim would also not have been unsympathetic to the rebels of 1381 who identified so strongly with the figure of Piers Plowman from William Langland's fourteenth-century poem *Piers Plowman*, a figure at least sometimes in Anne Bradstreet's period with associated with the Plowman of the pseudo-Chaucerian Lollard tale or even with Chaucer himself.

Piers Plowman, and the figure of the Plowman more broadly, feature significantly in New World writers' mobilization of the Chaucerian tradition in the service of their religious and political aims. Indeed, one iteration of the Plowman traveled to New England on the same ship as Anne Bradstreet, daughter of Thomas Dudley.[18] Anne Dudley married

Simon Bradstreet, son of a Puritan vicar from Lincolnshire, in 1628. In March of 1630, Anne and Simon, along with Anne's parents, Thomas and Dorothy Dudley, sailed for New England aboard the *Arbella*.[19] Significantly, Thomas Dudley brought books with him to New England, including a copy of Robert Crowley's edition of *Piers Plowman*.[20]

Robert Crowley strongly links *Piers Plowman* with reformed religion, positioning the author as Wycliffe's contemporary. He considers the author of *Piers Plowman* and the Oxford theologian to be "twin precursors of the Protestant Reformation."[21] Crowley attributes the authorship of *Piers Plowman* to "Roberte langelande, a Shropshere man borne in Cleybine, about viii. Myles from Maluerne hille."[22] He likely made this assertion of authorship based on information he took from John Bale. Though Crowley does not assign authorship of *Piers Plowman* to Chaucer, evidence exists that in his period and for many years afterward some readers connected the figure of Piers Plowman, and in some cases the poem *Piers Plowman* itself, with Chaucer, as Lawrence Warner has demonstrated in recent work.[23] For example, John Leland attributed "Petri Aratoris fabula" to Chaucer, and Alexandra Gillespie and John Carley have provided strong evidence that the text Leland had in mind in making this claim was not, as was long assumed, the pseudo-Chaucerian Plowman's Tale, but in fact the poem *Piers Plowman* itself.[24] Furthermore, as Warner has shown, there is also an extant copy of Crowley's first, 1550 edition that—in spite of what Crowley himself says about authorship—associates the text with Chaucer. This copy is Cambridge University Library Syn. 7.55.12, and it is "signed 'Ez. Johnson' in a seventeenth- or eighteenth-century hand."[25] Johnson has written on the title page, "The Vision of Pierss Plowman sd to be wrote by Chaucer some say by a Wickliffian about Rc 2d time."[26] By the time Thomas Dudley brought his copy of Crowley's text to New England, there was, then, an established tradition conflating the poem *Piers Plowman*, the figure of Piers Plowman, the pseudo-Chaucerian Plowman's Tale, and the figure of Chaucer, all of which merged into a kind of aggregate fourteenth-century proto-Protestantism.

We cannot be sure whether or not Thomas Dudley or Anne Bradstreet was aware of the associations among Chaucer, the figure of the Plowman, and Crowley's *Piers Plowman*. It is certainly possible that they did know this textual tradition, however. Equally, we can only speculate about whether Anne Bradstreet read her father's copy of Crowley's *Piers Plowman*. Bradstreet had, however, an exceptionally strong education, education her father encouraged, so she may well have done so. Simon and Anne Bradstreet's large library was destroyed in a fire (a fire Anne Bradstreet made the subject of one of her poems), and we do not know its full contents, but it even seems plausible to imagine that they even had their own copy of Crowley's *Piers Plowman* on the shelf, along with the works of the Protestant literary stars Philip Sidney, Edmund Spenser, and Guillaume de Salluste du Bartas— among others—who feature in Anne Bradstreet's poetry.

Mather devotes a fairly extended passage to Anne Bradstreet in his biography of Thomas Dudley, emphasizing her learning and situating her in relation to a European tradition of women's writing. He traces the contours of a history of Old World female authorship beginning with classical figures to place Bradstreet in an established lineage. He states, "*America* justly admires the Learned Women of the other *Hemisphere*," mentioning such classical women as Hypatia; Sarocchia; "the Three *Corinne's* which equal'd, if not excell'd, the most celebrated *Poets* of their Time" (2:17); moving then to the "Empress *Endocia*, who Composed Poetical Parahprases in Divers Parts of the *Bible*, and . . . *Rosuida*, who wrote the *Lives* of Holy Men; and *Pamphilia*, who wrote other Histories" (2:17). He concludes by praying that into "Catalogues of *Authoresses*" there may be "a room now given unto Madam Ann Bradstreet, the Daughter of our Governour *Dudley*, whose *Poems*, divers times Printed, have afforded a grateful Entertainment unto the Ingenious, and a Monument for her Memory beyond The Stateliest *Marbles*" (2:17). Though Chaucer does not appear in Mather's all-female list of European writers, the Chaucerian tradition (particularly the Plowman branch of that tradition) and the England of Chaucer's and *Piers Plowman*'s time have important roles to play in Bradstreet's "*Poems*, divers times Printed," as she seeks to advance the English Protestant cause while at the same time establishing an independent, distinctive colonial voice and identity. [27]

It is a commonplace in criticism of Bradstreet's poetry to divide her work into the categories of "public" and "private." The "public" poems include those published in the 1650 edition of *The Tenth Muse* and are typically considered less than successful poetic efforts, even though the collection evidently sold well when it was initially published. The volume appears in William London's 1657 *Catalogue [of] the Most Vendible Books in England* as follows: "Mrs. Bradstreet. The 10. Muse, a Poem. 8o." While we do not have specific data on print runs for Bradstreet's publications, it is possible to approximate this information by comparing accounts for similar volumes. Research on publishing records for colonial literary texts demonstrates that in the early and middle eighteenth century, it was not uncommon to see print runs of three hundred to five hundred copies. Because Bradstreet's first and second editions of *The Tenth Muse* were published in the seventeenth rather than the eighteenth century, these comparative data apply most aptly to the third edition, which appeared in 1758. However, Pattie Cowell indicates that according to what we know of market factors, the print runs of Bradstreet's first and second editions would likely have been at least as large.[28] Bradstreet's "private" poetry, which has received greater literary acclaim, includes the poems about domestic life, her relationship with her husband, and her roles as wife and mother, poems added to those originally published in the 1650 edition when it was published again in Boston, Massachusetts, in 1678. More recent work on Bradstreet has sought to break down these categories, and in her own period the circumstances of her poetry's first publication, combined with the content of the poems themselves, indicate that from the outset her poetry exhibits a complicated interplay of the personal and the political, the domestic and the public.

One poem that illustrates the ways in which the public and the private, the religiopolitical and the domestic, are not separate but rather mutually informing in *The Tenth Muse* is "A Dialogue between Old England and New, concerning their Present Troubles, Anno 1642."[29] Bradstreet frames the poem as an intimate conversation between the figures of Old England as a mother and New England as a daughter. The content of this domestic tete-à-tete is, though, explicitly political. The two female figures explore the dynamic interplay of the past, present, and desired future for reformed religion in relation to the political events in England during the 1630s and early 1640s. The political dimensions of this poem, and of *The Tenth Muse* as a whole, are highlighted by the fact that the publisher who brought out *The Tenth Muse* in London in 1650 was Stephen Bowtell, who was known as a publisher of political books.[30] The likely process by which the poems that were published as *The Tenth Muse* came to England is itself entwined in religiopolitical affairs. John Woodbridge likely took Bradstreet's manuscripts to Britain in 1647.[31] Woodbridge was Anne Bradstreet's brother-in-law; he married her sister Mercy in 1639, and he was quite active in both the religious and political spheres in both the Old and New Worlds. He immigrated to Massachusetts in 1634, leaving his education for the ministry at Oxford after Archbishop Laud instituted severe penalties for nonconformity, and he was ordained in Boston, Massachusetts, in 1645. He then helped found the new settlement of Andover, serving as its first minister.[32] When he returned to England in 1647, likely bearing Bradstreet's poems with him, he became chaplain to the Commissioners of Parliament. The Commissioners were sent to the Isle of Wight in December 1647 to negotiate with Charles I.[33] The efforts at negotiation failed, because Charles was already plotting with envoys from Scotland to try to gain support for efforts to restore him to the throne.[34] Furthermore, "A Dialogue" undoubtedly helps illustrate why *The Tenth Muse* was included in a collection of Civil War and Commonwealth political texts compiled by the London bookseller George Thomason between 1641 and 1662.[35]

In Bradstreet's "Dialogue," the figure of New England laments and criticizes Old England's contemporary state before visualizing a glorious future. New England expresses a desire for the end of destructive civil war while sounding a clarion call for reformed religion. As New England diagnoses Old England's troubles and develops a picture of an optimistic future, a recursive mode emerges reminiscent of Mather's typological methodology in the *Magnalia*.[36] In looking to the past to understand the present and envision the future, New England turns to iconic moments of early modern English history, moments typically characterized by their own turns further to the past, to medieval texts, history, and cultural phenomena.

Historical recursivity appears early in the poem, when, in asking Old England "What ayles the" (141), New England asks, in effect, whether a series of events from England's medieval history have recurred:

What, hath some *Hengist*, like that *Saxon* stout,
By fraud, and force, usurp'd thy flowring crown,
And by tempestuous Wars thy fields trod down?
Or hath Canutus, that brave valiant *Dane*,
The regall, peacefull Scepter from thee tane?
Or is't a *Norman*, whose victorious hand
With *English* blood bedews thy conquered Land?
Or is't intestine Wars that thus offend?
Doe *Maud*, and *Stephen* for the Crown contend?
Doe Barons rise, and side against their King?
And call in Forreign ayde, to help the thing?
Must *Edward* be depos'd, or is't the houre
That second *Richard* must be clapt I'th'Tower?
Or is it the fatall jarre againe begun,
That from the red, white pricking Roses sprung?
Must *Richmonds* ayd, the Nobles now implore,
To come, and break the tushes of the Boar?

(142)

Old England responds by denying that contemporary versions of any of these situations are the cause of her current distress. She, too, though, introduces medieval history into the conversation as she denies that her problems are iterations of earlier political traumas:

Nor is it *Alcies* Son, and *Henries* Daughter,
Whose proud contention cause this slaughter;
Nor Nobles siding, to make *John* no King,
French *Lewis* unjustly to the Crown to bring;
No *Edward*, *Richard*, to lose rule, and life,
Nor no *Lancastrians*, to renew old strife;
No Crook-backt Tyrant, now usurps the Seat,
Whose tearing tusks did wound, and kill, and threat:
No Duke of *York*, nor Earl of *March*, to soyle
Their hands in Kindreds blood, whom they did foyle:
No need of *Tudor*, Roses to unite,
None knows which is the Red, or which the White.

(142–43)[37]

While Old England's problems are not recurrences of medieval acts of usurpation, manifestations of tyranny, or rival claims to the throne, Old England indicates that the cause of her current predicament is something else strongly associated with one dominant early modern, Protestant characterization of the Middle Ages: popery. Old England tells New England that "the cause" of her suffering is "my Sins, the breach of sacred Lawes" (143), and enlarges:

> Idolatry, supplanter of a Nation,
> With foolish superstitious adoration;
> And lik'd, and countenanc'd by men of might,
> The Gospel is trod down, and hath no right;
> Church Offices are sold, and bought, for gaine,
> That Pope, had hope, to find *Rome* here againe.
> (143)

The solution to Old England's predicament, too, lies, from New England's perspective, in yet another early modern characterization of the Middle Ages, one consolidated in the Elizabethan era and typified by Foxe's Chaucer the "right Wicclevian" and Crowley's Piers Plowman—that is to say, Lollard-style anticlericalism, iconoclasm, and rejections of prelacy.

Another important vector is involved in transmitting this tradition of fourteenth-century proto-Protestantism to the seventeenth century: the Martin Marprelate pamphlets, which were produced between 1588 and 1590 by one or more Puritan writers to skewer the episcopacy and the Elizabethan Religious Settlement. Many of the pamphlets feature "a country bumpkin, jabbering clown, or a naïve but earnest observer" who satirizes and criticizes the established church.[38] One such rustic figure is none other than Piers Plowman, as the tracts draw both upon William Langland's *Piers Plowman* and the pseudo-Chaucerian Lollard Plowman's Tale. Indeed, the second edition of the Protestant polemical text *I Playne Piers* includes a proclamation on the title page linking Piers Plowman and the Marprelate pamphlets. The title character, Piers, assumes the authorial role and declares, occupying the place of an authorial signature, "if any my name doo craue, I am the Gransier of Martin Mareprelitte."[39]

Particularly apposite to my purposes is the Marprelate tract *A Dialogue Wherein Is Plainly Layd Open the Tyrannicall Dealing of Lord Bishops against Gods Children*, since this text, first published in 1589, was reprinted in 1640 as part of an anti-episcopal campaign.[40] In this *Dialogue*, a Puritan figure, falling into conversation with a character called Jacke, who has been at Orléans in France, says, "I pray you, if you came from *Orleans*, there they have the masse, for they are of the league; & then I suppose you have bin partaker of their Idolatrie" (A1b). Once an Anglican minister joins the conversation, the Puritan character discourses at length on "the vnlawefulnesse of Lord Bb" (Bishops) (A2b). He later describes contemporary England to a Catholic who joins the group as "a land sore troubled with these treacherous *Papists*, and filthy *Atheists*, and our church pestered with the Bishops of the Diuel, nonresidents, Popish priests, and dumbe dogs" (D2a).

New England's speech in Bradstreet's "Dialogue" resembles the language and rhetoric of the Marprelate tradition as characterized in the *Dialogue*. For instance, her antiprelatical polemic recalls the speech of the Puritan to the Papist mentioned above, echoing as well the language of the vestarian controversy of the 1560s that helped spur on the Martin Marprelate pamphleteers. New England proclaims:

These are the dayes, the Churches foes to crush
To root out Prelates, head, tail, branch, and rush.
Let's bring Baals vestments out, to make a fire,
Their Myters, Surplices, and all their tire,
Copes, Rochets, Crossiers, and such trash,
And let their names consume, but let the flash
Light Christendome, and all the world to see,
We hate Romes Whore, with all her trumperie.

(147)

New England calls not only for iconoclasm and the destruction of all traces of popery but also for military crusade. In doing so, she reanimates more than just the early modern proto-Protestant fourteenth century as embodied in Foxe's Wycliffite Chaucer, Crowley's Lollard Piers Plowman, and the construal of Piers Plowman as Martin's "grandsire." She also reembodies Elizabeth I, in whose reign these early modern textual revivals of the Middle Ages circulated. Before outlining her final vision of a happy ending for Old England—which looks to be a return to what Bradstreet calls, in the opening of the very next poem in *The Tenth Muse*, England's "Halson dayes" in Elizabeth's reign—New England exclaims:

> When thus in Peace: thine Armies brave send out,
> To sack proud Rome, and all her vassals rout:
> There let thy name, thy fame, thy valour shine,
> As did thine Ancestours in Palestine. . . .
>
> . . . .
>
> This done, with brandish'd swords, to Turky go,
> (For then what is't, but English blades dare do)
> And lay her wast, for so's the sacred doom,
> And do to Gog, as thou hast done to Rome.
>
> (148)

Bradstreet's perspectives on monarchical rule, and on Elizabeth I in particular, are somewhat difficult to pin down (of course, there are always dangers in assuming one can ever pin down an author's political views from literary works). Clearly, in the "Dialogue" New England looks back to Elizabeth I's reign approvingly, and Bradstreet praises the period, and its Protestant heroes, in her poem on Philip Sidney. Her poem on Elizabeth herself, too, is quite positive, defending the queen's legacy even as she writes a defense of women more broadly construed. Elizabeth Wade White advances a theory that Anne Bradstreet (in spite of the praise for Parliament that appears in the "Dialogue") was one of those who mourned Charles I's death under Cromwell's Protectorate but had to conceal their feelings or to express them in coded, secret fashion.[41] She grounds this argument in an interpretation of Bradstreet's "David's Lamentation for Saul and Jonathan," which, she argues, was not taken to England in the original batch of poems to be published but rather was composed in 1649 and then sent to England to Woodbridge, or possibly to Nathaniel Ward, as "an elegy in scriptural disguise for the king."[42]

However, there is a moment in the "Dialogue" that potentially suggests very different political attitudes toward Charles and perhaps toward the monarchy as an institution. New England proclaims:

Go on brave *Essex*, shew whose son thou art,
Not false to King, nor Countrey in thy heart,
But those that hurt his people and his Crown,
By force expel, destroy, and tread them down.

(147)

The Essex in question is Captain General and Chief Commander of the Parliamentary Army. He is the son of Robert Devereux, second earl of Essex and favorite of Elizabeth I. Suggesting that this Essex resembles—perhaps even is a new iteration of—his father introduces a note of ambiguity into the poem that is quite Chaucerian, quite reminiscent, in fact, of the linguistic cleverness that characterizes the Wife of Bath's Prologue and Tale, where the Wife seems to say one thing only to mean another, or where she wields double entendres with ease. The lines emphasize Essex's loyalty to king and crown, calling to mind the second earl's long loyal service to Elizabeth I. However, the second earl of Essex was also the instigator of the famous "Essex Rebellion" against Elizabeth, a rebellion for which, as I mention above, he set the stage with a performance of Shakespeare's *Richard II*. So, is New England urging further action against the king—even rebellion and deposition, if not outright regicide—under cover of lines emphasizing Essex's loyalty to the monarch? Does New England see Charles, as Elizabeth I is reported to have seen herself, as Richard II, or as Mather saw Elizabeth, an inadequate supporter of religious reform? This argument seems possible, albeit somewhat unlikely; at the least, though, these lines present a complication, even if perhaps an unintended one, to the praise lavished on Elizabeth elsewhere in Bradstreet's poetry.

Whatever Queen Elizabeth may have meant to Anne Bradstreet personally, in *The Tenth Muse* Elizabeth features as an Amazon or virago who prefigures the character of New England. In speaking her belligerent lines about crusading against Roman popery and "Gog," New England calls to mind Bradstreet's description of Elizabeth I as "Feirce

Tomris (Cirius Heads-man, Sythians Queen)." Bradstreet's Elizabeth and her New England are warriors for the reformed cause; New England's call to arms in the "Dialogue" evokes the queen as she is poised to defeat the Armada of Catholic Spain, whom Bradstreet describes in her poem "In Honour of That High and Mighty Princess, Queen Elizabeth of Most Happy Memory" as "Our Amazon I'th' Campe at Tilberry" (157).[43] In the future New England outlines for Old England, reformed religion will triumph by both the Word and the sword as a militant woman leads the way.

THE PLOWMAN MEETS THE WIFE OF BATH: NATHANIEL WARD AND ANNE BRADSTREET

Perhaps the earliest American literary reference to Chaucer by name, one that predates Mather's 1702 *Magnalia*, occurs in the paratextual material incorporated in *The Tenth Muse*. The volume includes a series of commendatory verses, one of which was written by Bradstreet's neighbor in Ipswich, Massachusetts, Nathaniel Ward. Ward's poem includes a brief reference to Chaucer, and, though it is brief, around this Chaucer reference coalesce ideas that resonate with Bradstreet's interests in the "Dialogue" as well as with Mather's aims in the *Magnalia*. In Ward's poem, as in the militant closing scene of the "Dialogue," gender, political power, and reformed religion are all at play. A similar interrogation of gender, religious reform, and mid-seventeenth-century political turmoil in England characterizes Nathaniel Ward's longer and better-known work, *The Simple Cobler of Aggavvam in America*, published in 1647 by Stephen Bowtell, the same publisher who in 1650 would publish *The Tenth Muse*.[44] This longer text helps shed light on the implications of Ward's invocation of Chaucer in the commendatory poem in *The Tenth Muse*.

Ward was a Puritan minister who, prior to his ordination in 1618, pursued a legal career in England. He was member of the circle of Thomas Hooker, a group opposed to Archbishop Laud's attempts to standardize the Church of England.[45] In England Ward was closely connected with John Cotton, Cotton Mather's maternal grandfather, and he immigrated to Ipswich, Massachusetts, in 1634 after Archbishop Laud expelled him from his pulpit at Stondon. He later moved to Boston, where he worked with John Cotton to draft the law codes for Massachusetts. In 1645, Ward began writing *The Simple Cobler of Aggavvam*, which he sent to his brother John in England. In 1646, Nathaniel Ward himself returned to England, and *The Simple Cobler* appeared in print a year later.

James Egan has argued persuasively that the joking tone, rhetorical strategies, and literary tropes of *The Simple Cobler* draw upon the Martin Marprelate tracts. As we have seen, the Marprelate *Dialogue* was reprinted in 1640, and Egan notes that the Marprelate tradition had a robust presence in the pamphlet exchanges that characterized the period of the Civil War and Interregnum.[46] Ward's simple cobbler is another naïve rustic like Piers Plowman, jestingly speaking truth to power. One of the most strikingly Marprelate-inflected sections of *The Simple Cobler* comes when Ward embarks upon an excursus on fashion. In a somewhat forced connection, Ward links contemporary arguments for religious toleration (which he opposes mightily) to what he sees as English women's equally foolish desires for up-to-the-minute attire. Expressing from a very different religious stance the same sort of antipathy toward novelty that William Forrest proclaims in his writings, Ward says, "If all be true we hear Never was any people under the Sun, so sick of new Opinions as *English-men*; nor of new-fashions as *English-women*: if God help not the one, and the devil leave not helping the other, a blindman may easily foresee what will become of both."[47] Joining his criticism of English women's frivolous concerns with new modes of dress with his hostility toward the French, Catholic queen Henrietta Maria, Ward, in full Marprelate spate, opines: "When I heare a nugiperous Gentledame inquire what dresse the Queen is in this week; what the nudiustertian fashion of the Court; I mean the very newest: with egge to be in it in all haste, what ever it be; I look at her as the very gizzard of a trifle, the product of a quarter of a cypher, the epitome of nothing, fitter to be kickt, if shee were of a kickable Substance, than either honoured or humoured" (BIVb). He further claims that English women's adoption of courtly fashions "not only dismantles their native lovely lustre" but also transforms them into "gant bar geese, ill-shapen shotten shell-fish, Egyptian Hieroglyphicks, or at the best into French flurts of the pastery, which a proper English woman should scorn with her heels" (BIVb). Finally, he laments, "I speak sadly; mee thinks it shold break the heartes of English-men, to see so many goodly English-women imprisoned in French Cages" (CIb). Ward follows his tirade on feminine foolishness and excess in dress with a critique of men who wear their hair long, presumably in stereotypical Cavalier fashion, saying, "I am sure men use not to weare such manes" (CIIb).

Just as Ward draws upon the Marprelate pamphlets—texts with ties to the Piers Plowman/Chaucerian tradition—in *The Simple Cobler* to address issues of religious reform and political conflict obliquely via a discussion of fashion trends, so too he turns to Chaucer in his commendatory poem in Bradstreet's *The Tenth Muse*. Here also the speaker adopts a satirical, humorous tone resembling that of the narrator of the Marprelate tracts and *The Simple Cobler* as he confronts the conundrum posed by the phenomenon of a female author. Furthermore, in the poem a critique of women's clothing is, as in *The Simple Cobler*, a vehicle to carry the tenor of a message with much greater stakes. In the commendatory poem, Ward creates a scene in which Mercury shows Apollo a volume of poetry by the French Protestant writer du Bartas, while Minerva shows him Bradstreet's volume, which was inspired in part by the French poet. Apollo is then charged with judging which poet is superior. Ward writes that Apollo finds himself in something of a predicament:

He view'd, and view'd, and vow'd he could not tell.
They bid him Hemisphear his mouldy nose,
With's crackt leering-glasses, for it would pose
The best brains he had in's old pudding-pan,
Sex weigh'd, which best, the Woman, or the Man?
He peer'd, and por'd, and glar'd, and said for wore,
I'me even as wise now, as I was before:
They both 'gan laugh, and said, it was no mar'l
The Auth'resse was a right Du Bartas Girle.

Since Bradstreet is "Du Bartas' Girl" and Apollo need not judge between them, Ward has Apollo close with a mocking remark about women writers' emasculating potential, a remark that, like the criticisms offered by the simple cobbler, especially targets women's dress:

Good sooth quoth the old Don, tel, ye me so,
I muse whither at length these Girls wil go;
It half revives my chil frost-bitten blood,
To see a woman once do, ought that's good;
And chode buy Chaucer's Boots, and Homers Furrs,
Let men look to't, least women weare the Spurs.

The reference to Chaucer combined with a reference to women wearing the spurs immediately calls to mind none other than the Wife of Bath, who, as we know from the General Prologue, famously has "on hir feet a paire of spores sharpe."[48]

On the one hand, Ward's lines represent a venture into the domain of the *querelle des femmes* (a quarrel of women), echoing the satirical, joking tone of the *Simple Cobler*'s account of foolish women's devotion to court trends and French fashion. He suggests that Anne Bradstreet, or indeed any woman writer who inserts herself into the male poetic tradition, is adopting male drag. She may thus be seen as a later incarnation of Chaucer's outspoken, male-dominating, emasculating Wife of Bath—perhaps a particularly distressing figure in an era of long-haired, insufficiently masculine men, men in danger, from a Protestant point of view, of falling under the feminizing influence of the Roman faith practiced by the French Catholic queen.[49]

On the other hand, there is, interestingly, a sort of Matheresque typological truth, or an evocation of the historical recursivity of the "Dialogue," in the equivalence Ward suggests between Bradstreet and the Wife of Bath. If one hears in the Chaucerian tradition the strains of social and religious reform that Mather seems to have heard, if one considers the Wife of Bath in her guise of the Lollard-like vernacular preacher and critic of the ecclesiastical establishment, then linking Anne Bradstreet to the Wife of Bath at the beginning of *The Tenth Muse* is quite appropriate to her project. Indeed, in the "Dialogue," the figure of

New England not only provides a "back to the future" vision of Elizabeth I and the Elizabethan era, but she also draws into the poem's present another female figure from England's past. We might well see in the figure of New England a type of the rebellious, quasi-Lollard Wife of Bath with whom I began this project in the introduction. New England is a preaching daughter who calls for her mother to return to an era in which the true, reformed English religion—the religion that began in the days of "Wycliffite" Chaucer and the Lollard Plowman—first triumphed over "popery." Thus, though it may not have been Ward's intention, Chaucer, and particularly the Wife of Bath, end up serving for Bradstreet's spiritual and political aims the same sort of legitimating function they serve for Mather. Chaucer gives new-world religious reform an authentic, and authoritative, source in the English past. He enables American efforts to distinguish New England from contemporary England through reference to "old England" and to comment pointedly on religiopolitical tumult that characterized England in the 1630s and 1640s.

NOTES

1. By the Chaucerian tradition I mean such works as the Plowman's Tale attributed to Chaucer but not actually written by him as well as works by such "next generation" writers as Thomas Hoccleve, John Lydgate, and Osbern Bokenham who fashioned themselves in a Chaucerian vein.

2. Geoffrey Chaucer, *The Canterbury Tales*, in *The Riverside Chaucer*, ed. Larry Benson, 3rd ed., (Boston: Houghton Mifflin, 1987), fragment III, lines 10–13 (hereafter in this introduction, the *Tales* are cited parenthetically by fragment and line number).

3. On the Wife of Bath and female preaching, see Alistair Minnis's recent work, in particular, chapters 3 and 4 of *Fallible Authors: Chaucer's Pardoner and the Wife of Bath* (Philadelphia: University of Pennsylvania Press, 2008). He considers the ways in which Chaucer's depiction of the Wife of Bath intersects with clerical concerns about orthodox women's religious teaching and speech as well as with ecclesiastical fears about the purported authority to teach, preach, and perform the sacraments afforded to women by the Lollards (authority that, as Minnis shows, existed more in the imaginations of nervous clerics than in actual Lollard thought or practice). On the Wife of Bath and Lollardy, see also Alcuin Blamires, "The Wife of Bath and Lollardy," *Medium Aevum* 68 (1989): 224–42.

4. Alison Wiggins observes that these texts were both "highly valued as dense repositories of *sententiae*, proverbs, and memorable phrases, and . . . regularly annotated with dots, ticks, manicules, or clover leaves to indicate notable lines" ("What Did Renaissance Readers Write in Their Printed Copies of Chaucer?," *The Library*, 7th ser., 9, no. 1 [March 2008]: 16). The sort of pattern of annotation that Wiggins discusses is evident in a copy of the 1532 edition of *The Workes of Geffray Chaucer Newly Printed* in the Harry Ransom Center library at the University of Texas (PR1850 1532; this is not the same copy of the works that I discuss below). Numerous passages in the Wife of Bath's Prologue are underlined or bracketed, and in the section of the wedding night speech on

poverty, several couplets are underlined, bracketed, or both: "The poore man whan he bothe by the way / Byforne theues he may synge and play" (underlined); "Pouert is al though it seme elenge / Possession that no wyght wol challenge" (underlined and bracketed); "Pouert a spectacle as thynketh me / Through whiche one may his very frendes se" (underlined and bracketed) (fol. xlvi r).

5. Quoted from the version archived in the English Broadside Ballad Archive, EBBA ID 32447, University of California, Santa Barbara, http://ebba .english.ucsb.edu/ballad/32447/xml. The version archived is from a ballad sheet printed between 1790 and 1818; however, the ballad is considerably older. On June 25, 1600, for instance, "three men were heavily fined for printing and selling a 'disorderly' ballad. The entry in the *Stationers' Register* is as follows: 'Yt is ordered touching a Disorderly ballad of *the wife of Bathe*. Printed by Edward aldee and William white and sold by Edward white: That all the same ballates shalbe brought in and burnt / And that either of the printers for theire Disorders in printing yt shall pay vs A pece for a fine.'" (Ernest Kuhl, "The Wanton Wife of Bath and Queen Elizabeth," *Studies in Philology* 26, no. 2 [1929]: 177–83, quote from 177).

6. As Helen Cooper points out, this ballad was, "to judge from its publishing history, . . . found deeply subversive. . . . The subversiveness of the broadside is due to its picking up the Wife's attacks, not on her husbands, but on the patriarchs and saints. She spends much of the first part of her *Prologue* in vigorous debate with St. Paul, St. Jerome and assorted other antifeminist or pro-celibacy writers. . . . She herself admits to preferring the text to the commentary. . . . Once the boundaries of licit or authorized biblical interpretation are transgressed, pious orthodoxy—and especially celibate orthodoxy—is going to have a hard time. The broadside, like the *Prologue*, is concerned with overstepping these bounds" ("The Shape-Shiftings of the Wife of Bath, 1395–1670," in *Chaucer Traditions: Studies in Honour of Derek Brewer*, ed. Ruth Morse and Barry Windeatt [Cambridge: Cambridge University Press, 1990], 168–84, quote from 180). Cooper further observes that both Chaucer's Wife and that of the ballad "may select what suits their own arguments, but orthodoxy can scarcely claim that it does otherwise" (181).

7. James Simpson, *Reform and Cultural Revolution* (Oxford: Oxford University Press, 2004), 41.

8. John Foxe, *The Unabridged Acts and Monuments Online*, or *TAMO* (1570 edition) (Sheffield: HRI Online Publications, 2011), https://www.john-foxe.org/index.php?realm=text&gototype=&edition=1570&pageid=1, accessed September 20, 2012. Hereafter I cite this text parenthetically by book and page number from this edition.

9. Private correspondence with Mark Rankin. Thanks also to Hope Johnson for help with this passage.

10. Private correspondence with Mark Rankin.

11. *Oxford English Dictionary*, online edition, s.v. "gear."

12. Private correspondence with Mark Rankin.

13. *Oxford English Dictionary*, online edition, s.v. "gear."

14. In the famous passage from the preface of the *Fables*, Dryden writes, "In the first place, as he is the Father of *English* Poetry, so I hold him in the same Degree of Veneration as the *Grecians* held *Homer*, or the *Romans Virgil*" (John Dryden, *Fables Ancient and Modern*, in *The Works of John Dryden*, ed. Vinton Dearing, vol. 7, *Poems, 1697–1700* [Berkeley and Los Angeles: University of California Press, 2002], 33).

CHAPTER I. Female Spirituality and Religious Controversy
in *The Canterbury Tales*

1. William Kamowski presents a useful survey of scholarly perspectives on Chaucer and Wycliffe and offers a persuasive reading of the "substantive affinities between John Wycliffe and the Chaucer of the *Canterbury Tales*" ("Chaucer and Wycliffe: God's Miracles against the Clergy's Magic," *Chaucer Review* 37, no. 1 [2002]: 5–25, quote from 5). The following sources, though far from an exhaustive list of critical treatments of Chaucer, Wycliffe, and Lollardy, afford a range of perspectives on Chaucer's relationship to, and possible alignments with, the emergent heresy: Paul A. Olson, *"The Canterbury Tales" and the Good Society* (Princeton: Princeton University Press, 1986); Peter Brown and Andrew Butcher, *The Age of Saturn: Literature and History in "The Canterbury Tales"* (Oxford: Oxford University Press, 1991); Peggy Knapp, *Chaucer and the Social Contest* (New York: Routledge, 1990)—although she does not wish to consider Wycliffe's direct influence on Chaucer; David Aers and Lynn Staley, *The Powers of the Holy: Religion, Politics, and Gender in Late Medieval English Culture* (University Park: Pennsylvania State University Press, 1996); Paul Strohm's essay "What Can We Know about Chaucer That He Didn't Know about Himself?," in his collection of essays *Theory and the Premodern Text*, Medieval Cultures 26 (Minneapolis: University of Minnesota Press, 2000), 165–81; and most recently and extensively Alastair J. Minnis, *Fallible Authors: Chaucer's Pardoner and the Wife of Bath* (Philadelphia: University of Pennsylvania Press, 2008).

2. For work on Continental influences on Margery Kempe generally, see Ute Stargart, "The Beguines of Belgium, the Dominican Nuns of Germany,

and Margery Kempe," in *The Popular Literature of Medieval England*, ed. Thomas J. Heffernan (Knoxville: University of Tennessee Press, 1985), 277–83; Susan Dickman, "Margery Kempe and the Continental Tradition of the Pious Woman," in *The Medieval Mystical Tradition in England*, ed. Marion Glasscoe (Cambridge: Brewer, 1984), 150–68; Kate Parker, "Lynn and the Making of a Mystic," in *A Companion to The Book of Margery Kempe*, ed. John H. Arnold and Katherine J. Lewis (Cambridge: Brewer, 2004), 55–73. On Margery Kempe and St. Birgitta in particular, see Nanda Hoppenwasser and Signe Wegener, "Vox Matris: The Influence of St. Birgitta's *Revelations* on *The Book of Margery Kempe*: St. Birgitta and Margery Kempe as Wives and Mothers," in *Crossing the Bridge: Comparative Essays on Medieval European and Heian Japanese Women Writers*, ed. Barbara Stevenson and Cynthia Ho (New York: Palgrave, 2000), 61–85; Nanda Hoppenwasser, "The Human Burden of the Prophet: St. Birgitta's *Revelations* and *The Book of Margery Kempe*," *Medieval Perspectives* 8 (1993): 153–62; Liam Peter Temple, "Returning the English 'Mystics' to their Medieval Milieu: Julian of Norwich, Margery Kempe, and Bridget of Sweden," *Women's Writing* 23, no. 2 (2016): 141–58.

3. Though at first glance the Prologues and Tales of these professed women would seem to have little in common with those of the much married, happily lusty Wife of Bath, there are important areas of overlap. In an early essay influenced by feminist theory, Robert S. Sturges suggests common concerns shared by Chaucer's three female narrators in *The Canterbury Tales*. He observes, "All three are concerned with the kinds of power or authority women can attain, and, perhaps more significantly, each of the three women narrators attempts in her prologue and tale to create, not merely a single authoritative female figure, but a whole female tradition of authority in which powerful women are invoked to pass their authority to other women, including the narrator herself" ("The *Canterbury Tales'* Women Narrators: Three Traditions of Female Authority," *Modern Language Studies* 13, no. 2 [1983]: 41–51, quote from 41). Alistair Minnis has also masterfully examined a constellation of issues similar to those that in this chapter concern me vis-à-vis Chaucer's female monastic pilgrims. See his study of the Wife of Bath and the anxiety-producing figure of the Lollard female preacher in chapters 3 and 4 of *Fallible Authors*.

4. Anthony Tuck, "Carthusian Monks and Lollard Knights: Religious Attitudes at the Court of Richard II," *Studies in the Age of Chaucer* (1985): 149–61.

5. See Gail McMurray Gibson, *The Theater of Devotion: East Anglian Drama and Society in the Late Middle Ages* (Chicago: University of Chicago Press, 1989).

6. On Chaucer, Norwich, and the wool trade, see Mary Giffin, *Studies on Chaucer and His Audience* (Hull, Québec: les Editions l'Eclair, 1956), 36. Indeed, Giffin observes that Chaucer's "writings show detailed knowledge of Norfolk towns and villages." She goes on to detail several other Chaucerian ties to the region of East Anglia: "In the *Astrolabe* there is mention of the calendar of Friar Nicholas of Lynn, which was made in 1386 for John of Gaunt and is preserved in MSS Arundel 207 and 347. Chaucer in 1386 was mainpernor for his friend, Sir William Beauchamp, a benefactor of Norwich Cathedral, when Beauchamp received the custody of Pembroke estates in Norfolk, within which was located Baldeswelle, the home of the Reeve. When Chaucer requested a deputy to the customs in 1383, Richard Baldeswelle was one of his mainpernors" (*Studies*, 36).

7. Sherry Reames has admirably clarified the textual sources for the Second Nun's Tale. See "The Sources of the Second Nun's Tale," *Modern Philology* 76 (1978): 111–35; Reames, "A Recent Discovery concerning the Sources of Chaucer's 'Second Nun's Tale,'" *Modern Philology* 87 (1990): 337–61.

8. Sherry Reames indicates that Wycliffe "cited Cecilia's example as proof that the laity could perform minor sacraments like consecrations" ("Recent Discovery," 344); for Wycliffe's discussion of St. Cecilia, see *Trialogus cum Supplemento Trialogi*, ed. Gotthardus Lechler (Oxford: Oxford University Press, 1869, 280).

9. Kamowski, "Chaucer and Wycliffe," 22.

10. Lynn Staley Johnson, "Chaucer's Tale of the Second Nun and the Strategies of Dissent." *Studies in Philology* 89, no. 3 (1992): 314–33; see especially 332–33

11. Sturges briefly suggests a connection between St. Birgitta and the Second Nun's Tale. He writes, "That spiritual power in a political sphere was available to fourteenth-century women, as it is to the Second Nun's heroine St. Cecilia, is demonstrated by the political influence of such figures as St. Catherine of Siena and St. Bridget of Sweden" ("*Canterbury Tales*' Women Narrators," 42–43). He does not, though, go on to explore connections between the Brigittine tradition and the Second Nun's Tale, indicating instead that "even more interesting than these authoritative individuals, however, is the phenomenon of the béguinage" ("*Canterbury Tales*' Women Narrators," 43).

12. F. R. Johnston, "The English Cult of St. Bridget of Sweden," *Analecta Bollandiana* 103 (1985): 75–93, quote from 78. Italics in this and subsequent quotations from primary sources are original unless otherwise noted.

13. David Wallace, *Chaucerian Polity: Absolutist Lineages and Associational Forms* (Stanford: Stanford University Press, 1999), 13–14.

14. Lynn Staley Johnson says that Chaucer was in Milan "at the time of the announcement of the election of Clement VI" ("Chaucer's Tale," 320); Clement VI was elected September 30, 1478. Chaucer was in Milan, as Wallace indicates, to negotiate with the English mercenary John Hawkwood (Wallace, *Chaucerian Polity*, 33).

15. Wallace, *Chaucerian Polity*, 13.

16. Johnston, "English Cult," 83.

17. Giffin, *Studies*, 38.

18. Anne Hudson, introduction to *Selections from English Wycliffite Writings* (Cambridge: Cambridge University Press, 1978), 10.

19. *Registrum Johannis Trefnant episcopi herefordensis*, ed. W. W. Capes, Canterbury and York Society 20 (London: Canterbury and York Society, 1916), 364, no. 30; quoted in Margaret Aston, "Lollard Women Priests?," in *Lollards and Reformers: Images and Literacy in Late Medieval Religion* (London: Hambledon, 1984), 52. The Latin reads, "Asserere pertinaciter quod mulieres habent potestatem at auctoritatem predicandi and conficiendi corpus Cristi et quod habent potestatem ecclesia clavium, ligandi et solvendi, est heresis" (*Registrum Johannis Trefnant*, 364; online via Hathi Trust).

20. On the question of Lollard women priests, and on Lollard women and preaching, see Aston, "Lollard Women Priests?," 49–70.

21. James Alan Schmidtke, "Adam Easton's Defense of St. Birgitta from Bodleian MS Hamilton & Oxford University" (PhD diss., Duke University, 1971), 197.

22. Eric Colledge, "*Epistola solitarii ad reges*: Alphonse of Pecha as Organizer of Brigittine and Urbanist Propaganda," *Medieval Studies* 43 (1956): 19–49, quote from 43.

23. Schmidtke, "Adam Easton's Defense," 171; the translation is from ibid., 45.

24. For Easton's comparison of St. Birgitta and St. Cecilia, see MS Hamilton 7 fol. 232, Bodleian Library, Oxford; quoted in translation in James A. Schmidtke, "'Saving' by Faint Praise: St. Birgitta of Sweden, Adam Easton, and Medieval Antifeminism," *American Benedictine Review* 33, no. 2 (1982): 149–61, quote from 159.

25. Schmidtke, "Adam Easton's Defense," 189; translation from ibid., 64; here and elsewhere brackets in the translation are present in the original.

26. Schmidtke, "'Saving' by Faint Praise," 157. Interestingly, in making his refutation of the argument that St. Birgitta violated prohibitions on female religious instruction and speech, Easton in a sense undercuts his own point by comparing Birgitta's utterances to those of Mary Magdalene, who is specifi-

cally designated as a woman who preaches: "Unde et Maria Magdalena apostola provincie predicatur ratione predicacionis fidei et doctrine et conversionis infidelium in hac plebe. Quare ergo devota domina Birgitta non potuit unam regulam a Christo dictatam pro monialibus domestice promulgare non video ratione consonum nec ab apostolis reprobatum." (Therefore Mary Magdalene was proclaimed an apostle in order to preach and convert infidels. Wherefore, [that] Birgitta was not able to privately promulgate a rule dictated by Christ does not appear consonant with reason or worthy or rejection by the apostle.) (Schmidtke, "Adam Easton's Defense," 186–87; translation from ibid., 61.)

27. Schmidtke, "'Saving' by Faint Praise," 157. The passage in the *Defensorium* on this point reads, "Sed moniales seu mulieres sunt inbecilles intellectu et rudes ad capiendum subtilia legis Dei, ergo regula vivendi talibus debet sub stilo grosso ac facili tradi atque rudi secundum capacitatem congruam eorundem." (But nuns or women are weak in intellect and unskilled in grasping the subtleties of the law of God. Therefore, the rule for living should be general [gross] in style, easily transmitted and rude according to the proper capacity.) (Schmidtke, "Adam Easton's Defense," 181; translation from ibid., 55–56.)

28. Marguerite Tjader Harris, ed. and trans., *Birgitta of Sweden: Life and Selected Revelations* (Mahwah, NJ: Paulist Press, 1990), 177.

29. Harris, *Birgitta of Sweden*, 179.

30. Roger Ellis, ed., *The Liber Celestis of St. Bridget of Sweden*, Early English Text Society 291 (Oxford: Oxford University Press, 1987), 1.

31. I undertake a much more detailed analysis of the role and status of the vernacular in Brigittine spirituality in chapter 2 of *Spiritual Economies: Female Monasticism in Later Medieval England* (Philadelphia: University of Pennsylvania Press, 2001).

32. John Henry Blunt, ed., *The Myroure of Oure Ladye: Containing a Devotional Treatise on Divine Service, with a Translation of the Offices Used by the Sisters of the Brigittine Monastery of Sion, at Iselworth, during the Fifteenth and Sixteenth Centuries*, Early English Text Society, extra series 19 (London: Kegan Paul, Trench, and Trübner, 1873), 19.

33. Blunt, *Myroure of Oure Ladye*, 104.

34. Ellis, *Liber Celestis*, 63.

35. Russell Peck, "The Ideas of 'Entente' and Translation in Chaucer's Second Nun's Tale," *Annuale mediaevale* 8 (1967): 17–37, quote from 22. Peck notes that the Second Nun's translation of the life of St. Cecilia is situated "in a sequence of transmission of primary truth, a chain that goes back to the archetypal translator, Mary. Mary inspired Cecile . . . who in turn inspired the first author, who inspired the rest, etc." (23). A holy female genealogy of mothers,

a chain of virtuous women, correspondingly glorifies translation both linguistic and corporeal when, in her invocation, the Second Nun requests aid from Mary, called "Thow Cristes mooder, doghter deere of Anne" (VIII 70). Sturges similarly observes of this passage that the "lines establish once again a tradition of women: a female storyteller calls on a female Muse for the poetic authority to tell the story of a female saint. Cecilia is referred to as 'thy' maiden, Mary's suggesting a direct connection between the two, a connection strengthened by the references to virginity. . . . A community of virgins, united despite their temporal distance from one another, has been established" (49).

36. Peck, "Ideas of 'Entente' and Translation," 32.

37. For instance, Lisa Lampert observes, "As the Prioress attempted to shut down the proliferation of meaning created by the Shipman's pun, the Second Nun demonstrates an ability to create a proliferation of holy meanings, much as her protagonist performs a kind of 'spiritual procreation'" (*Gender and Jewish Difference from Paul to Shakespeare* [Philadelphia: University of Pennsylvania Press, 2004], 163–64). See also Johnson, "Chaucer's Tale," 326, on the "spiritual fecundity" of St. Cecilia in the Second Nun's Tale.

38. Interestingly, virgins who "reproduce" by their verbal labors are also praised by the Lollard Walter Brut, who lauds "holy virgins" who "steadfastly . . . have preached the word of God and converted many to the faith" (Aston, *Lollards and Reformers*, 444). The Latin from the *Episcopi Herefordensis* reads "cum mulieros, sancta virgines, constanter predicarunt verbum Dei et multos ad fidem converterunt sacerdotibus tunc non audentibus loqui verbum" (345).

39. Ann Astell sees the Second Nun's representation of Christ's female genealogy (what she calls the St. Anne Trinity) in her Prologue as quite different from the other invocation of the same paradigm in *The Canterbury Tales* by the Man of Law. In the Second Nun's Tale, Astell sees Anne as Mary representing "the older ideal of virginal holiness" ("Chaucer's 'St. Anne Trinity': Devotion, Dynasty, Dogma, and Debate," *Studies in Philology* 94 [1997]: 395–416, quote from 405), whereas in the Man of Law's Tale, she finds "an ideal of sanctity that would have appealed to the Ricardian nobility and to the London merchant class" (404). Quoting Clarissa Atkinson, she argues, "'Through the cults of the great mother-saints'—among them Elizabeth of Thuringia (d. 1231), Birgitta of Sweden, and Anne—'the gulf between physical and spiritual motherhood began to be repaired,' so much so that physical maternity could actually assist, rather than impede, a woman in her quest for sanctity" (Astell, "Chaucer's 'St. Anne Trinity,'" 405). I would argue, however, that the Invocacio section of the Prologue demonstrates a very Brigittine focus on bodily as well as spiritual maternity; for the Second Nun, as for St. Birgitta, the corpo-

real, incarnational work of maternal "translation" is central to female holiness and indeed to salvation.

40. Johnson, "Chaucer's Tale," 44.

41. For instance, in addition to the instructions given to Bishop Bernard de Rodez discussed previously, St. Birgitta had well-known and widely disseminated revelations concerning the Hundred Years' War addressed to the kings of England and France (for example, *Liber celestis*, book 4, chapter 105). She also addressed revelations about the Avignon papacy, which she abhorred, to Urban V and Gregory XI (for example, *Liber celestis*, book 4, chapters 137–39).

42. Harris, *Birgitta of Sweden*, 175. Christ furthermore gives Birgitta a list of fourteen enumerated instructions for Queen Joanna, directing her to, among other things, "make a clean confession of all that she has done from her youth," to "grant her gifts with discretion and according to her means, not oppressing some while making others rich," and to "acquire greater humility and contrition for her sins because, in my eyes, she is a predator of many souls, a prodigal squanderer of my goods, and a rod of tribulation to my friends" (Harris, *Birgitta of Sweden*, 174–75).

43. On Arundel's Constitutions, see Nicholas Watson, "Censorship and Cultural Change in Late-Medieval England: Vernacular Theology, the Oxford Translation Debate, and Arundel's Constitutions of 1409," *Speculum* 70, no. 4 (1995): 822–64. Chaucer's translating, teaching nun demonstrates that there are women (and St. Birgitta was one of them, since we know she learned at least some Latin) who will not easily be taken in by self-interested renderings of Latin like Chauntecleer's and like those of some clerics, desirous of maintaining the social privilege and political clout that stemmed from their monopoly on access to Scripture. In Archbishop Gregersson's life of St. Birgitta from the *Officium Sanctae Birgittae* as translated into Middle English we are told that Birgitta "couthe vndirstand and speke wele Latin" (Ellis, *Liber Celestis*, 4)— charmingly, thanks to the aid of St. Agnes who "oft time teched her" (ibid.).

44. The Second Nun's Tale's presentation of equally important roles for men and women in salvation history is also, I would note, quite suggestively Brigittine; as I discuss in the next section of this chapter, in Brigittine spirituality both the Virgin Mary and St. Birgitta participate actively and importantly in salvific, redemptive work.

45. Lampert observes, "With the gospel 'in mind,' as Cecilia's (written and translated) story shows, she understands fully the terms of her faith and its rewards and risks; she combined belief with understanding" (*Gender and Jewish Difference*, 164).

46. As Lampert notes, this saint's life "focuses on a model of ideal Christian identity that defies prohibitions against women's preaching and teaching and presents a world in which men and women play not only complementary, but equally important roles in salvation history" (*Gender and Jewish Difference*, 166).

47. See John Livingston Lowes, *Convention and Revolt in Poetry* (Boston and New York: Houghton Mifflin, 1919); Lowes, "Simple and Coy": A Note on Fourteenth-Century Diction," *Anglia* 33 (1910): 440–51. Far too much has been written on the anti-Semitism of the Prioress's Tale to cite all such studies comprehensively, but for some representative examples see Jessica Fenn, "Apostrophe, Devotion, and Anti-Semitism: Rhetorical Community in the Prioress's Prologue and Tale," *Studies in Philology* 110, no. 3 (2013): 432–58; Albert Friedman, "The Prioress's Tale and Chaucer's Anti-Semitism," *Chaucer Review* 9, no. 2 (1974): 118–29; Merrall Llewelyn Price, "Sadism and Sentimentality: Absorbing Antisemitism in Chaucer's Prioress," *Chaucer Review* 43, no. 2 (2008): 197–214. Lawrence Besserman provides a perspective contrary to Friedman, arguing that Chaucer himself was unlikely to have held the anti-Semitic views of the Prioress; see "Chaucer, Spain, and the Prioress's Antisemitism," *Viator* 35 (2004): 329–53.

48. See Sister Mary Madeleva, "Chaucer's Nuns," in *Chaucer's Nuns, and Other Essays* (New York: Appleton, 1925), 1–42.

49. Hardy Long Frank, "Chaucer's Prioress and the Blessed Virgin," *Chaucer Review* 13, no. 4 (1979): 346–62, quote from 347.

50. Indeed, in Chaucer's lifetime there were as yet no Brigittine nuns in England, and none in areas where Chaucer traveled on the Continent, though the Brigittine rule was approved by Pope Urban V in 1370 and the existence of the order was certainly known in Italy.

51. Marie Hamilton, "Echoes of Childermas in the Tale of the Prioress," *Modern Language Review* 34 (1939): 1–8, quote from 3. Lee Patterson also discusses the presence of language for the Mass of the Holy Innocents in the Prioress's Prologue and Tale. See "'The Living Witnesses of Our Redemption': Martyrdom and Imitation in Chaucer's Prioress's Tale," *Journal of Medieval and Early Modern Cultural Studies* 31, no. 3 (2001): 507–60.

52. Benedicta Ward, *Miracles of the Medieval Mind: Theory, Record, and Event, 1000–1215* (Philadelphia: University of Pennsylvania Press, 1987), 163.

53. Patterson, "Living Witnesses," 517.

54. Ellis, *Liber Celestis*, 1.

55. Ibid., 15.

56. Ibid., 63.

57. Ibid.

58. Ibid., 4.

59. *The Revelations of Saint Birgitta*, ed. William Patterson Cumming, Early English Text Society 178 (London: Oxford University Press, 1929), 117.

60. Ibid., 117.

61. Ibid., 119.

62. Ibid., 120–21.

63. Ibid., 121.

64. Hamilton, "Echoes of Childermas," 3.

65. For an overview of the broad range of interpretations critics have assigned to the "greyn," see Kathleen Oliver, "Singing Bread, Manna, and the Clergeon's 'greyn,'" *Chaucer Review* 31 (1997): 357–64. Oliver interprets the "greyn" as either manna or a eucharistic wafer, and as Shannon Gayk notes in her essay "'To Wonder upon This Thyng': Chaucer's Prioress's Tale," the association of the "greyn" with the Eucharist "seems to be the most widely accepted interpretation" (*Exemplaria* 22, no. 2 [2010]: 138–56, quote from 153n1). Sister Nicholas Maltman discusses the "greyn" in relation to the commemoration of St. Thomas in the second vespers of Holy Innocents. See "The Divine Granary, or the End of the Prioress's 'Greyn,'" *Chaucer Review* 17, no. 2 (1982): 163–70. Maltman argues that in this service "a responsory, a prosa, and a carol" associated with the martyr Thomas of Canterbury all "contain the figures of the grain, and in such instance the grain symbolizes the martyr's soul purged from the body and transported to the divine granary" (166).

66. Patterson, "Living Witnesses," 512.

67. Birgitta of Sweden, *Revelations* 6.88.7, quoted from Claire Sahlin, *Birgitta of Sweden and the Voice of Prophecy* (Woodbridge: Boydell, 2001), 1. The Latin reads, "Nam sicut pater et mater senescientes et quiescentes imponunt nurui onus et dicunt ei ea, que sunt facienda in domo, sic Deus et ego in cordibus hominum sense et frigidi a caritate eorum indicare volumus amicis nostris et mundo per te voluntatem nostrum" (Sahlin, *Birgitta*, 1n2).

68. Helen Barr also reads the Prioress's Tale as a sort of hybrid text that at the same time presents orthodox Marian devotion and a Lollard-inflected critique of what she calls "blind, ignorant devotion" with particular connection to "Wycliffite criticisms of the way in which song (including hours of the Virgin), invented by sinful men, impedes proper understanding of the meaning of the words" ("Religious Practice in Chaucer's Prioress's Tale: Rabbit and/or Duck," *Studies in the Age of Chaucer* 32 [2010]: 39–65, quote from 51). Barr's arguments and mine are complementary rather than directly overlapping. She is also, interestingly, the only critic whom I have encountered to consider the Brigittine

tradition in relation to the Prioress's Tale, though she does so quite briefly, referring to a passage from the *Myroure of Oure Ladye* concerning the need for true
devotion in the heart while singing the liturgy (59; see Blunt, *Myroure*, 22).

69. Blunt, *Myroure*, 77.

CHAPTER 2. Chaucer, the Chaucerian Tradition,
and Female Monastic Readers

1. Quoted from British Library Catalogue of Illuminated Manuscripts,
accessed September 6, 2013, http://www.bl.uk/catalogues/illuminatedmanu-
scripts/record.asp?MSID=7286&CollID=20&NStart=327.

2. Osbern Bokenham, "Life of St. Margaret," in *Legendys of Hooly
Wummen*, ed. Mary S. Serjeantson, Early English Text Society, original series,
206 (London: Early English Text Society, 1938), lines 414–17.

3. David Lorenzo Boyd, "Compilation as Commentary: Controlling
Chaucer's *Parliament of Fowls*," *South Atlantic Quarterly* 94 (1992): 945–64,
quote from 952.

4. Derek Pearsall, "Lydgate as Innovator," *Modern Language Quarterly*
53, no. 1 (1992): 5–22, quote from 15; Walter F. Schirmer, *John Lydgate: A
Study in the Culture of the Fifteenth Century* (Berkeley and Los Angeles: University of California Press, 1961), 64.

5. John Lydgate, *Lydgate's Siege of Thebes*, ed. Axel Erdmann and Eilert
Ekwall, Early English Texts Society, extra series 125 (London: Oxford University Press, 1930), lines 40–47.

6. Charlotte D'Evelyn, ed., *Peter Idley's Instructions to His Son* (Boston:
D. C. Heath; London: Oxford University Press, 1935), 49.

7. Charles F. Briggs, *Giles of Rome's "De Regimine Principum": Reading and Writing Politics at Court and University, c. 1275–c. 1525* (Cambridge:
Cambridge University Press, 1999), 21.

8. Catherine Nall, *Reading and War in Fifteenth-Century England from
Lydgate to Malory* (Woodbridge: D. S. Brewer, 2012), 11.

9. M. C. Seymour indicates that at least eight folios have been lost following fol. 289, so Laud misc. 416 most likely originally contained the full text
of *The Parliament of Fowls* (*A Catalogue of Chaucer Manuscripts: Volume I,
Works before the Canterbury Tales* [Aldershot: Scholar Press, 1995], 25).

10. The full inscription reads: "Istum librum dominus Richardus Wygyngton, capellanus, dedit prioresse et conuenti monasterii Ambrosii Burgi in vig-
ilia natiuitatis beate Marie uirginis Anno Domini m<illesim>o quingentesimo

octaua, ut ipse ex caritate orent pro ipso et amicis suis. Et si aliquis istum librum a monasterio alienauerit, anathema sit" (Richard Wygyngton, chaplain, gave this book to the prioress and convent of the monastery of Amesbury on the vigil of the Feast of the Nativity of the Virgin Mary in the year of Our Lord 1508; for this out of charity may they pray for him and his friends. And if anyone removes this book from the monastery, let him be cursed.) (fol. 99v; quoted in David Bell, *What Nuns Read: Books and Libraries in Medieval English Nunneries* [Kalamazoo, MI: Cistercian Publications, 1995], 104).

11. Bell, *What Nuns Read*, 103.

12. Nall, *Reading and War*, 23.

13. Ibid., 21.

14. Seymour, *Catalogue of Chaucer Manuscripts*, 26.

15. Ibid.

16. Linda Clark, "Tiptoft, John, first Baron Tiptoft (*c.* 1378–1443)," in *Oxford Dictionary of National Biography*, ed. H. C. G. Matthew and Brian Harrison (Oxford: Oxford University Press, 2004); online ed., ed. Lawrence Goldman, May 2005, http://www.oxforddnb.com/view/article/27470.

17. Benjamin G. Kohl, "Tiptoft, John, first earl of Worcester (1427–1470)," in *Oxford Dictionary of National Biography*, online ed., ed. Lawrence Goldman, May 2006, http://www.oxforddnb.com/view/article/27471.

18. Ibid.

19. Bell, *What Nuns Read*, 190.

20. Ibid., 195.

21. Rebecca Krug, *Reading Families: Women's Literate Practice in Late Medieval England* (Ithaca, NY: Cornell University Press, 2002), 191. Krug observes that the nuns of Syon "came from the same social milieu that produced wives of great landholders" and that they "shared the literate interests and understandings of the aristocratic and highborn laywomen who were their mothers, sisters, and cousins" (191). Krug refers specifically to Brigittine monastic culture, but I see no reason not to extend this assessment to the mutually informing dimensions of monastic culture and lay culture of other female communities, given the well-established permeability of the convent wall in the later medieval and early modern periods.

22. See Krug, *Reading Families*; Claire Walker, *Gender and Politics in Early Modern Europe: English Convents in France and the Low Countries* (New York: Palgrave Macmillan, 2003); Nicky Hallett, *Lives of Spirit: English Carmelite Self-Writing of the Early Modern Period* (Aldershot: Ashgate, 2007).

23. Mary C. Erler, *Women, Reading, and Piety in Late Medieval England* (Cambridge: Cambridge University Press, 2002), 95–95.

24. Krug, *Reading Families*, 155.

25. Erler, *Women, Reading, and Piety*, 95.

26. Michael Hicks, "Hungerford, Robert, third Baron Hungerford and Baron Moleyns (*c.* 1423–1464)," in *Oxford Dictionary of National Biography*, online ed., ed. Lawrence Goldman, May 2010, http://www.oxforddnb.com/view /article/14178.

27. Virginia Bainbridge, "Syon Abbey: Women and Learning, c. 1415– 1600," in *Syon Abbey and Its Books: Reading, Writing and Religion, c. 1400– 1700*, ed. E. A. Jones and Alexandra Walsham (Woodbridge: Boydell, 2010), 82–103, quote from 90.

28. Bainbridge, "Syon Abbey," 90.

29. Ibid., 88.

30. On the textual cultures of the English Benedictine nunneries at Cambrai and Paris, see chapter 2 of Nancy Bradley Warren, *The Embodied Word: Female Spiritualities, Contested Orthodoxies, and English Religious Cultures, 1350–1700* (Notre Dame, IN: University of Notre Dame Press, 2010).

31. There has been considerable debate concerning Margaret More Roper's authorship of this letter. It exists in two manuscript copies: Bodleian MS Ballard 72 and British Library MS Royal 17D xiv. The letter was also printed with Thomas More's correspondence in 1557. From this publication in 1557 it was attributed to Thomas More rather than to Margaret, even though the letter states she is the author. As Nancy E. Wright notes, "The methods and concepts of textual criticism can establish a definitive text of the letter to Alice Alington but cannot definitely attribute it to either More or Margaret on the basis of external evidence or extant sixteenth-century texts" ("The Name and the Signature of the Author of Margaret Roper's Letter to Alice Alington," in *Creative Imitation: New Essays on Renaissance Literature in Honor of Thomas M. Greene*, ed. David Quint et al. [Binghamton, NY: Medieval and Renaissance Texts and Studies, 1992], 239–57, quote from 241). Wright compellingly outlines the social forces at work in the 1550s that prevented Margaret's authorship from being acknowledged. Though the question of attribution is currently unresolvable, Kara Doyle points out that

> it is worth exploring the hypothesis that Margaret had some role in the letter's composition. We may speculate that she agreed, tacitly or otherwise, to help circulate and clarify her father's views. Along with Margaret's biographer, E. E. Reynolds, we may envision a scenario in which Margaret and More discussed his response to the concerns of Lord Chancellor Aubrey and More's other friends . . . a discussion that Margaret then wrote up and sent to her sister, which was later copied (perhaps without

the salutation and whatever else may have preceded the reported conversation), preserved, and eventually published in 1557. ("Criseyde Reading, Reading Criseyde," in *New Perspectives on Criseyde*, ed. Cindy L. Vitto and Marcia S. Marzec [New York: Pegasus Press, 2003], 105)

Furthermore, even if Thomas More did write the letter, it tells us something worth considering about gender and textual culture that he found it to be plausible to depict his daughter referring knowledgeably to *Troilus and Criseyde* in this particular situation.

32. Doyle, "Criseyde Reading," 102.

33. Thomas More, *The Correspondence of Sir Thomas More*, ed. Elizabeth Frances Rogers (Princeton: Princeton University Press, 1947), 549.

34. More, *Correspondence*, 549.

35. Geoffrey Chaucer, *Troilus and Criseyde*, III 929–31, in *Riverside Chaucer*.

36. Doyle, "Criseyde Reading," 107.

37. Wright, "Name and the Signature," 255.

38. Criseyde says, "O, rolled shal I ben on many a tonge! / Thorughout the world my belle shal be ronge! / And wommen moost wol haten me of alle" (Chaucer, *Troilus and Criseyde*, V 1061–63).

39. Richard Firth Green, *Poets and Princepleasers: Literature and the English Court in the Late Middle Ages* (Toronto: University of Toronto Press, 1980), 189.

40. As Nigel Mortimer observes, "Exciting as the emergence of this portrait of Lydgate's intelligent and occasionally daring political understanding has been, the tantalizing tension between cloister and court seems to have been resolved, with the Monk of Bury of fifteenth-century readers becoming a civil servant for their modern successors" (*John Lydgate's Fall of Princes: Narrative Tragedy in Its Literary and Political Contexts* [Oxford: Clarendon, 2005], 52).

41. MS Bodleian Laud misc. 416 fol. 255r.

42. D'Evelyn, *Peter Idley's Instructions to His Son*, 19.

43. John M. Bowers, "Thomas Hoccleve and the Politics of Tradition," *Chaucer Review* 36, no. 4 (2002): 352–69, quote from 355.

44. Hoccleve, "To Sir John Oldcastle," lines 194–200, in F. J. Furnivall, ed., *Hoccleve's Works: The Minor Poems*, vol. 1, Early English Text Society, extra series 61 (Oxford: Oxford University Press, 1892).

45. John Tiptoft was married for a time to Cecily, widow of Henry Beauchamp, duke of Warwick, whose aunt Cecily was wife of Richard, duke of York, and when Edward IV ascended the throne in 1461, Tiptoft "was appointed to the king's council" (Kohl, "Tiptoft, John, first earl of Worcester").

46. See Nancy Bradley Warren, *Spiritual Economies: Female Monasticism in Later Medieval England* (Philadelphia: University of Pennsylvania Press, 2001), 124–30.

47. Thomas Hoccleve, *Thomas Hoccleve: The Regiment of Princes*, ed. Charles R. Blyth (Kalamazoo, MI: Medieval Institute Publications, 1999), line 1960, available online as part of the TEAMS Middle English Text Series (Rochester, NY: University of Rochester), accessed August 12, 2013, http://www.lib .rochester.edu/camelot/teams/hoccint.htm.

48. See Charles R. Blyth, introduction to *Thomas Hoccleve: The Regiment of Princes.* The passage reads:

> My deere maistir, God his soule qwyte,
> And fadir, Chaucer, fayn wolde han me taght,
> But I was dul and lerned lyte or naght.
>
> Allas, my worthy maistir honurable,
> This landes verray tresor and richesse,
> Deeth by thy deeth hath harm irreparable
> Unto us doon; hir vengeable duresse
> Despoillid hath this land of the swetnesse
> Of rethorik, for unto Tullius
> Was nevere man so lyk amonges us.
>
> Also who was heir in philosophie
> To Aristotle in our tonge but thow?
> The steppes of Virgile in poesie
> Thow folwedist eek. Men woot wel ynow
> That combreworld that thee, my maistir, slow.
> Wolde I slayn were! Deeth was to hastyf
> To renne on thee and reve thee thy lyf.
>
> Deeth hath but smal consideracioun
> Unto the vertuous, I have espyed;
> No more, as shewith the probacioun,
> Than to a vicious maistir losel tryed
> Among an heep. Every man is maistried
> With here, as wel the poore as is the ryche;
> Leered and lewde eek standen alle ylyche.
>
> Shee mighte han taried hir vengeance a whyle
> Til that sum man had egal to thee be—

Nay, let be that! Shee knew wel that this yle
May nevere man foorth brynge lyk to thee;
And hir office needes do moot shee.
God bad hir so, I truste, as for thy beste;
O maistir, maistir, God thy soule reste!
                    (2077–2107)

49. The *Secretum secretorum* was the most popular *speculum princeps* in
the Middle Ages, followed closely by Giles of Rome's *De regimine* (Briggs,
Giles of Rome's "De regimine principum," 21). As we have seen, the scribe of
Add. 18632 connects Hoccleve's *Regiment* with Giles of Rome's *De regimine*.

50. Hoccleve, *Regiment of Princes*, lines 1961–64.

51. Ibid., lines 4992–98.

52. Ibid., lines 5006–7.

53. Ibid., lines 5008.

54. Ibid., lines 4999–5005.

55. Jeanne E. Krochalis, "Hoccleve's Chaucer Portrait," *Chaucer Review*
21, no. 2 (1986): 234–45. Such valorization of Chaucer as a saintly figure might,
I would suggest, have served to influence nuns, as well as those who, like
Richard Wygyngton, gave to nuns books in which Chaucerian texts were included, to believe that Chaucer's writings and texts in the Chaucerian tradition
were appropriate reading material for women religious.

56. Krochalis, "Hoccleve's Chaucer Portrait," 240.

57. See chapter 5 of Warren, *Spiritual Economies*. The original location
for Syon was near the royal manor at Sheen, a location closely associated with
Richard II, who had the manor of Sheen destroyed after Queen Anne's death.
Henry's choice of this particular location for what has been described as "a gi-
gantic chantry for the House of Lancaster" helped him forge a connection with
Richard II, glossing over his father's (Henry IV) deposition of Richard II and
his usurpation of the throne (see A. Jeffries Collins, *The Bridgettine Breviary
of Syon Abbey*, Henry Bradshaw Society 96 [Worcester: Henry Bradshaw Society, 1969], 11n1). Furthermore, the foundation charter for Syon, in addition
to creating a connection to Richard II, also emphasizes that Henry V is son and
heir of Henry IV, who had been interested in the Brigittine order. Henry IV
had written in 1408 to the Brigittine authorities in Vadstena to notify them that
he had given permission for Sir Henry FitzHugh to keep two monks from
Vadstena at Cherry Hinton. He also indicated that he wanted "to be the special
friend and protector of the order," and he petitioned the pope (albeit unsuc-
cessfully) to be allowed to found a Brigittine house in York (Neil Beckett,

"St. Bridget, Henry V, and Syon Abbey," in *Studies in St. Birgitta and the Brigittine Order*, 2 vols., ed. James Hogg [Salzburg: Institut für Anglistik und Amerikanistik, 1993], 2:125–50, quote from 127).

58. Margaret, Lady Hungerford was the daughter of William, Lord Botreaux, and married Robert, Lord Hungerford. Their eldest son, Robert, "was summoned to parliament from January 1445 as Lord Moleyns . . . a signal mark of royal favour" that "probably implies an earlier intimacy with Henry VI" (Hicks, "Hungerford, Robert"). Margaret's son Robert also was a member "of the royal council opposed to the duke of York's rebellion in 1452" (Ibid.).

59. British History Online (London: Institute of Historical Research, University of London), accessed July 14, 2014, http://www.british-history.ac.uk/report.aspx?compid=36534.

60. Ibid.

61. Ibid.

62. Ibid.

63. On the time Margaret, Lady Hungerford, spent at Syon, see Michael Hicks, *Richard III and His Rivals: Magnates and Their Motives in the Wars of the Roses* (London: Hambledon Press, 1991), 105. On her time at Amesbury, see British History Online, accessed July 14, 2014, http://www.british-history.ac.uk/report.aspx?compid=36534.

64. Hicks, *Richard III and His Rivals*, 105.

65. Robert returned to fight in other battles on the Lancastrian side; he was attainted in 1461 and executed in May 1464.

66. Greg Walker, *Writing under Tyranny: English Literature and the Henrician Reformation* (Oxford: Oxford University Press, 2007), 11.

67. Walker, *Writing under Tyranny*, 12.

68. See chapter 6 of Nancy Bradley Warren, *Women of God and Arms: Female Spirituality and Political Conflict, 1380–1600* (Philadelphia: University of Pennsylvania Press, 2005).

69. In the 1520s, the English Brigittines were very active in opposition to Henry VIII's declaration of supremacy and his efforts to obtain a divorce from Katherine of Aragon, and they expressed this opposition in some quite overt ways. As Alexandra Da Costa observes, "Once the visitations began in 1534, the letters of the king's commissioners are filled with reports of resistance to the king's supremacy within Syon" ("The King's Great Matter: Negotiating Censorship at Syon Abbey, 1532–34," *Review of English Studies* 62 [2011]: 15–29, quote from 19). In a well-known instance of the nuns' expression of their opposition to the king's divorce and remarriage, the sisters of Syon refused Anne Boleyn entry to their choir. As William Latimer reports, the nuns "denied her

highness entry," going so far as to lie on the floor "with their faces downeward to the grownde" (Oxford, Bodleian Library MS Donc 42 fol. 31r; quoted in Da Costa, "King's Great Matter," 18).

70. Alexandra Da Costa, *Reforming Printing: Syon Abbey's Defense of Orthodoxy, 1525–1534* (Oxford: Oxford University Press, 2012), 119. See also chapter 5 of Warren, *Women of God and Arms*.

71. As Da Costa observes, "Hugh Riche, the Observant Friar, showed her revelations regarding the King to Confessor-General John Fewterer, Abbess Agnes Jordan, the proctors, Brother William, and some other ladies at the Abbey. The Bridgettines also invited [Thomas] More to meet Elizabeth Barton so as to give them his opinion, and she seems to have stayed there for a while, before being invited to see the Lady of Horsley in Surrey. Although it is often noted that Syon stopped short of wholehearted acceptance of Barton . . . their support was perceived as instrumental in spreading her influence" (17–18). Henry Golde indicated that he, his brother, and others "were persuaded to her cause 'by means of the firm credence that I and other religious persons of Syon, Schene, and Richmond . . . did give her'" (Da Costa, "King's Great Matter," 18).

72. L. E. Whatmore, "The Sermon against the Holy Maid of Kent and Her Adherents, Delivered at Paul's Cross, November the 23rd, 1533, and at Canterbury, December the 7th," *English Historical Review* 58 (1943): 467.

73. Thomas Malory's *Morte Darthur* famously described Guinevere's resorting to Amesbury. On this subject, see Virginia Blanton, "'. . . The Queen in Amysbery, Nunne in Whyght Clothys and Blak . . .': Guinevere's Asceticism and Penance in Malory's *Le Morte D'Arthur*," *Arthuriana* 20 (2010): 52–75.

74. James Gairdner, *Letters and Papers Illustrative of the Reigns of Richard III and Henry VII* (London: Longman, 1861), 1:407–8.

75. David M. Head, "Howard, Thomas, second duke of Norfolk (1443–1524)," in *Oxford Dictionary of National Biography*, online ed., ed. Lawrence Goldman, September 2012, http://www.oxforddnb.com/view/article/13939.

76. Ibid.

77. Ibid.

78. Colin Richmond, "Mowbray, John (VII), fourth duke of Norfolk (1444–1476)," in *Oxford Dictionary of National Biography*, online ed., ed. Lawrence Goldman, May 2006, http://www.oxforddnb.com/view/article/19455.

79. Ibid.

80. Comparing the contents of MS Bodleian Laud misc. 416 with those of all the other surviving texts from Syon's library is beyond the scope of this chapter. Syon clearly had an extraordinary library; both the nuns and brothers had their own collections, and from the nuns' library, approximately forty-eight

manuscripts and printed books survive that can be definitively connected with the sisters. Though counts of manuscripts and printed books associated with the Syon nuns' library differ somewhat, the number of volumes known to be still extant constitute "just under a third of all the nuns' books which survive."

81. Significantly, Bell observes that in addition to the wealthy and educationally renowned nunneries of Syon, Barking, and Dartford, "more nuns than we suppose might have been able to construe a Latin text, and more nunneries than we suspect might have taught the language" (Bell, *What Nuns Read*, 63).

82. Oxford, All Souls College MS 6, a mid-thirteenth-century manuscript, is called the "Amesbury psalter" and, as Erler indicates, "has long been associated with this house." Erler continues, "The case pro and con is most recently summarized by Watson, who concludes: 'In spite of the absence of firm evidence an Amesbury connection of some kind seems probable' (*Medieval Manuscripts*, 14)'" (*Women, Reading, and Piety*, 145). See Andrew G. Watson, *A Descriptive Catalogue of the Medieval Manuscripts of All Souls College Oxford* (Oxford: Oxford University Press, 1997). There are also extant fragments of two breviaries as well as an imperfect liturgical manuscript containing material from the fourteenth and the fifteenth centuries (Oxford, Bodleian Library Liturg. misc. 407).

83. Inscription quoted in Bell, *What Nuns Read*, 104.

84. Erler, *Women, Reading, and Piety*, 36.

85. See "Houses of Benedictine Nuns: Abbey, Later Priory, of Amesbury," in *A History of the County of Wiltshire* (1956), 3:242–259, British History Online, accessed August 28, 2014, http://www.british-history.ac.uk/report.aspx ?compid=36534.

86. Interestingly, there is some final evidence worth considering to flesh out more fully my representations of Syon and Amesbury as monastic communities in which women religious were interested in the politics of advice and engaged with a didactic, politically inflected Chaucerian tradition. There was at least one more politically oriented text with a connection to Chaucer (in addition to the ones in Laud misc. 416) that was read by at least one Syon nun during the period when Anne Coville and Clemencia Thraseborough were inscribing their names in Laud misc. 416. Margaret Windsor, who was prioress from 1513 to 1539, was given as a gift a printed French translation of Boccaccio's *De casibus virorum illustrium*, and she claimed ownership of the text twice, once in English and once in French (Ann Hutchison, "What the Nuns Read: Literary Evidence from the English Bridgettine House, Syon Abbey," *Mediaeval Studies* 57 [1995]: 205–22, quote from 215). The *De casibus virorum* is Lydgate's chief source for his *Fall of Princes*, and it is a text to which Chaucer

gestures in his Monk's Tale. Margaret Windsor, like her fellow Syon nun Anne Coville, comes from a family with ties to the court and the world of politics. Andrew, Lord Windsor, Syon's steward, was her brother; he was "a renaissance scholar and favoured courtier of Henry VIII" (Bainbridge, "Syon Abbey," 89). Significantly, the Fettyplace women who were professed at both Syon and Amesbury, too, came from a family in which the provision of political advice was an important literary concern. Their half-brother Thomas Elyot was the author of *The Book Named the Governour* (1531). This text was dedicated to Henry VIII and is designed, as Elyot says in the dedication, with "the intent that men which wil be studious about the weale publike may fynde the thinge therto expedient compendiously written. And for as moch as this present boke treateth of the education of them that hereafter may be demed worthy to be gouernours of the publike weale under your hyghnesse . . . I therefore haue named it The Gouernour" (Thomas Elyot, *The Boke Named the Gouernour Deuised by Sir Thomas Elyot, Knight*, 1531, Internet Archive, accessed October 20, 2015, http://archive.org/stream/bokenamedgouerno01elyouoft/boke-namedgouerno01elyouoft_djvu.txt).

87. MS Oxford, Jesus 39, has a connection with Laud misc. 416 discussed above. As Michael Sargent points out, "Jesus College 39 was both written and annotated by the scribe and annotator of the Laud misc. 416 copy of the *Cursor Mundi*, which was owned by sister Anne Colvylle" ("A New Manuscript of *The Chastising of God's Children* with an Ascription to Walter Hilton," *Medium Aevum* 46, no. 1 [1977]: 60).

88. Lee Patterson, *Negotiating the Past: The Historical Understanding of Medieval Literature* (Madison: University of Wisconsin Press, 1987), 117–18. Bodleian Laud misc. 99 is later, dating to around 1500. Jones observes, "Paleographic evidence . . . points to a date for the manuscript after 1470, and the artificiality of the main hand suggests that it is significantly later. Malcolm Parkes has dated the manuscript to the turn of the century" (E. A. Jones, ed., *The 'Exhortacion' from "Disce Mori" Edited from Oxford, Jesus College MS 39* [Salzburg: Universitätsverlag Winder Heidelberg, 2006], xix, hereafter cited parenthetically).

89. Patterson, *Negotiating*, 117–18.

90. The compiler adds a comment to a discussion of true freedom taken from the *Miroir du monde* stating the king "might not be 'parfite lorde of hymself'" (Jones, *Exhortacion*, xxvii). This addition might reflect the situation in the last years of Henry VI's reign, when he experienced both physical and mental illness. During this period, the duke of York was twice named protector (March 1454 through early 1455, and November 1455 through February

1456). Jones further notes, "The compiler's allusion might suggest that *Disce Mori* was written, if not during one of York's protectorates, then at least towards the beginning of the period 1453–1464, when their memory was still fresh" (*Exhortacion*, xxvii–xxviii). Dating MS Oxford, Jesus 39, on paleographic evidence, Jones generally agrees with Patterson in assigning the manuscript to the mid-fifteenth century, stating, "The text hand is an elegant and well-formed Secretary of the mid-fifteenth century, which becomes somewhat more current as the long manuscript progresses. The use of unlooped w indicates a date after c. 1430. There is none of the accentuation of the splay of the script, nor of the attention to calligraphic details such as the horns of certain letters, characteristic of hands of the second half of the century" (*Exhortacion*, xv).

91. Patterson, *Negotiating*, 298.

92. Patterson calls the text a "handbook for nuns" and interprets the "well beloved sister Dame Alice" mentioned in the compiler's envoy as a Syon nun (*Negotiating*, 142). Jones argues that the *Disce mori* "never in fact addresses itself to a Sister Alice, and many of the details given in the first chapter of the 'Exhortacion' are inconsistent with monastic discipline of any kind, let alone that of the strictly enclosed Bridgettine order" (*Exhortacion*, xxix). Jones argues that the Dame Alice to whom the envoy directs the text was perhaps one of the vowesses with whom Syon had connections. He writes, "A plausible hypothesis of the genesis of the *Disce Mori* might be that it was commissions from a brother of Sheen or Syon around the time of her profession by a vowess as a one-volume guide to her new vocation; that she received the archetype while the compiler retained a copy (J [that is, MS Oxford, Jesus 39], which he (or another) then used as the basis for *Ignorancia Sacerdotum*, and which afterwards served novices of the Brigittine order (Dorothy Slyght among them) as a vade mecum during their probationary year, and / or (mutatis mutandis) as improving reading thereafter" (Jones, *Exhortacion*, xxx). For my purposes, what matters most is that Syon nuns read the work, as is strongly suggested by the inscription of Dorothy Slyght's name in the manuscript, no matter who the original intended audience for the text might have been. Dorothy Slyght was the widow of a merchant of St. Albans, and, in addition to signing the manuscript of the *Disce mori*, she wrote her name in a fifteenth-century processional and signed a will upon entering Syon (Bainbridge, "Syon Abbey," 85). When Syon was dissolved in 1539, Dorothy Slyght's name appeared on the list of sisters, and she returned to the community under the Marian restoration of 1557. The Syon Martyrology indicates that "Dorothea Slithe" died before 1576 (George James Aungier, *The History and Antiquities of Syon Monastery, the Parish of Isleworth, and the Chapelry of Hounslow* [London: J. B. Nichols, 1840], 89).

93. Patterson, *Negotiating*, 119.

94. In addition to including the stanza from *Troilus and Criseyde*, the compiler may echo Chaucer's text in his accounts of the third and fourth tokens of fleshly love (Jones, *Exhortacion*, 98n60/30–31 and n60/45). As Jones observes, the compiler includes in his account of the third token of fleshly love a passage reminiscent of Criseyde's lines from book 5, when she says, "O Troilus, what dostow now? . . . Lord, Wheyther thow yet thenke upon Criseyde?" (V 734–35). The compiler, imagining the laments of the woman unable to see her beloved and thus experiencing "þe inquietude þat þees fleshly lovynge hertes suffer," writes, "A, where is now my deere loue? What euer he do now? Wheþer he þenke now on me, as I now do on hym" (Jones, *Exhortacion*, 60). Additionally, the compiler's reference to "eny poynte of vnloue" in his account of the fourth token of fleshly love, which is "hasty ire and inpacience" (Jones, *Exhortacion*, 60), might "plausibly have been suggested by Troilus's despairing 'I ne kan nor may, / for al this world, withinne myn herte fynde / To unloven yow a quarter of a day!' (V 1696–98)" (Jones, *Exhortacion*, 98n60/45), since the noun "unlove" is does not appear in the *Middle English Dictionary* (University of Michigan, https://quod.lib.umich.edu/m/med/) and is "not in OED before 1611, and rare thereafter" (Jones, *Exhortacion*, 98n60/45).

95. Indeed, Patterson posits that though "*Troilus and Criseyde* is not about saints and their doctrine, it does aim to distinguish true from false, good from evil, vice from virtue" (*Negotiating*, 145).

96. In *Pasquill the Playne*, Pasquill says to Gnato, "What a gods name haue ye a booke in youre hand? A good feloweshyp whereof is it? Let me se *Nouum stestamentum* [sic]. . . . But what is this in your bosom? An other booke. . . . Let se, what is here? Troylus & Chreseid? Lorde what discord is bytwene these two bokes" (quoted from Derek Brewer, *Geoffrey Chaucer: The Critical Heritage*, vol. 1, *1385–1837* [London: Routledge, 1978], 90).

97. Chaucer, *Troilus and Criseyde*, II 1176, 118.

98. Chaucer, *Troilus and Criseyde*, II 100–105.

99. Ibid., II 750–54.

100. The compiler of the *Disce mori* and Margaret More Roper were not alone in discerning spiritual value of a sort in Chaucer's *Troilus and Criseyde*. As Thomas Heffernan points out, "John of Ireland, a fifteenth-century member of the faculty of philosophy at the University of Paris, mentions approvingly a passage concerning God's providence and free will in the *Troilus* (IV, 953–1085) in his *Meroure of Wisdom*" ("Aspects of the Chaucerian Apocrypha: Animadversions on William Thynne's Edition of the *Plowman's Tale*," in *Chaucer Traditions: Studies in Honour of Derek Brewer*, ed. Ruth Morse

and Barry Windeatt [Cambridge: Cambridge University Press, 1990], 155–67, quote from 158).

101. Patterson, *Negotiating*, 147.

102. E. Talbot Donaldson states, "The *moralitee* of *Troilus and Criseyde* (and by the morality I do not mean 'ultimate meaning') is simply this: that human love, and by a sorry corollary everything human, is unstable and illusory. I give the moral so flatly now because . . . I shall be following the narrator in his endeavor to avoid it, and indeed shall be eagerly abetting him in trying to avoid it, and even pushing him away when he finally accepts it. . . . The meaning of the poem is not the moral, but a complex qualification of the moral" (*Speaking of Chaucer* [London: Athlone Press, 1970]).

103. Blunt, *Myroure*, 66.

104. Chaucer, *Troilus and Criseyde*, II 118.

105. Patterson, *Negotiating*, 150.

106. Blunt, *Myroure*, 60.

107. Jones designates this scribe's hand Jc and writes, "It is a Secretary of similar duct and date to the main text hand, but of greater currency. Distinctive features include the consistent use of the 'horned' secretary g, a widely splayed v-shaped r, and a willingness to use secretary s in word-initial position as well as elsewhere" (*Exhortacion*, xv–xvi).

108. James Perrot was the illegitimate son of Sir John Perrot. He was "the author of a number of political and devotional works printed between 1596 and 1630" (Jones, *Exhortacion*, xvii). As Jones observes, Perrot may have acquired the manuscript that he donated to Oxford "directly from Syon between 1589, when his father purchased the Crown lease of the house from the Earl of Essex (whose sister had married Sir John's legitimate son Thomas), and 1594, when it passed, on the remarriage of Thomas's widow, to her second husband" (Jones, *Exhortacion*, xvii). That Perrot advanced an appreciation for any aspects of the *Disce mori* at all is perhaps somewhat surprising, given his strong anti-Catholic leanings. He was adamantly opposed to the plan to marry the Prince of Wales to the Infanta of Spain (the so-called Spanish Match); as Andrew Thrush notes, Perrot believed "the newfound boldness of the papists" was "closely connected to the negotiations for a Spanish bride for Prince Charles" (Andrew Thrush, "Perrot, Sir James (1571/2–1637)," in *Oxford Dictionary of National Biography*, online ed., ed. Lawrence Goldman, January 2008, http://www.oxforddnb.com/view/article/21985). However, in Parliament in April 1624, "he probably astounded many of his colleagues . . . when, during a debate on recusant officeholders, he admitted that his wife of twenty years was a papist" (ibid.).

109. San Marino, Huntington Library HM 148; quoted from Andrew Kraebel, page 19 of the manuscript version of his forthcoming edition of Rolle's *English Psalter*.

110. Roger Ellis, *"Viderunt Eam Filie Syon": The Spirituality of the English House of a Medieval Contemplative Order from Its Beginnings to the Present Day* (Salzburg: Institut für Anglistik und Amerikanistik, 1984), 28–29.

111. Sten Eklund, *Den Heliga Birgitta Opera Minor I: Regula Salvatoris*, SFSS, ser. 2, Latinska Skrifter (Uppsala, 1975), 167.

112. Krug, *Reading Families*, 157.

113. Ibid., 192.

114. Chaucer, *Canterbury Tales*, VII 3441–43.

CHAPTER 3. Competing Chaucers

1. The only manuscript of Forrest's *History* is what evidently was the presentation copy for Mary. W. D. Macray, the editor of the 1875 edition of the *History*, which is the only edition of the entire text available, writes, "*The History of Grisilde the Seconde* exists amongst the MSS of Ant. À Wood in the Bodleian Library, No. 2 in that collection which was bought by the University after his death. It is evidently the copy presented by the author to Queen Mary, being beautifully written on fine vellum, and having been originally 'bound in laced satin.' Nearly all the lace has now disappeared, and the satin is tattered and faded. It has clasps, and brass bosses with the words, 'Ave Maria, Gracia Plena' at each corner, as well as a center boss" (introduction to *The History of Grisild the Second: A Narrative in Verse of the Divorce of Queen Katharine of Aragon*, by William Forrest, ed. W. D. Macray [London: Chiswick, 1875], xix–xi). I cite the *History* parenthetically by page number from this edition, since lines are not numbered. For a range of discussions of early modern Chaucer reception and the identification of Chaucer and the Chaucerian tradition as proto-Protestant in addition to sources cited below, see Thomas Heffernan and Andrew N. Wawn, "Chaucer, *The Plowman's Tale* and Reformation Propaganda: The Testimonies of Thomas Godfrey and *I Playne Piers*," *Bulletin of the John Rylands Library* 56 (1973): 174–92; Alice S. Miskimin, *The Renaissance Chaucer* (New York: Yale University Press, 1975); A. C. Spearing, "Renaissance Chaucer and Father Chaucer," *English: The Journal of the English Association* 34 (1985): 1–38; essays in Theresa M. Krier, ed., *Refiguring Chaucer in the Renaissance* (Gainesville: University Press of Florida, 1998).

2. James Gairdner, *Letters and Papers Foreign and Domestic, Henry VIII* (London: Longman, 1880), vol. 5, no. 1023.

3. Walker, *Writing under Tyranny*, 32.

4. Heffernan, "Aspects of the Chaucerian Apocrypha," 159.

5. Ibid.

6. Walker, *Writing under Tyranny*, 47–48.

7. Heffernan, "Aspects of the Chaucerian Apocrypha," 160.

8. Walker, *Writing under Tyranny*, 32.

9. Ibid., 49.

10. Ibid., 66.

11. Ibid., 85.

12. Ibid., 81–82.

13. Andrew Higl, "Printing Power: Selling Lydgate, Gower, and Chaucer," *Essays in Medieval Studies* 23 (2006): 55–77, quote from 67.

14. Quoted in Kathleen Forni, *The Chaucerian Apocrypha: A Counterfeit Canon* (Gainesville: University Press of Florida, 2001), 93.

15. James Simpson, *Burning to Read: English Fundamentalism and Its Reformation Opponents* (Cambridge, MA: Harvard University Press, 2010), 238.

16. John Guy, *Thomas More* (New York: Oxford University Press, 2000), 119.

17. Alistair Fox, "Chaucer, More, and English Humanism," *Parergon* 6 (1988): 63–75, passage from 65–66.

18. Alistair Fox, "Thomas More's *Dialogue* and the *Book of the Tales of Caunterbury*: 'Good Mother Wit' and Creative Imagination," in *Familiar Colloquy: Essays Presented to Arthur Edward Barker*, ed. Patricia Brückmann (Ottawa: Oberon, 1978), 15–24, quote from 20. In addition to the Chaucer allusions and references in the *Dialogue*, the editors of the Yale edition of More's complete works find, as Fox indicates, "several occasions when More had *The Parliament of Fowls* and the *House of Fame* strongly in mind (*Complete Works*, VIII, III, 1463, 1576, 1644, 1649)" (23n7).

19. Thomas More, *A Dialogue concerning Heresies*, in *The Complete Works of Thomas More*, ed. Thomas M. C. Lawler, Germain Marc'hadour, and Richard C. Marius (New Haven: Yale University Press, 1981), vol. 6, part 1, p. 98; see also vol. 6, part 1, p. 215; hereafter cited parenthetically by page number.

20. Fox, "Thomas More's *Dialogue*," 20.

21. Ibid., 20.

22. Anne Lake Prescott, "The Ambivalent Heart: Thomas More's Merry Tales." *Criticism* 45, no. 4 (2003): 417–33, quote from 422.

23. On "Mayster Chauncellour" as a protective fiction, see Dale B. Billingsley, "The Messenger and the Reader in Thomas More's *Dialogue concerning Heresies*," *Studies in English Literature, 1500–1900* 24, no. 1 (1984): 5–

22. Billingsley observes, "Within the fiction, the labor of transcription makes Mayster Chauncellour an amanuensis (like Morus in *Utopia*), and the judgment of the unnamed advisers relieves him of responsibility for errors in doctrine or decorum" (7–8).

24. Fox also notes the similarity of some of More's "merry tales" to Chaucer's fabliaux ("Thomas More's *Dialogue*," 20), and Prescott observes that some of More's anecdotes are sufficiently critical of the church that "one might have thought [they] would make Luther's strictures seem plausible" ("Ambivalent Heart," 423).

25. Thomas More, *The Apology*, vol. 9 of *The Complete Works of Thomas More*, 170.

26. Geoffrey Chaucer, *The Legend of Good Women*, in *Riverside Chaucer*, F 21, F 25.

27. The Wife of Bath says in her Prologue:

Telle me also, to what conclusion
Were membres maad of generacion,
And of so parfit wys a [wright] yroght?
Glose whoso wole, and seye bothe up and doun
That they were maked for purgacioun
Of uryne, and oure bothe thynges smale
Were eek to knowe a femele from a male,
And for noon oother cause—say ye no?
The experience woot wel it is noght so.
So that the clerkes be nat with me wrothe,
I sey this: that they maked ben for bothe;
That is to seye, for office and for ese
Of engendrure, ther we nat God displese.
(III 115–28)

28. Simpson, *Burning to Read*, 266.

29. Chaucer, *Canterbury Tales*, X p. 328; Simpson, *Burning to Read*, 271.

30. Chaucer, *Canterbury Tales*, X p. 328.

31. For information on the life of William Forrest, see Peter Holmes, "Forrest, William (*fl.* 1530–1576)," *Oxford Dictionary of National Biography*, online ed., ed. Lawrence Goldman, January 2007, http://www.oxforddnb.com /view/article/9892.

32. Macray, introduction, xiv.

33. Holmes, "Forrest, William."

34. See chapter 3 of Warren, *Women of God and Arms*.

35. Thomas Betteridge, "Maids and Wives: Representing Female Rule during the Reign of Mary Tudor," in *Mary Tudor: Old and New Perspectives*, ed. Susan Doran and Thomas S. Freeman (New York: Palgrave 2011), loc. 3179 of 8022, Kindle.

36. Amanda Holton, "Chaucer's Presence in *Songes and Sonettes*," in *Songes and Sonettes in Context*, ed. Stephen Hamrick (Aldershot: Ashgate, 2013), 87–110; see especially 89.

37. Chaucer, *Canterbury Tales*, IV 213.

38. The italics in this and subsequent quotations form Forrest's *History of Grisild the Second* are original unless otherwise noted.

39. Betteridge, "Maids and Wives," loc. 3066 of 8022. On other readings of the Griselda story that also include discussions of Forrest's text, see Lee Bliss, "A Renaissance Griselda: A Woman for All Seasons," *Viator* 2 (1992): 301–43; Ursula Potter, "Tales of Patient Griselda and Henry VIII," *Early Theatre* 5, no. 2 (2002): 11–28.

40. Chaucer, *Canterbury Tales*, IV 1175–76.

41. In other writings Forrest does mention Chaucer as an authoritative predecessor, as many early modern writers do. For example, in his *History of Joseph*, he includes a conventional statement of authorial modesty, writing:

I wote this hathe not the florischinge veyne
Of *Gowers* phrase, adorned in suche sorte.
Oather of *Chaucer*, that Poete souerayne,
To aske their counsaylles I came all to shorte.

42. Chaucer, *Canterbury Tales*, II 158.

43. Ibid., I 3081.

44. Ibid., IV 1142–44.

45. Ibid., IV 1145–46.

46. Ibid., IV 1164–65.

47. Vives's text was translated into Spanish, French, and English. It became "the leading theoretical manual on women's education in the sixteenth century" (Diane Bornstein, introduction to *Distaves and Dames: Renaissance Treatises for and about Women* [Delmar, NY: Scholars' Facsimile and Reprints, 1978], xviii). See also Juan Luis Vives, *The Education of a Christian Woman: A Sixteenth-Century Manual*, ed. and trans. Charles Fantazzi (Chicago: University of Chicago Press, 2000).

48. This quasi-canonization of Chaucer's heroine as embodied in Katherine of Aragon also resonates with the (possible) Marian translation by Nicholas Brigham of Chaucer's body and the creation of a new tomb for him in 1556

in order "to 'fix' the resting place of Chaucer as that of a 'Catholic' poet" and to give his body a status something like that of a saint's relics (Thomas Prendergast, *Chaucer's Dead Body: From Corpse to Corpus* [New York and London: Routledge, 2004], 46). Prendergast usefully outlines the uncertainties about what actually happened with Chaucer's body and the religious as well as the literary implications.

49. Juan Luis Vives, *Instruction of a Christian Woman*, trans. Richard Hyrd, facsimile printed in Bornstein, *Distaves and Dames*, h2v. Since Hyrd died in 1528, his translation had to be made between 1523 and 1528.

50. Joseph Patrick Keena, *An Edition of the Marian Poems of the Recusant Writer William Forrest from MS Harleian 1703* (PhD diss., University of Notre Dame, 1960), v.

51. Keena, *Edition of the Marian Poems*, v.

52. Griselda/Katherine uses imagery suggestive of the garden of Eden in her deathbed speech to Mary. She describes her marriage to Henry in horticultural terms, using the image of the Tudor rose and the pomegranate of Aragon and recalling

florischige yeares, when hee was content
With the Pomegarnet on stawlke to bee fownde,
Till serpentine shakynge loased the grounde,
Dysceauerynge vs muche myserablye. (108)

The reference to "serpentine shakynge" that destroys their union further suggests a parallel between Walter's/Henry's rejection of Griselda/Katherine and the fall.

CHAPTER 4. "Let Chaucer Also Look to Himself"

1. John Spurr, "The Piety of John Dryden," in *The Cambridge Companion to John Dryden*, ed. Steven N. Zwicker (Cambridge: Cambridge University Press, 2004), 237–58, quote from 250.

2. Though there is some controversy about the authorship of *The Roman Church's Devotions Vindicated* (some attribute it to Abraham Woodhead, while others attribute it to Cressy himself), the authorship is not of primary concern for my purposes.

3. See Jennifer Summit, "From Anchorhold to Closet: Julian of Norwich in 1670 and the Immanence of the Past," in *Julian of Norwich's Legacy: Medieval Mysticism and Poet-Medieval Reception*, ed. Sarah Salih and Denise N. Baker (New York: Palgrave, 2009), 32.

4. Summit, "From Anchorhold to Closet," 32.

5. This is a dynamic that, I have argued elsewhere, also emerges in writings of Margaret Gascoigne, in which through reading Julian's text she reincarnates Julian's experience of the divine. Recall, too, the evocative lines from the end of Julian's revelations that "this boke is begonne by Goddes gifte and his grace, but it is not yet performed" (*The Writings of Julian of Norwich: A Vision Showed to a Devout Woman and a Revelation of Love*, ed. Nicholas Watson and Jacqueline Jenkins [University Park: Pennsylvania State University Press, 2006], 379; unless otherwise noted, I cite Julian's writings, Cressy's edition, and Stillingfleet's *Discourse* parenthetically from the selections included in this text).

6. In his epistle to the reader, too, Cressy highlights the affective dimension of textual encounter and the performance of past experience in the reader's present enabled by reading: "And now, since she her self professes, that the Lights and Torches which God was pleased to give her, were intended not for her self alone, but for the Universality of God's true Servants, for whose benefit also she wrote them, the Devout Reader will, I hope, think himself obliged not to content himself with a fruitless admiring, but will, after her example, aspire to alike affectuous operative Contemplation of the meer Nothingness of Creatures, of the inconceivable ugliness of Sin, of the infinite tenderness and indefectibility of God's Love to his Elect, and of the Omnipotency of Divine Grace working in them" (Watson and Jenkins, *Writings*, 451).

7. Interestingly, in an anti-Quaker text from 1673 called *Quakerism no Christianity* (Wing 2nd ed. F302; accessed via Early English Books Online), John Faldo draws extensively upon Stillingfleet to illustrate "the third *Fundamentil* common to the *Papists* and *Quakers*, viz. immediate revelations and *divine Inspirations*" (59). Faldo cites Stillingfleet's examples involving the revelations of St. Catherine of Siena and St. Birgitta of Sweden, and he writes, "Let us cite a little of the doctrine and phrases, some of which are pretended from Inspiration by the Popish Votaries, and first of Mother *Juliana*" (60).

8. Edward Stillingfleet, *A Discourse concerning the Idolatry Practised in the Church of Rome* (London, 1671), 340; accessed via Early English Books Online. Similarly, in the *Discourse* Stillingfleet highlights both St. Birgitta of Sweden and St. Catherine of Siena before he trains his sights on Julian. As evidence of Catholic fanaticism, he cites "*Of the Revelations pleaded for the immaculate Conception. The Revelations of* S. Brigitt *and* S. Catharin *directly contrary in this point, yet both owned in the Church of* Rome. *The large approbations of S.* Brigitts *by Popes and Councils; and both their revelations acknowledged to be divine in the lessons read upon their dayes.* S. Catharines *wonderful faculty of smelling souls . . .*" (Watson and Jenkins, *Writings*, 451).

9. William Guild, *Anti-Christ Pointed and Painted Out* . . . (Aberdeen, 1655), Wing/G2203, 162; accessed via Early English Books Online. Walter Pope, "The Catholic Ballad: or an Invitation to Popery on Considerable Grounds and Reasons" (London, 1674), Wing/P2906; accessed via Early English Books Online.

10. Pope, "Catholic Ballad." Pope further picks up on the association of Catholicism with femininity, falsity, and (in keeping with the personification of the Catholic Church as the Whore of Rome), female sexual transgression, writing:

And ye sweet-natured Women, who hold all things common,
My addresses to you are most hearty,
And to give you your due, you are to us most true
And I hope we shall gain the whole party.
If you happen to fall, your Penance shall be small,
And although you cannot forgo it,
We have for you a cure, if of this you be sure,
To confess before you go to it.

11. In Walter Pope's satiric "Catholic Ballad" the Latin of Catholic prayers is feminized and made into a kind of debased "mother" tongue that contrasts to the authoritative English Protestant (scriptural) vernacular. Imagining England as once again a Catholic realm, he writes:

Then Shall Traffic and Love, and whatever can move
Be restor'd again to our Britain,
And Learning so common, that every old woman
Shall say her Prayers in Latin.

The reference to Latin learning becoming "common," paired with the attribution of Latinity to old women, also gives the language of Catholic prayer a tinge of sexual promiscuity, fitting with Pope's earlier account of the attractions of Catholicism for women who "fall."

12. Edward Stillingfleet, *An Answer to Several Late Treatises, Occasion'd by a Book Entitled "A Discourse concerning the Idolatry Practised in the Church of Rome, and the Hazard of Salvation in the Communion of It* (London, 1673), 11; Wing/S5559; accessed via Early English Books Online.

13. Stillingfleet, *An Answer*, 58.

14. Manuscript version; my thanks to Vickie Larsen for sharing this work in progress.

15. Larsen, manuscript.

16. Stillingfleet, *An Answer*, 16.

17. Serenus Cressy, *Fanaticism Fanatically Imputed to the Catholick Church by Doctour Stillingfleet and the Imputation Refuted and Retorted / by S.C. a Catholick* (Douai?, 1672), 64; Wing/C6898; accessed via Early English Books Online.

18. Ibid., 65.

19. Ibid.

20. Ibid., 63.

21. *The Roman Church's Devotions Vindicated from Doctor Stillingfleet's Mis-Representation, by O.N. a Catholick* (n.p., 1672); Wing/W3454; accessed via Early English Books Online.

22. Ibid., 87–88.

23. Ibid., 22.

24. Ibid., 23.

25. Ibid., 5–6.

26. Ibid., 6–7.

27. Ibid., 48. This bolstering of the legitimacy of Julian's experiences and its textual representation through association with a wealth of male exemplars and predecessors represents a massive expansion of a technique also employed by Cressy himself in his epistle to the reader, where he seems eager to forestall an association of Julian's revelations with "Curiosity" or "strange things" ("To his most Honoured Lady," A2r). In the epistle to the reader, he states that the "Manner of these Revelations" was "the same of which we read in innumerable Examples, both among Ancient and Modern Saints" (A3v).

28. Cressy, *Fanaticism Fanatically Imputed*, 68

29. Ibid., 69.

30. Ibid., 41.

31. Ibid., 41–42.

32. Ibid., 42.

33. *Roman Church's Devotions*, 17. Another Catholic contributor to the debate makes a similar point. In *Doctor Stillingfleet against Doctor Stillingfleet* (London, 1671), John Warner writes, "And I am confident that Dr. *Still* might produce out of the *Canticles*, the *Revelations* of S. *John, Ezechiel*, and other Prophets, and out of other Books of Scripture, as strange and extraordinary expressions, and practises, as any he alleges out of the Revelations of S. *Brigit*, and Mother *Juliana*, or out of the lives of the founders of religious Orders approv'd by the *Roman* Church" (p. 9; Wing/W909; accessed via Early English Books Online).

34. *Roman Church's Devotions*, 17. In the margin, O. N. includes the following references to Bible verses: "Gal. 2.20. 4. 19. I. Cor.15.10, 2. Cor. 4. 16."

35. *Roman Church's Devotions*, 18. O. N. notes in the margins here the following Biblical references: "2. Pet 1.4. Phil 4.7. Eph. 3. 17. 18. 19. 20. 2. Cor. 4. 18. 2. Cor. 6. 16. 17" (18).

36. In another Catholic refutation of Stillingfleet, Thomas Godden counters Stillingfleet's denigration of Julian's language by turning Stillingfleet's criticism back on Stillingfleet's own writing, choosing, significantly, a passage in which Stillingfleet seeks to discredit transubstantiation to make his point. Godden writes, "*For I do verily believe that neither Harphius nor Rusbrochius, nor the profound Mother Juliana have any thing in their writings so seemingly unintelligible, and contradictory, as this discurse of the Doctor's is really* such. For (beside the hard words of *hypostatical union*, consecrated *Elements*, *Conversion into the Person of Christ*, &c, . . .) *First*, He will have it to be the *same Body*. . . . Then he will have it *not* to be the *same Body*. . . . And then again it must be the *same Body*." (*Catholicks No Idolators, or A Full Refutation of Doctor Stillingfleet's Unjust Charge of Idolatry against the Church of Rome* [1672; Wing/G918; accessed via Early English Books Online], 241).

37. Stillingfleet, *Discourse*, 341–42; *Roman Church's Devotions*, 112.

38. As Anne Cotterill points out, "One popular theme of contemporary response was the susceptibility of Dryden's conscience to wifely wish and female art—'his fond uxorious vice.' A typical anonymous pamphlet scolded Dryden for falling prey 'To Midianitish Gods and Wives' and associated the 'soft bewitching Arts' of *The Hind and the Panther* with the decadent wiles of Feminized Egypt, Babylon, and Balaam" ("'Rebekah's Heir': Dryden's Late Mystery of Genealogy," *Huntington Library Quarterly* 63 [2000]: 201–26, quote from 201). The pamphlets Cotterill quotes are *The Weesils: A Satyrical Fable, Giving an Account of Some Argumental Passages Happening in the Lion's Court about Weesilion's Taking Oaths* (London, 1691), 2; and *The Murmurers* (London, 1689), 14. On Chaucer and Dryden, see also Stephanie Trigg, *Congenial Souls: Reading Chaucer from Medieval to Postmodern* (Minneapolis: University of Minnesota Press, 2002), 144–56.

39. Charles E. Ward, ed., *The Letters of John Dryden with Letters Addressed to Him* (Durham, NC: Duke University Press, 1942), 123. See also letter 74 for another instance of Dryden's juxtaposition of an account of the process of writing the *Fables* with a discussion of religiopolitical affairs. In this letter, written to Mrs. Steward on March 12, 1699, Dryden writes about his dedicatory poem to his cousin John Driden and then moves immediately to

lamenting the statute of 11 and 12 William III, which prohibited Catholics who had not taken the Oath of Allegiance from holding property or inheriting.

40. Ward, *Letters of John Dryden*, 123.

41. John Dryden, *Fables Ancient and Modern*, in *The Works of John Dryden*, ed. Vinton Dearing, vol. 7, *Poems, 1697–1700* (Berkeley and Los Angeles: University of California Press, 2002), 41. Hereafter I cite from this edition parenthetically by page number (for prose) or line number (for verse).

42. Sean Walsh, "'Our Lineal Descents and Clans': John Dryden's *Fables Ancient and Modern* and the 1690s" (Ph.D. diss., University of Oxford, 2006).

43. James A. Winn, "Past and Present in Dryden's *Fables*," in *John Dryden: A Tercentenary Miscellany*, ed. Susan Greene and Steven N. Zwicker (San Marino, CA: Huntington Library, 2001), 167. He observes, "Chaucer is the 'first' of the line of British poets, but the song that he 'Tun'd to his *British* Lyre' is 'ancient.' The poem is one 'which *Homer* might without a Blush rehearse,' not one that he might *have* rehearsed. Homer is treated as if he were alive, as if he came later than Chaucer. The poem 'leaves a doubtful Palm in *Virgil's* Verse' [present tense]; Chaucer 'match'd' [past tense] the 'Beauties' of Homer and Virgil 'where they most excel' [present tense]" ("Past and Present," 167).

44. Cotterill, "Rebekah's Heir," 2–3.

45. In the letter to the Duke of Ormond that precedes the preface, Dryden opens by emphasizing the duke's own place in a distinguished and virtuous exclusively male lineage of patrons. Dryden writes, "I am not vain enough to boast that I have deserv'd the value of so Illustrious a Line; but my Fortune is the greater, that for three Descents they have been pleas'd to distinguish my Poems from those of other Men; and have accordingly made me their peculiar Care. May it be permitted me to say, That as your Grandfather and Father were cherish'd and adorn'd with Honours by two successive Monarchs, so I have been esteem'd, and patronis'd, by the Grandfather, the Father, and the Son, descended from one of the most Ancient, most Conspicuous, and most Deserving Families in *Europe*" (17).

46. Dearing, *Works of John Dryden*, 7:631–32n30.

47. Cedric Reverand II writes: "In a poem that insists on his relationship to Chaucer, why would Dryden liken the Duchess to somebody not at all connected to Chaucer? Dryden is writing to the wife of his patron? Who is the most famous wife of Chaucer's best-known patron? I would argue that Walter Scott was right in the first place: the fairest nymph is Blanche, Duchess of Lancaster, whom Chaucer memorialized in The Book of the Duchess, written after her death in 1369. For one thing, one cannot help noticing that besides being the wife of Chaucer's patron, John of Gaunt, Blanche was also a duchess. That

Dryden had a duchess parallel to Chaucer's duchess is a coincidence that is unlikely to have escaped his notice. That one was married to John of Gaunt while the other was descended from him would only have reinforced the parallel in Dryden's mind. Is Blanche of equal kindred to the throne? Like the Duchess of Ormond, Blanche too is directly descended from an English monarch, being the great-great-granddaughter of Henry III, which also makes her a Plantagenet" ("Dryden's 'To the Duchess of Ormond': Identifying Her Plantagenet Predecessor," *Notes and Queries* 54 [2007]: 57–60, quote from 59).

48. Mary Somerset's Plantagenet genealogy is specifically a Catholic genealogy, not only in the fourteenth century but also more proximately to Dryden's time. As Cotterill observes:

> Mary's father, Henry Somerset, was created the first duke of Beaufort by Charles II in 1682 in part because of "his noble descent from King Edward III by John de Beaufort, eldest son of Joan of Gaunt, duke of Lancaster, by Catherine Swinford, his third wife." Raised a Catholic, he had conformed during the Interregnum but with the Restoration provided a firm supporter of the court party. He voted against Exclusion, bore the queen's crown at the coronation of James II, was appointed a gentleman of the bedchamber, and refused to swear the oath of allegiance to William. (Cotterill, "Rebekah's Heir," 213)

Mary Somerset, duchess of Ormond, represents "divine poetry with its venerable lineage from an earlier age; of ancient Roman Catholicism; of a royal race yet to be restored" (Cotterill, "Rebekah's Heir," 217).

49. Ward, *Letters of John Dryden*, 107–8.

50. Cotterill, "Rebekah's Heir," 204. Dryden's poem "To the Pious Memory of . . . Anne Killigrew" demonstrates that he could imagine a place for women in a poetic lineage. He writes:

> If by Traduction came they Mind,
> Our Wonder is the less to find
> A Soul so charming from a Stock so good;
> Thy Father was transfus'd into thy Blood:
> So wert thou born into the tuneful strain,
> (An early, rich, and inexhausted Vain).
> But if thy Praeexisting Soul
> Was form'd, at first, with Myriads more,
> It did through all the Mighty Poets roul,

Who Greek or Latine Laurels wore,
And that was Sappho last, which once it was before.

(23–33)

In these lines Dryden expresses the idea that a single poetic soul passes through generations, to become embodied in male and female poets alike. In the final line, he gives an image of female doubling in which Anne Killigrew reincarnates Sappho, rather like the way in which he envisions the duchess of Ormond reincarnating her Plantagenet ancestor as a source of poetic inspiration.

51. He goes so far in focusing on the duchess's frailty that, as Cotterill observes, he "almost lay[s] to rest the duchess of Ormond" ("Rebekah's Heir," 206). This poem is one in a series of what she calls "epitaphs, elegies, and elegy-like poems to saintly ladies" written between 1689 and 1700, poems that exhibit a "suspicious pattern, a match of deceased lady and buoyant male survivor" (206).

52. The Plantagenet legacy from the duchess's side is particularly important for the imagined heir to possess, because the royal legacy available from the *duke* of Ormond comes from the lineage of the hated William III. The duke of Ormond's mother was Emilia de Beverweert, who had "the same great-grandfather as William III. They were both descended, each through at least one illegitimate child, from William I of Nassau and Orange, 'William the Silent' (1533–84)" (Cotterill, "Rebekah's Heir," 213). As Cotterill argues, "The poem subtly suggests that the duchess's background and proper world is Chaucerian and kingly, like that of the poet. She has the richer blood in the marriage, and her family represents the oldest tradition of English monarchy" (215).

53. The frontispiece (fig. 1) contains the signatures of Pierre La Vergne and one of the brothers Van der Gucht (Jan or Gerard).

54. Janine Barchas, *Graphic Design, Print Culture, and the Eighteenth-Century Novel* (Cambridge: Cambridge University Press, 2003), 25.

55. In the famous passage from the preface, Dryden writes, "In the first place, as he is the Father of *English* Poetry, so I hold him in the same Degree of Veneration as the *Grecians* held *Homer*, or the *Romans Virgil*" (33).

56. C.66/3119, no. 6, August 18, 1670; quoted in Eleanore Boswell, "Chaucer, Dryden, and the Laureateship: A Seventeenth-Century Tradition," *Review of English Studies* 7 (1931): 338.

57. Cotterill, "Rebekah's Heir," 213.

58. See Caroline Walker Bynum, *Fragmentation and Redemption: Essays on Gender and the Human Body in Medieval Religion* (New York: Zone Books, 1991).

59. Greg Clingham says, "Metonymically, the presence of the Holy Spirit (the fire essential in the process of translation) in the Eucharist, linking the celebrant with the universal church back to Christ (the Logos), is acknowledged and recreated in the translator's containment of the genius of the Other" ("Another and the Same: Johnson's Dryden," in *Literary Transmission and Authority: Dryden and Other Writers*, ed. Earl Miner and Jennifer Brady [Cambridge: Cambridge University Press, 1993], 149–50).

60. "To Dr. Samuel Garth, occasioned by the much Lamented Death of John Dryden, Esq.," in *Luctus Britannici, or the Tears of the British Muses for the Death of John Dryden, Esq.* (London: Henry Playford, 1700), 55; accessed via Early English Books Online.

61. On this tradition, see chapter 3 of Prendergast, *Chaucer's Dead Body*, especially 57–64.

CHAPTER 5.   "Flying from the Depravities of *Europe*,
to the *American Strand*"

1. Cotton Mather, *Magnalia Christi Americana* (London, 1702). The "General Introduction" lacks pagination. Hereafter citations are given parenthetically by book and page number.

2. As Sarah Kelen points out, "The Plowman's Tale was first included in the Chaucer canon in Thynne's 1542 edition of Chaucer's *Works*, and it remained there until it was removed by Tyrwhitt in 1775" (*Langland's Early Modern Identities* [New York: Palgrave Macmillan, 2007], 66).

3. As a medievalist, I initially found the territory of early American literary studies nearly as foreign in some ways as the colonialists must have found the woods of New England. I am very grateful to have had as a colleague at Florida State University Joseph McElrath, one of the leading scholars and editors of the work of Anne Bradstreet. Conversations with him were invaluable as I took my first tentative steps developing this essay, and his edition of Bradstreet's poetry has been a welcome resource. I am also grateful to Dennis Moore, another former colleague at Florida State, who helped me immensely with suggestions for secondary reading as I started working on what seemed at the time the somewhat unlikely topic of Chaucer and Cotton Mather.

4. N. H. Keeble, "Bradstreet [*née* Dudley], Anne (1612/13–1672)," *Oxford Dictionary of National Biography*, online ed., ed. Lawrence Goldman, September 2004, http://www.oxforddnb.com/view/article/3209 (accessed December 20, 2012).

5. Candace Barrington, *American Chaucers* (New York: Palgrave Macmillan, 2007), 4.

6. Ibid., 5.

7. Ibid.

8. Ibid.

9. Foxe, *Unabridged Acts and Monuments Online.* Hereafter I cite this text parenthetically by book and page number from this edition.

10. As Sacvan Bercovitch notes, "Mather and Foxe have much in common as biographers: the long heritage of ecclesiastical hagiography; the pronounced influence of Eusebius, who fathered the typological approach to history; an obsession with the millennial calendar . . . and the idea of the hero as representing a corporate mission" (*The Puritan Origins of the American Self* [New Haven and London: Yale University Press, 1975], 72–73).

11. Chaucer, *Canterbury Tales*, III 905 (hereafter cited parenthetically by fragment and line number).

12. D. Andrew Penny, "Bradford, John (c. 1510–1555)," *Oxford Dictionary of National Biography*, online ed., ed. Lawrence Goldman, September 2004, http://www.oxforddnb.com/view/article/3175 [accessed July 12, 2013]. If William Bradford and John Bradford are kin, I have as yet been unable to determine what the relationship between them might be.

13. Bercovitch, *Puritan Origins*, 73.

14. Thomas Steele, "The Biblical Meaning of Mather's Bradford," *Bulletin of the Rocky Mountain Modern Language Association* 24, no. 4 (1970): 147–54, quote from 148.

15. In 1601, on the eve of his rebellion against Queen Elizabeth, the earl of Essex commissioned the Chamberlain's Men to perform Shakespeare's *Richard II*. According to the Elizabethan historian William Lambarde, Elizabeth is purported to have remarked, "I am Richard II, know ye not that?" (quoted in E. K. Chambers, *William Shakespeare: A Study of Facts and Problems*, 2 vols. [Oxford: Clarendon Press, 1930], 2:327).

16. William Camden, *Reges, reginae, nobiles, at alij in ecclesia collegiata B. Petri Westmonasterij sepulti* (London, 1606), 66, 67; see Thomas Wright, *Literary Culture in Early New England* (New Haven: Yale University Press, 1920), 148n34.

17. On the Wife of Bath and the Lollard movement, see Blamires, "Wife of Bath and Lollardy." See also chapters 3 and 4 of Minnis, *Fallible Authors.*

18. Interestingly, when introducing Thomas Dudley, Mather reiterates the alignment of nobility with character rather than birth put forth in the introduction to book 2 in his citation of "Old Chaucer." Mather writes: "Among

the Judges of Areopagus, none were admitted . . . unless they were Nobly Born, and Eminently Exemplary for a Virtuous and Sober Life. The Report may be truly made concerning the Judges of New-England, tho' they were not Nobly Born, yet they were generally Well Born, and by being Eminently Exemplary For a Virtuous and Sober Life, gave Demonstration that they were New-born" (2:15).

19. Keeble, "Bradstreet [*née* Dudley], Anne."

20. Mary Rhinelander McCarl, ed., *The Plowman's Tale: The c. 1532 and 1606 Editions of a Spurious Canterbury Tale* (New York and London: Garland, 1997), 9.

21. John M. Bowers, *Chaucer and Langland: The Antagonistic Tradition* (Notre Dame, IN: University of Notre Dame Press, 2007), 65.

22. William Langland, *Piers Plowman*, ed. Robert Crowley (London, 1550), quoted in Bowers, *Chaucer and Langland*, 64.

23. I want to thank Lawrence Warner for his generosity and kindness in sharing his own work in progress on *Piers Plowman* and the Chaucerian tradition. His immense knowledge about *Piers Plowman* and the early modern print history of the poem have been invaluable resources. Thanks are also due to Sarah Kelen, who also has provided very helpful suggestions and ideas about the early modern print tradition of *Piers Plowman*, both in her book *Langland's Early Modern Identities* and in conversation and correspondence.

24. For Leland's attribution of "Petri Aratoris fabula" to Chaucer, see *De Uiris Illustribus: On Famous Men*, ed. James P. Carley (Toronto: University of Toronto Press, 2010), 708–9; see also Carley, appendix 4, in Leland, *De Uiris Illustribus*, 844; Alexandra Gillespie, *Print Culture and the Medieval Author: Chaucer, Lydgate, and Their Books, 1473–1557* (Oxford: Oxford University Press, 2006), 199. For an illuminating discussion of this evidence illustrating that the text Leland had in mind was in fact *Piers Plowman* and not the Plowman's Tale, see Lawrence Warner, "The Vision of Piers Plowman, Said to Be Wrote by Chaucer: Leland's *Petri Aratoris Fabula* and Its Descendants Revisited," *Chaucer Review* 48, no. 1 (2013): 113–28, reference to 115–16.

25. Warner, "Vision of Piers Plowman," 118.

26. Cambridge University Library Syn. 7.55.12, quoted in Warner, "Vision of Piers Plowman," 118.

27. As Katharine Gillespie notes, Bradstreet's poem "Elegie upon That Honourable and Renowned Knight Sir Philip Sidney" "praises Sidney's literary record and his participation in the battle . . . at Zutphen, and it notes her own blood connection to the Sidney family"; however, "Bradstreet also constructs her difference from her English Protestant poetic lineage even as she

inscribes herself within it" ("'This Briny Ocean Will O'erflow Your Shore': Anne Bradstreet's 'Second World' Atlanticism and National Narratives of Literary History," *Symbiosis* 3, no. 2 [1999]: 99–118, quote from 103). Anne Bradstreet's genealogical connection with the Sidney family is through her birth family the Dudleys. Sir Philip Sidney's maternal grandfather was John Dudley, duke of Northumberland. Similarly, Andrew Hiscock points out that there are "many examples" in Anne Bradstreet's poetry "in which 'Britain' becomes a slippery term undergoing constant processes of masking and elision" ("'A Dialogue between Old England and New': Anne Bradstreet and Her Negotiations with the Old World," in *Mighty Europe*, ed. Andrew Hiscock [Berlin: Peter Lang, 2007], 185–220, quote from 203). Hiscock argues that in the poems added to the 1678 edition of Bradstreet's volume of poetry one finds that "from within the focus of close affective ties, for the first time Bradstreet may be seen to construct a clear oppositional discourse between a New England *home* and a British (or English) Other." He also points out, however, that in Bradstreet's poem "To the Memory of My Dear and Ever Honoured Father Thomad Dudley Esq. Who Deceased, July 31, 1653, and of His Age 77," she "is clearly exploring the possibilities of cultural integrity for a New England which may now begin to compose its own heroic lineages" (216–17). I would argue that the "Dialogue" suggests some thinking along similar lines considerably earlier in her poetic career.

28. Pattie Cowell, "The Early Distribution of Anne Bradstreet's Poems," *Critical Essays on Anne Bradstreet*, ed. Pattie Cowell and Ann Stanford (Boston: Hall, 1983), 270–79, quote from 271.

29. All quotations from Anne Bradstreet's poetry are taken from Joseph R. McElrath and Allan P. Robb, eds., *The Complete Works of Anne Bradstreet* (Boston: Twayne, 1981). Because this edition does not mark line numbers, my citations give only page numbers.

30. Elizabeth Wade White, *Anne Bradstreet: The Tenth Muse* (Oxford: Oxford University Press, 1972), 252.

31. Hiscock, "A Dialogue," 189.

32. White, *Anne Bradstreet*, 223.

33. Ibid., 246.

34. Ibid. Anne Bradstreet's "Dialogue" was written at a time when many like John Woodbridge who had come to New England fleeing religious persecution returned to England as the political tide turned for the nonconformists and Parliamentarians. As David Cressy points out, "The early 1640s may have been the only time in New England history when immigrants were outnumbered by people returning in the opposite direction" (*Coming Over: Migra-*

tion and Communication between England and New England in the Seventeenth Century [Cambridge: Cambridge University Press, 1987], 201).

35. White, *Anne Bradstreet*, 251. According to Stephanie Jed, Thomason purchased *The Tenth Muse* for this collection "a few days after its issue" ("The Tenth Muse: Gender, Rationality, and the Marketing of Knowledge," in *Women, "Place," and Writing in the Early Modern Period*, ed. Margo Hendricks and Patricia Parker [London: Routledge, 1994], 195–208, quote from 203). This collection of seventeenth-century texts is now known as the Thomason Tracts.

36. As Andrew Hiscock observes, in the "Dialogue," as in Bradstreet's poems on Philip Sidney and Queen Elizabeth I, "there is an affirmation of a more classicized, cyclical notion of time" rather than a strict reliance on "a Judeo-Christian construct of time in which the linear, the providential and the apocalyptic become the organizing principles" (202).

37. Old England does, though, give an approving mention of medieval English monarchs' triumphs during the Hundred Years' War in also denying the suggestion that France might be the cause of her woes, saying, "France knows, how of my fury she hath drunk; / By Edward third, and Henry fifth of fame" (14).

38. James Egan, "Nathaniel Ward and the Marprelate Tradition," *Early American Literature* 15, no. 1 (1980): 59–71, quote from 61.

39. The title page of *I Playne Piers* is quoted in Kelen, *Langland's Early Modern Identities*, 65.

40. The 1589 edition is STC (2nd edition) 6805; accessed via Early English Books Online from the Henry E. Huntington Library's copy. All quotations, hereafter cited parenthetically, are from this edition. The 1640 edition is STC (2nd edition) 6805.3.

41. White, *Anne Bradstreet*, 248.

42. Ibid., 246.

43. Bradstreet refers to the famous scene when, on August 9, 1588, Elizabeth addressed the troops at Tilbury, reportedly clothed in armor. It is in this speech that she made her famous remark that though she was a "weak and feble woman," she had the "harte and stomack of a kinge" (quoted in Janet M. Green, "'I My Self': Queen Elizabeth I's Oration at Tilbury Camp," *The Sixteenth Century Journal* 28, no. 2 (1997): 421–45, quote from 429). This essay provides an excellent summary of the critical debate concerning whether or not Elizabeth actually delivered the speech attributed to her; Green provides convincing evidence for its authenticity.

44. I am grateful to my colleague Dennis Berthold for encouraging me to consider Ward's *The Simple Cobler* as I developed this essay. I am also grateful

to his helpful suggestions about primary and secondary sources to consult as I worked to orient myself in the unfamiliar landscape of early American literature. His intellectual generosity in reading and providing useful comments on a draft of this essay, and his willingness to chat about early American religion over lunch, are much appreciated.

45. Baston, "Ward, Nathaniel."

46. Egan, "Nathaniel Ward," 59.

47. Nathaniel Ward, *The simple cobler of Aggavvam in America Willing to help mend his native country, lamentably tattered, both in the upper-leather and sole, with all the honest stitches he can take. And as willing never to be paid for his work, by old English wonted pay. It is his trade to patch all the year long, gratis. Therefore I pray gentlemen keep your purses. By Theodore de la Guard* (London, 1647), BIIIb (Wing 2nd ed. W786, accessed via Early English Books Online). Hereafter I cite this text parenthetically from this edition.

48. Chaucer, *Canterbury Tales*, I 473.

49. On Catholicism as a feminizing force, see, for example, Frances E. Dolan, *Whores of Babylon: Catholicism, Gender, and Seventeenth-Century Print Culture* (Notre Dame, IN: University of Notre Dame Press, 1999), especially chapter 3, "The Command of Mary: Marian Devotion, Henrietta Maria's Intercessions, and Catholic Motherhood."

CPSIA information can be obtained
at www.ICGtesting.com
Printed in the USA
LVHW050050050219
606418LV00002B/4